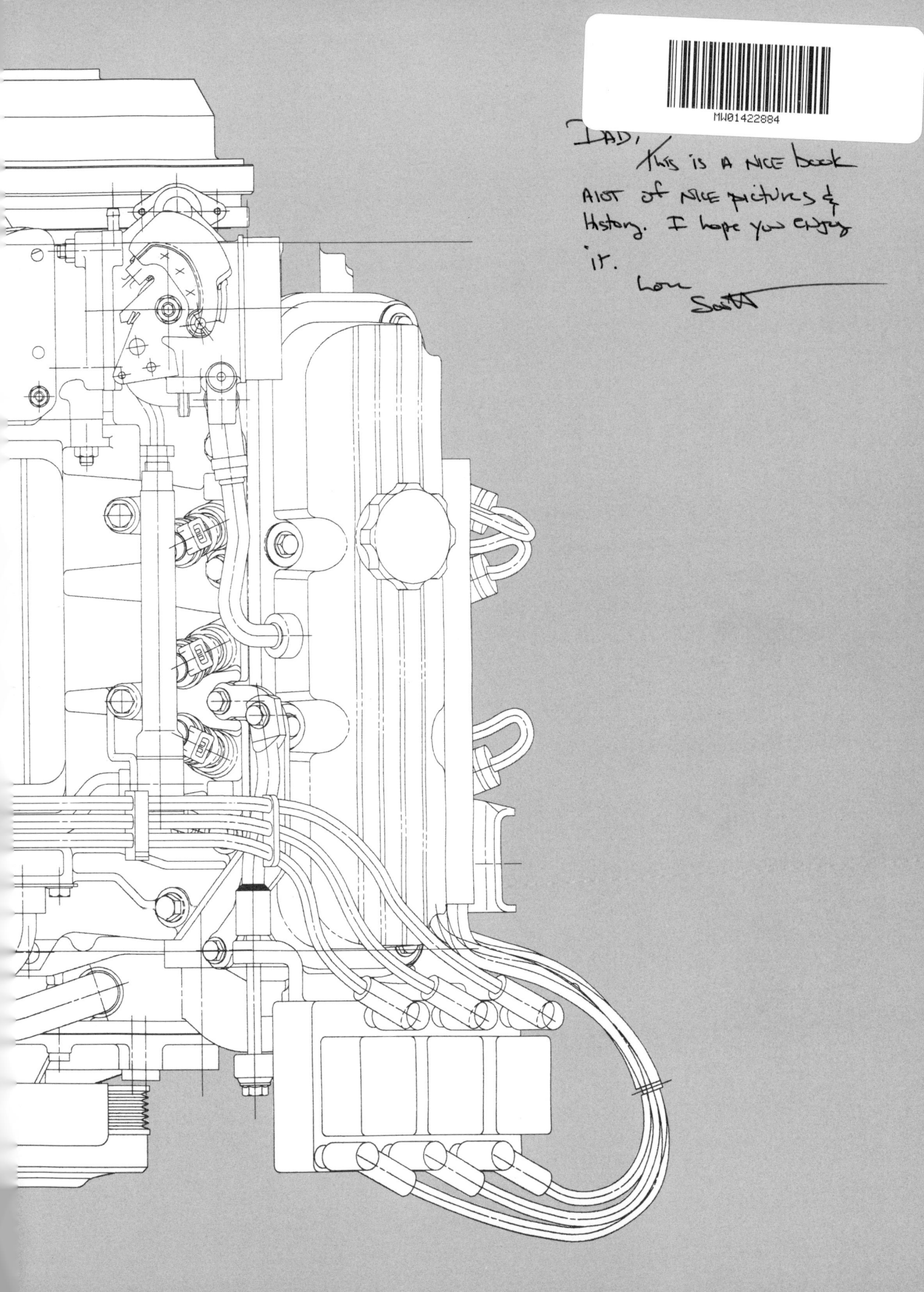

Dad,
This is a nice book. A lot of nice pictures & History. I hope you enjoy it.
Love
Scott

PROJECT VN

An Australian car for the 1990s

by Pedr Davis and Tony Davis

**The design, development,
manufacture and marketing of the new
Holden Commodore and Calais**

MARQUE
PUBLISHING COMPANY

Acknowledgments

It would not be possible to write a book such as this without the cooperation and unstinted support of the people who had planned, designed, engineered and developed the car. And of course we also talked at length to the very cooperative teams who now manufacture and market the VN Commodore. Several hundred people within Holden's Motor Company (now General Motors-Holden's Automotive Ltd) and Holden's Engine Company provided us with assistance well beyond the call of duty, often working in their own time to make sure we received as complete and accurate a picture as they could paint.

From the first day when we arrived at the Fishermans Bend and Elizabeth plants, tape-recorders and notebooks at the ready, we encountered nothing but whole-hearted enthusiasm from Holden people at the shop floor to boardroom level. Many were so keen to help that we could have filled five times as many pages as we have with the material thrust upon us. Time after time, we felt slightly guilty because space dictated we should leave out material which someone had laboured over for hours especially to help us.

The photos in this book were taken under the supervision of Ken Jacoby. The photographers included Ken, Philip Martin, Steve Cooper, Ken Redpath and others.

We would also like to acknowledge the work of the Marque Publishing production team for providing their usual highly professional services. Thank you Irene Meier, Anne Sahlin and all those at Macarthur Press.

Pedr Davis
Tony Davis
August 1988

Project VN — An Australian Car For the 1990s
was first published in 1988 by Marque Publishing Company Pty Ltd, PO Box 203, Hurstville NSW 2220.

Text © Copyright 1988 by Marque Publishing Company Pty Ltd.

The National Library of Australia Cataloguing-in-Publication.
Davis, Pedr.
    Project VN, an Australian car for the 1990s.

    Includes index.
    ISBN 0 947079 05 X.
    ISBN 0 947079 06 8 (pbk.).

    1. Automobiles — Australia — Design and construction.
    2. Holden Commodore automobile. 3. Holden Calais
    automobile. I. Davis, Tony. II. Title.

Proudly produced wholly within Australia.

Production by Tony Davis and Irene Meier.
Design and layout by Irene Meier.
Copy editing by Anne Sahlin.
Typeset by Photoset Computer Service
Wholly set up and printed in Australia by Macarthur Press (Sydney).

All rights reserved. No part of this publication may be reproduced, stored in retrieval form or transmitted in any form, or by any means, without written permission from the publisher.

All specifications relating to the VN in this book were supplied to Marque Publishing Co by GMHA and were correct at the time of going to press. However, like all car companies, Holden's reserves the right to change or improve the specifications or equipment levels at any time.

Foreword

The design, development and manufacture of a new car anywhere in the world is a fascinating story.

'Project VN', the model designation for the new-generation Holden Commodore and Calais, is a story about a brand-new car, an event which occurs in Australia once in every ten years.

It takes you behind the scenes, into the design and planning areas, into engineering, into proving grounds, even into the Boardroom where critical decisions are made which shape the financial destiny of a company for the next decade.

The new VN Commodore and Calais are designed specifically for Australian conditions. They are products of a new era of technology and sophisticated manufacturing techniques.

As we move into the nineties and look even further ahead, the critical importance of building quality into manufactured goods is perhaps the biggest challenge facing industry in Australia. It is the challenge of being able to compete successfully in world markets with quality Australian products.

Within Australia too, being able to meet the demand for quality products and services will determine future business success, and the dedicated men and women behind the VN project had quality as one of their major objectives.

In the following pages, the story of how this was accomplished is told.

With the original Commodore in 1978, Holden set out to establish a new standard in Australian motoring. I believe Project VN has produced a vehicle which deserves to rank with the best volume-produced cars in the world. It shares the same advanced design and manufacturing techniques introduced by General Motors into other major countries and tailored to suit Australia.

It is a car Australians can be truly proud of.

John G. Bagshaw
Managing Director
General Motors-Holden's Automotive Ltd

August 1988

Contents

FOREWORD
... by Holden's Managing Director John Bagshaw   7

1
MEMO TO BOSS: HERE'S A $51 MILLION QUESTION
... planning the completely new car   14

2
IT MUST BE SEEN TO BE BIG
... the design story   34

3
TECHNOLOGY ORCHESTRATED
... engineering for Australia   55

4
COMPRESSING THE YEARS
... durability, reliability and road testing   69

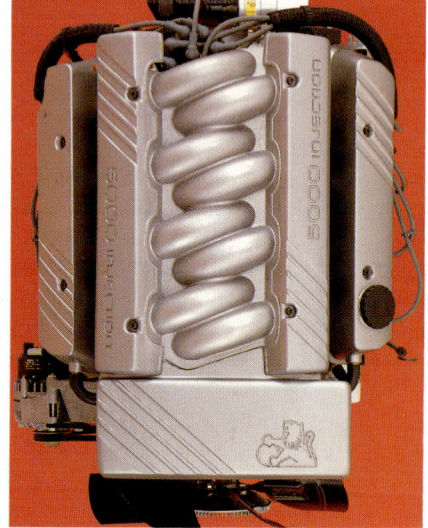

5
VEE POWER
... the new six and eight   91

6
PUTTING IT TOGETHER
... building cars in the new age 103

7
POWERFUL FRIENDS
... worldwide support 121

8
TO MARKET, TO MARKET
... selling the product 128

9
GETTING ON TRACK
... motor sport and special vehicles 151

10
THE END RESULT
... specification details 164

APPENDIXES:
1. THE HOLDEN HERITAGE ... a chronology 172
2. FORTY YEARS OF FAMILY HOLDENS
    ... models leading to the VN 185
INDEX 208

Memo to Boss:
Here's a $51 million question

At 8.30 on a sunny Saturday morning in July 1984, a white Ford Falcon cruised along Beach Road, Port Melbourne. Three men occupied the rear seat — C.S. (Chuck) Chapman, John Loveridge and Joe Whitesell. They stretched and wriggled, made notes and passed good-humoured comments about each other's size and shape. They peered at the instrument panel, looked at the roof lining and scrutinised every facet of the interior.

The car headed toward the town of Mordialloc and, after 30 kilometres, stopped to let the men out. Their places were immediately taken by another group who emerged from a nearby sedan. More banter followed and the newcomers repeated a similar procedure. In due course, the car stopped again and a third group took the back seat.

Any passers-by would have been further puzzled had they known that the nine men using the Falcon comprised almost the entire board of directors of General Motors-Holden's (later Holden's Motor Company). Even more curious was that the Falcon's interior was unlike any which Ford had built. The normal rear seat, headlining and trim had been replaced by a fibreglass shell trimmed in vinyl.

After nearly two hours, the Falcon returned to Fishermans Bend to be closeted in Holden's top-security area. The directors went home happy in the knowledge they had the answer to a haunting problem. They had lived with it since the day Chuck Chapman had received a memo which said in effect: 'Dear Boss, We want to widen the proposed car by 38 mm — but it will cost $51 million'.

Nearly two years earlier, on 9 July 1982, those same directors had met with a number of other key players in Holden's plush conference room in its Fishermans Bend headquarters near Melbourne. The task was to discuss the new full-size car needed to take Holden into the 1990s.

These members of the key Product Strategy Committee were under great pressure. The demand for six-cylinder cars had fallen from 50 per cent of the passenger car market in the early 1970s to 33 per cent in the 1980s. Market-forecast experts said it could go as low as 20 per cent by 1990. Furthermore, Holden's own sales had fallen steadily and were hovering around 22.5 per cent of the new car market. This was a far cry from the early 1960s when Holden dominated the field to such an extent that half of all new vehicles carried a Holden badge.

Present at that fateful meeting were 11 executives representing the design, engineering, manufacturing, finance, quality control, styling, marketing, materials management and planning departments. The then Managing Director, Chuck Chapman, took the chair and the then Director of Planning, Ray Grigg, addressed the group.

He did not need to remind those present that whatever they decided would be expensive. It would also drastically affect the company's financial and sales performance for years to come.

Events beyond the company's control had already delivered a serious blow. Australians have a strong preference for sedans wide enough to seat three adults comfortably across the back seat. Almost half of all six-cylinder cars are bought by middle-aged couples with teenage children, and they expect plenty of room. The VB Commodore series, launched in

Opposite:
Reams of drawings were produced during the development of the VN shape, ranging from the fanciful [above] to those shaped around much tighter parameters [below].

Below left:
Another early theme drawing.

Below right:
A 1980 proposal for the 'V replacement' was based on the smaller front-drive Camira. It was at a time when fuel supplies were uncertain and the experts were tipping that Camira would become Australia's top-selling car.

1978, had been conceived at a time of rapidly increasing fuel prices and a worldwide trend toward smaller cars.

Its reduced size proved the perfect recipe for the late 1970s but the market changed abruptly with the easing of the fuel crisis. Ford, which had not downsized the Falcon, had a distinct marketing advantage when buyers rushed back to larger cars. Suddenly, Falcon was in the box seat. The six-cylinder Commodore was uncomfortably positioned halfway between the bigger Ford and the four-cylinder intermediate cars — and the intermediates were growing larger with each new model.

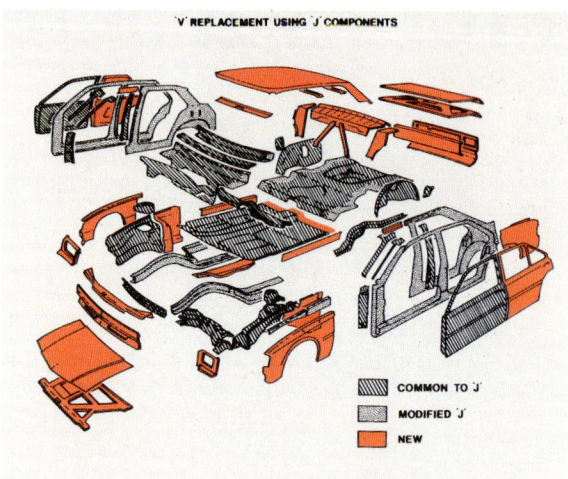

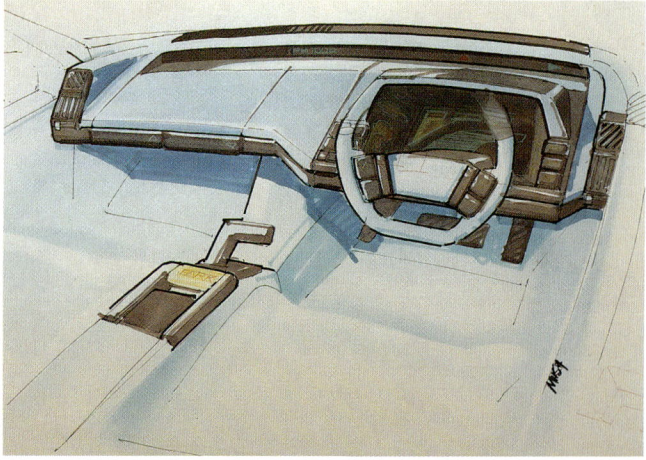

Above left and right:
Early interior theme sketches.

Ray Grigg and his department had been working on the problem for over 12 months. The planning job is to define precisely the type and size of vehicles the company should produce and what variations and options should be offered. The task becomes more difficult by the year. Cars have become so sophisticated that it takes a long incubation period and a tremendous amount of money to develop a completely new model. Compared with sharing a model program with an overseas affiliate, it would have taken an additional year plus an extra $100 million to design, engineer and tool a Holden unique to Australia.

Faced with this prospect, the company had to explore other options. The least expensive was to prolong the life of the current Commodore by means of a facelift and appropriate engineering changes — but this would not overcome the drawback of size. The other route was to search the world for a new model program which could be shared with Australia. The most promising possibility here was one offered by Opel, Holden's sister company in Germany. It was at Opel that the 1978 Commodore VB had been designed (in a program shared with Holden), and the German company was developing a new model based on the very latest technology.

A rendering of the proposed front-wheel drive 'Camira-based' Commodore (1980).

An interesting option — studied but never seriously considered — was what the industry euphemistically calls a 'do-nothing program'. Because of the competitive nature of the auto business, all models reach a point where maximum sales have been achieved. After this high point, the design is considered dated and sales begin to fall, no matter how clever the styling and mechanical updates may be.

Conventional wisdom says that a company can always lift sales by launching a new model — hence the relative frequency of styling changes made by most car firms — but the boost may be short lived. Facelifts cost money and the company needs an accurate forecast as to when sales will have dropped to the point where it can justify the large investment needed for a completely new replacement.

The do-nothing program involves a theoretical study which shows what would happen to sales if the model was not updated or replaced. It helps the bean-counters compare the cost of an investment program against the loss of revenue expected as sales fall. Balancing one factor against the other is a delicate but essential job which determines the optimum time to launch the replacement model. It also has a major influence on the firm's profit potential.

Holden's 'do-nothing' study revealed that Commodore sales would, by 1992, drop to 12 000 units a year unless a completely new model was introduced by 1987-88.

In October 1982, when the Strategy Committee met again, the Commodore VH was in production but the facelifted VK was being wrapped up for a 1984 release. Most details of the 1986 VL had also been settled, apart from the engine. The company required a new unit to handle unleaded fuel which was planned for introduction in Australia in mid-1985 and legislated to be compulsory for all cars built after January 1986. To best meet the challenge, Chuck Chapman insisted that Holden's make a leap forward in engine technology. Company engineers had considered the Buick V-6 and a number of other engines, including Jaguar and Opel designs. Eventually the matter was resolved in favour of the forthcoming 3-litre Nissan high-tech straight six. In January 1983, Holden's signed an agreement to buy the Nissan engine for use in the VL scheduled for release three years later.

The original plan had been to replace the VL in the third quarter of 1987, a decision based on the latest sales forecasts and industry rumours about the arrival date of the next Falcon model. Thanks to the new engine and improved styling, the VL was extremely well received and the resulting sales boost meant that the new model could be safely postponed until 1988. This in turn gave Holden engineers extra time to develop and refine the new model. As things turned out, they needed every bit of it.

When Chuck Chapman took the chair at the meeting to plan VL's successor, only one thing was certain — the model name. The proposed newcomer had been given two designations: 2158 and VN (there never was a

VM Commodore model but the designation was put aside in case an extra facelift of the original design was needed). The number 2158 was used far more than VN, especially on correspondence, hopefully to confuse prying eyes. Although it was issued because it happened to be next in the finance allocation book, it has a special attraction for lovers of trivia. The original Holden — introduced in November 1948 — was codenamed 215 and the VN was planned for release in 1988.

The 11 executives attending the meeting had more important things on their minds, of course. The preliminaries over, Ray Grigg reminded his colleagues that the original Commodore VB, which was based on Opel models, had done an excellent job and the company hoped to simply share in Opel's replacement program. As early as 1981, Holden's had considered this possibility and had sent Opel its reliability and durability testing standards requesting they be incorporated in the replacement design then under consideration (and later launched as the Omega and Senator ranges).

In all, Opel spent one billion dollars preparing the car for the market and was later able to claim it had the lowest aerodynamic drag factor in the world for the class — 0.28. By sharing the program, Holden's would gain the brilliant new technology at an affordable price and could also pick up future updates. It also allowed Australian buyers to benefit from the combined development expertise of the two companies.

From the word go, Holden executives were keen to share the program. Opel planned several versions, mainly for the European market, the body styles being a five-door station wagon, a sedan with four windows and a sedan with six windows. Holden's wanted a composite of the four-window and six-window designs.

The body design represented the latest in technology, including flush window glass to reduce aerodynamic drag and wind noise. Pleased though they were with the car's appearance, Holden's marketing executives had grave reservations about its size. They wanted a car which genuinely allowed three adults to sit in comfort in the rear seat. As the design concept progressed, the two firms moved closer and closer with one exception. Although Opel had widened the new car relative to the old, it was still not as wide as Holden's considered necessary for Australia. Opel was reluctant to make it any wider because of the effect on the aerodynamic drag. After an avalanche of messages, Opel said 'That's enough — we'll go no further'.

The decision sent shudders through Holden's management. The marketing people were emphatic that they needed a roomy car with ample shoulder room for burly adults, and this meant that the Opel was not the answer. When the bad news arrived, Leo Pruneau, Holden's former Director of Design (now stationed in the USA), was asked to review the Corporation's new model programs there to see if one was suitable for Australia. Leo looked at a promising front-wheel drive car — codenamed GM70 — which later emerged as the Buick Le Sabre, Pontiac Bonneville and Oldsmobile Delta. However, it did not excite him to the same extent as Opel's design had.

On 8 October 1982, Holden's strategic planning group met in the conference room on the second floor of the Fishermans Bend Technical Centre.

Below:
This 'tape' drawing, done in the very early 1980s, became the basis of a full-size clay model [above right].

The room is part of a top-secret work area which can only be penetrated by people wearing special security passes.

The group was told that sales of Falcon and Commodore were now level-pegging, reflecting the conservative estimates for full-size cars in the wake of the fuel crisis. They heard that the proposed Commodore VN would be built at an annual volume of 30 400 sedans and 7600 station wagons (this figure was subsequently increased substantially). Yet again, the marketing people identified their biggest handicap as the lack of interior width. Falcon offered 90 mm more shoulder room than Commodore — a major advantage when selling into the business and private markets.

Ray Grigg presented four possible scenarios:
(1) Holden's could adopt the Opel program in total, including the engine and transmission.
(2) The Opel body could be slit down the middle and widened locally.
(3) The existing Commodore could be redesigned with a view to better space packaging.
(4) The Opel body could be used in conjunction with existing Holden mechanical components.

Several executives spoke in favour of widening the Opel; others had reservations.

'The Opel design was so good', says Roger Gibbs who is now in charge of the Planning Department, 'that it seemed a touch like heresy to be talking about changing it'.

'But we had reviewed the position again and again in the months leading to the meeting. No matter which way we looked at it, it was going to be very hard to live with the width that Opel proposed. They wanted the best aerodynamic lines they could achieve, we needed that extra shoulder room and feeling of spaciousness.'

There was little support for the proposition that the existing Commodore be redesigned and this effectively reduced the options to three. The executives at the meeting were acutely aware that the plan to widen the Opel body would create an enormous amount of extra work and expense. They also knew that whatever decision was taken, it would set the company's course and profitability for years to come. After some debate, it was decided to accept the new Opel design in principle and to explore the feasibility of increasing the body width. There remained, however, the question

of whether to use Opel's new mechanical components or adapt existing Holden parts to the design.

Ed Jaworski, Manager of Forward Model Costing, took the floor and said that, as a reference for minimum capital investment, Holden's could take the existing Opel car and power train and assemble the VN here (with 50 per cent local content) and spend only $22 million. If they decided to use the Opel body but graft on the existing Commodore underbody and some Holden components, an investment of $110 million would give a vehicle with the desired minimum 75 per cent local content. Alternatively, the company could outlay $179 million and achieve 90 per cent local content.

Widening the Opel body was certain to be costly. Joe Whitesell, then Director of Engineering, calculated it would take 40 000 man-hours just for the design and drafting work. The other possible alternative — a major restyle of the existing VL Commodore — would require 61 000 man hours in design and drafting work. In addition, some $76 million (in 1982 dollars) would have to be spent in tooling and facilities. No matter what body was used, the company did not have the capacity to produce the tooling itself. To add to the problem, most spare capacity in Australia had already been taken by Ford, which was preparing the new Falcon for launch early in 1988. Holden's most likely source for the new tooling was therefore Japan.

At the time, the committee was blissfully unaware that Australia's currency was going to dive from 200 to 100 yen to the dollar. This fall was to have very serious repercussions on the whole program, doubling some areas of investment and making the prospect of an imported engine prohibitively expensive.

While work continued on refining the VN concept, the group studied the vexing question of the engine to be used in the yet-to-be-announced VL. This would have a major influence on VN as the intention, at the time, was to use the same unit in it. The ultimate decision was to import the Nissan 3-litre engine and transmission complete from Japan, and there was little doubt about its suitability for both VL and VN models. However, when the

group met on 14 October 1983, doubt was expressed whether the Nissan unit was a prudent choice for VN. While it was evident that it had ample power for both models, there were serious marketing reservations.

'Surely if we tell the public we have a much larger car, they will expect it to have a bigger engine', said the marketing people. Joe Whitesell pointed out that new design techniques meant that the enlarged VN would still weigh virtually the same as the car it replaced and therefore the power-to-weight ratio would be the same. (Ultimately the weight difference was a mere 15 kg — little more than carrying a big tool kit in the boot.)

Coupled with this news was concern that Ford would almost certainly continue with an engine around 4.1 litres in the next Falcon. This would leave Commodore with a distinct marketing disadvantage, because a 3-litre engine sounds to be a lesser unit than a 4.1, regardless of its technical merits.

The engine size was not the only worrying factor. Word had reached Holden's that a recent Ford styling clinic had revealed that traditional Falcon and Holden buyers rejected the highly aerodynamic shape then coming from Europe (as exemplified by the Audi 100). A Holden director wondered aloud whether the same rejection would apply to VN. The point was important because the aging Australian population meant that conservative buyers (35 to 45 years of age, many with teenage children) would remain a strong force in the market, accounting perhaps for 80 000 new cars a year. VN expected to capture up to 20 000 of these sales plus a further 20 000 from other buyer groups. This would happen only if the VN was perceived to be 'right' in appearance as well as size and specifications.

Not only was the Opel version of the proposed car more narrow than Falcon, its rounded lines made it appear to be even slimmer (and therefore less roomy) than it really was. The latest photographs of the prototype suggested it did not look substantially wider than the VL, whatever the actual dimensions.

Below and Previous Page:
Two 'Aero' Holden drawings done in 1984 provided some details which made their way into the final VN design.

A further concern came from an unexpected source. Nissan and Toyota were reported to be planning new entries into the six-cylinder market. If the reports were true, not only would the newcomers put further pressure on sales generally, but Holden's would be badly hurt if the proposed new Commodore proved to be less roomy than the Japanese sixes.

A top-level meeting was held on 17 November 1983 to hear the latest cost figures. An additional investment of $30 million would be required to fully manufacture the Opel vehicle locally, compared with Holden's developing a composite version using the Opel body and local components.

Once again, the question of body width dominated the meeting. A comparison chart was displayed showing key dimensions of the current Commodore and the proposed VL, along with those of the front-wheel drive GM70, which was substantially longer than the proposed Commodore. The possibility of redesigning the existing Commodore once again came into calculations.

But by February 1984 the strategic planning group had come to terms with some important facts: there was inherent danger in going it alone on a new car program, not just because of the costly technology involved, but because they would not be able to pick up changes from Opel if significant market shifts should occur.

At the same meeting, the company decided to investigate the space frame concept of body construction — a technique planned by the parent company for building several models then on the drawing boards. Essentially this involves constructing a steel framework and fixing to it panels made from plastic or other materials. This type of construction offered reduced cost, increased styling flexibility, improved panel fit, reduced corrosion and better resistance to minor parking damage.

After some study by the engineering and manufacturing departments, the committee decided it was premature to consider this technique for VN but that Holden's should stay in touch with developments for possible use in later models.

While the design and manufacturing departments explored the technology involved, the marketing group came up with some major recommendations. One was that VN should seat three adults in comfort in the rear seat

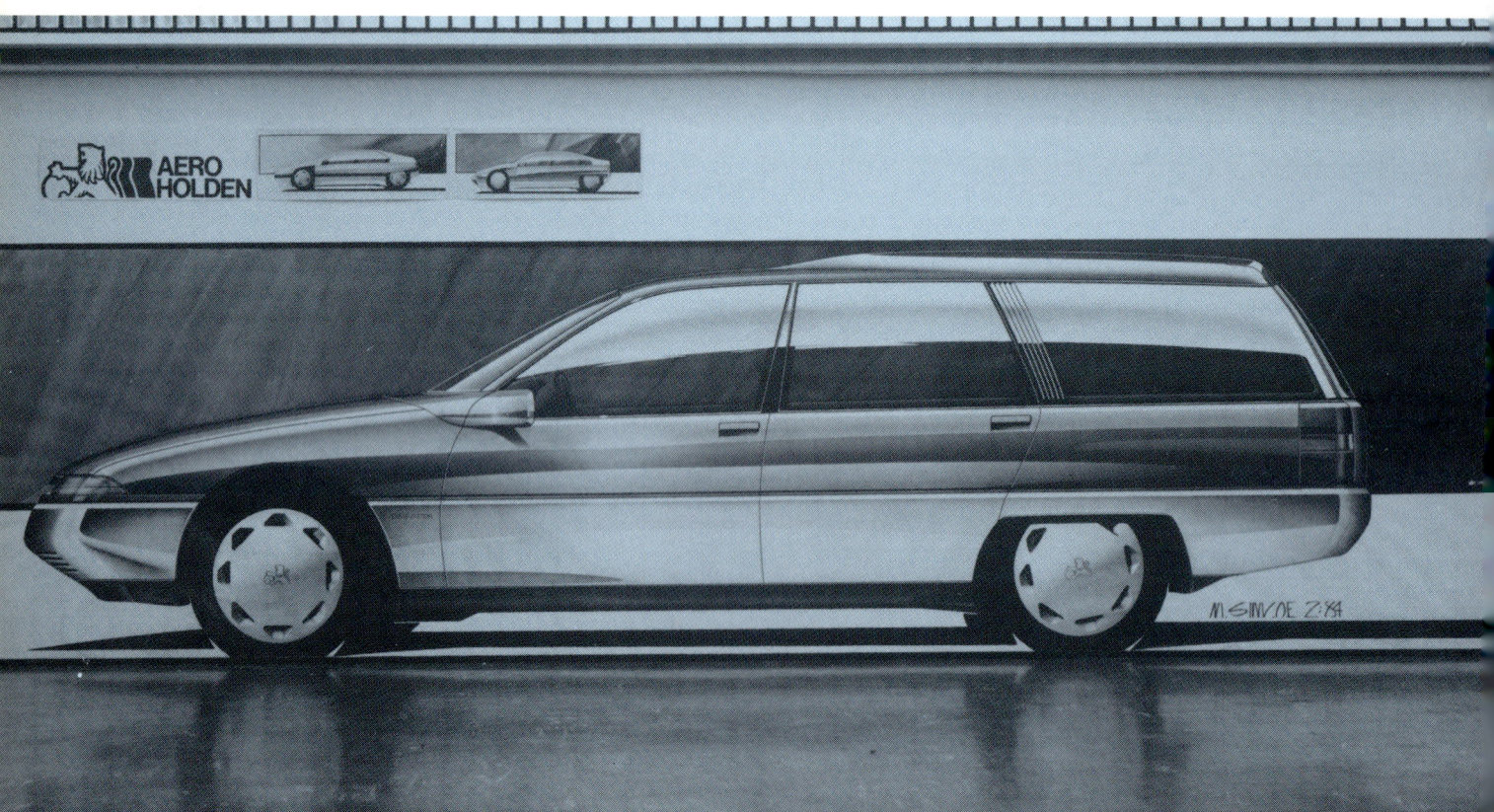

22

*Above and overleaf:
These full-sized 'tape' drawings of a car with a VL floor pan and an Opel-based body shell formed the basis of the first serious full-size VN clay model. The combination of an aggressive frontal treatment and a soft side appearance later gave way to an integrated form.*

and that the wagon variant should have a longer wheelbase than the sedan to provide a bigger 'black box'. In automotive language, a black box is like a large coffin, being the largest rectangular shape which can be pushed into the car from the back while still allowing the tailgate to be closed. The marketing department argued that the existing Commodore suffered in comparison with Falcon's interior space and this had allowed Ford to capture 63 per cent of the six-cylinder wagon market.

Although the proposed Opel-based station wagon had a good black box capacity, the marketing department felt it could not take the type of objects which Australians like to put into their cars. They therefore urged strongly that the VN wagon should be stretched to make it more directly competitive with Falcon.

Simple though it sounds, this idea created another problem. When a mock-up of the extended shape was made, it looked terrible.

'Our directors walked around the mock-up and said it would make a very good hearse', recalls Roger Gibbs.

'They were right and our design staff had to restyle the entire rear end so we could have a stylish appearance as well as the length we needed.'

Another difficulty was marketing's continuing recommendation that the engine should have a higher displacement than 3 litres. If Holden's presented a bigger car and did not change the engine size, they argued, potential customers would face a psychological barrier no matter how good the engine technology. After intensive discussion about possible power plants, the committee decided to review all forthcoming engines from the USA for possible use in the VN Commodore.

Despite the amount of work already done, the whole program was still in the melting pot. To help clarify matters, the planning department reiterated the three proposals for the Strategy Committee to study.

One was to reskin the VL, maintaining the same package size. Another was to develop a composite vehicle, using VL carry-over mechanicals and a widened Opel body. The third was to completely follow Opel's program apart from the power train.

It was much easier to decide how many variations on the basic body shape should be made. At the time (early 1984), sedans accounted for 76 per cent of new sales in this market segment. Station wagons came next (21.4 per cent), followed by coupes (2.2 per cent) and five-door hatchbacks (.04 per cent). The marketing people told the committee that they expected the trend to more aerodynamic shapes and folding rear seats to continue. However, the demand for six-cylinder wagons had fallen and was continuing to fall.

Since 1978, sales of large wagons had dropped at twice the rate of similar-sized sedans, mainly because of the growing popularity of forward control multiseat wagons — a factor which remained a continuing worry.

However, there was no question about the public's preference for spacious cars. A market research study revealed that 23 per cent of people who bought Falcon (and its stablemate Fairmont) chose the car because of its superior interior room or perceived riding comfort.

In March 1984, the finance group provided an investment update which showed that, by increasing the engineering expenditure to allow additional local design content, substantial savings would be made in the total tooling bill. Potentially, some $24 million would be saved and, more importantly, this approach gave the company greater flexibility to widen the body and extend the wheelbase of the station wagon.

Widening the body was a huge additional engineering burden and Chuck Chapman demanded convincing proof that it was necessary. The first step came on 8 March 1984 when the product strategy group met to review two clay models. One followed the Opel design with the six-window roof style. The other was a similar design, widened to provide the interior package dimensions of a Falcon with revised rear styling to emphasise the extra width. Seating bucks were provided so the group could assess the actual knee room, elbow room and shoulder width of each concept.

'Our design staff did a very good job and modelled up a buck which could represent both the original Opel design and a wider version', says Roger Gibbs.

'You can only judge roominess in the rear if you have the front seats in place with the instrument panel console and the roof properly installed.

'The exercise showed that the perception of a buck's roominess depends very much on the proportions of those who sit in them.

'Tall and well-built people had a satisfactory degree of shoulder comfort in the buck with Opel dimensions but were troubled by the proximity of the roof rail. This meant that the hip and eye room dimensions were really as important as the shoulder room in achieving perceived roominess.'

The seating buck had variable leg room and sides which could be moved in and out. It was also possible to adjust the location of the inner rear

wheel housing because this affects the flatness of the rear seat which is yet another factor in actual and perceived comfort.

'I guess we were fortunate in having directors built in assorted shapes and sizes', says Roger Gibbs.

'Hopefully, they represent the 98 percentile [an industry expression for size variations which accommodate 98 per cent of all adults]. John Loveridge, who was then Marketing Director, is very tall and we had Woody Leathley who is fairly short while Joe Whitesell has an ample girth.

'Less than one quarter of the key people who tried the bucks found in favour of the Opel width so we quickly agreed on the merits of the wheelbase, wheel housing position and body width.

'But once this was done, the Managing Director said: "That's all very well, but the buck is static. You would get a different perception if it was moving" '.

In response, Noel Bedford and Doug Mennie made a fibreglass mould from the buck in its wide position and created a shell which was built into a Falcon. The shell was trimmed to represent a real car and provided an interior width greater than Opel's version.

And so it was that at 8.30 am on a Saturday in July 1984, nine directors, four drivers and two observers assembled outside Holden's Fishermans Bend plant. They stepped into the modified Falcon, a standard Falcon sedan and the current VK Commodore. During an 80 km journey, the directors took turns sitting in the back of each car, occupying each of three possible seating positions for comparative purposes. An hour-long debriefing session followed the run and the nine directors allocated points on various comfort criteria. When totted up, these points indicated that the proposed VN buck was equal or superior to the current Falcon in all respects of interior seat room and comfort.

Above and opposite:
Opel developed the Omega (and Senator derivative) to replace the Rekord, on which the VB Holden Commodore had been based. The Omega was well received and gained the European 'Car of The Year' award. Although some Opel technology was incorporated in the 1988 Holden, the VN was eventually to differ in styling, dimensions, drive train and interior layout.

The unusual test also showed that the intrusion of the wheel house, and its effect on the seat back, is more critical than shoulder room in establishing satisfactory comfort for three passengers in the rear seat. The one disappointment was that Falcon had greater perceived headroom, and this was something to work on.

'We had an unexpected spin-off', says Tony Hope who drove the Falcon buck.

'I don't think our directors have sat in the rear seat very often, because they all complained their knees were hitting the window winders. It was decided to reposition them for all future Holden models!'

Roger Gibbs added: 'The mobile buck also gave us what we were looking for: the evidence needed to proceed with the costly exercise of widening the Opel body'.

'It told us, for example, that it was not necessary to widen the prototype by a full 28 mm to achieve the shoulder comfort we wanted, but it was necessary to ensure the occupant's eyes are sufficiently far from the body sides to convey a feeling of spaciousness.

'At the time, the proposed VN was 28 mm wider than the Opel but soon we received specific information on how the trim would be designed. When the trim creeps up in thickness, you start to lose the feeling of spaciousness as well. It was not until February 1985 that we had a final meeting on the subject and confirmed that the VN would actually be 38 mm wider than the forthcoming Opel.

'The exact width was becoming critical. Many dealers were aware of the basic VN proposals by this time, and some had expressed caution against widening it too much. It was therefore essential that we did not make it any larger than it had to be.'

While the car's exact size was being decided, considerable thought was given to the engine. The marketing department continued to stress the need for a bigger engine, especially as word had arrived that Ford was considering a 3.8-litre V-6 or a 4.1-litre overhead cam straight six for the forthcoming Falcon.

A meeting in April 1984 agreed that Nissan should be asked to provide details of any future plans for its 3-litre six and, in particular, to advise if a larger version was to become available. Nissan replied that the matter would be considered but the existing unit could only be increased by a nominal amount.

Apart from the engine, the VN concept was beginning to crystalise. At a meeting held in June 1984, the latest forecasts indicated that the direct tooling investment could be reduced by $30 million by producing a local adaptation of the Opel design and that such a program would be $39 million less than adopting the GM70 front-wheel drive model.

In July that year, Holden's directors agreed that work should proceed on the composite VN using a wider body than Opel's and a station wagon wheelbase extended by 91 mm. They also asked the Design department to implement styling changes which would further improve the car's perceived width. Those changes were to be submitted to a styling clinic scheduled for three months later.

Meanwhile, a different group — the Product Policy Committee — was considering a proposal that the station wagon should have a third seat to make it more competitive with the growing number of forward control wagons on sale. Several mock-ups of the three-seat wagon were built but the idea was eventually rejected. The designers found too many compromises were needed, affecting the leg room and ease of entry and exit.

It was not hard to reach a decision of a different kind. Opel intended having the complete instrument module assembled outside the car and glued into place as a structural member. The more the Holden people studied the idea, the more they liked it. The unusual technique would reduce the faults which sometimes arise during assembly because of the need to work in a restricted area behind the panel.

The original seating buck which Holden executives used to assess the extra comfort provided by the additional body width.

The styling clinic was held in October 1984 in Melbourne. A total of 800 people were invited to inspect eight different shapes including clay models of the proposed Commodore VL and VN designs and a Cadillac C car which had just been released in the USA. The Cadillac and the two clay models carried no form of identification. The other five exhibits were local sedans (including the current Commodore) carrying the normal badgewear but no insignia to indicate the engine size or equipment level. Selected because they were potential buyers in the Falcon/Commodore market segment, the participants were asked to record their preferences for a number of criteria or otherwise express a reaction to each car. They did not know who was conducting the clinic, so brand loyalty did not affect their thinking.

The VN scored well in some areas and was recognised as looking modern, even sporty, but the reactions were polarised. The results suggested that the design appealed to younger buyers but did not sufficiently penetrate its principal target market: middle-aged married couples with children. The design emerged with three shortcomings. The rear view found little favour, the interior was judged (from outside) as not being equal to Falcon's and some respondents felt that Falcon would be more costly to buy because its 'square' design made it appear to be larger. Holden's design staff then set about modifying the rear appearance to increase the perceived size without altering the sheet metal contours.

By now, Holden's had virtually finalised the VN design. There remained only one hurdle — the parent company had to approve the necessary capital investment.

THE GRIGG PRESENTATION

On 23 January 1985, Ray Grigg went to Detroit to present the proposed Holden VN program to a group of 25 top GM executives. Each man present was a Group Vice-President or Vice-President of General Motors and, collectively, they represented the highest-powered committee that the Corporation could muster. Among those present were Chairman, Roger Smith, Chief Operating Officer, F.J. McDonald, the now current President, Robert Stempel, and J.F. Waters, Vice-President and Group Executive of General Motors Overseas Corporation, Holden's direct parent company.

'This type of operation requires a professional and polished presentation, using immaculate 35 mm slides which lay out the key points as they are being explained', says Ray Grigg.

'I had been in Detroit a week or so earlier, going through the program with various department heads. One, the very able Howard Kehrl, had grave reservations about the project. He could not see why it was necessary for us to widen the Opel car. I had to go over the reasons point by point and I decided to make some last-minute changes to the official presentation

The 3-litre straight six engine fitted to the VL Commodore/Calais [below] once looked certain to be used in the VN. At one stage parallel development programs were being run with VN prototypes being powered by the straight six and the 3800 V-6.

to explain more fully the areas where Mr Kehrl had reservations. I sent this information back to Roger Gibbs in Melbourne for clarification and to have the necessary slides prepared in a great rush.'

Roger Gibbs says the next two days were frantic.

'We got to the point where agreement was reached on the revised written material', he said, 'but new photographic slides had to be prepared and despatched by air courier by next morning. No slides — no presentation!

'I was madly trying to work out how to meet the deadline when Rob McEniry (now Director of Marketing) told me his advertising agency could work overnight. I put my life in his hands and gave him my scripts. Next morning I received a box of the best slides I've ever seen, with beautiful computer-generated characters on pale blue backgrounds. Ray was delighted. The catch came three weeks later when Rob handed me a bill for $2000 covering the photographic work.'

Top:
Let the people decide! Many of those attending the first styling clinic, in 1984, preferred the crisp-edge styling of the then current Holden and Falcon to the soft form of the VN. This clinic included a Mitsubishi Galant Sigma, the basis of the 1985 Magna. The windows of the production cars were covered so that the VN clay model could be fairly compared.

Above:
When the square rear of the VN wagon was first produced in clay, there was concern that the resulting vehicle would be more popular with undertakers than the general public. A softer back was developed to give a more attractive and integrated appearance.

Meanwhile, back in Detroit, Ray Grigg was about to face the most decisive meeting he had ever attended. Three months earlier he had addressed a similar group in Detroit and outlined the key elements of Holden's new business strategy. This comprised several possible scenarios including joint-venture manufacturing, product sharing and maximising export credits. The Commodore 88V had been mentioned at that meeting but now Ray was about to spell out the details and seek formal approval for the Australian subsidiary to proceed. He knew it would not be easy and the outcome was crucial to Holden's future.

The meeting started at 8.00 am in GM's Technical Centre in Warren, Michigan. Several important matters were on the agenda ahead of the Holden presentation and, as a Corporation Vice-President, Chuck Chapman was present for the whole meeting. Ray, however, was asked to wait in an anteroom until they were ready for him.

For the best part of an hour he sat and nervously waited.

'I felt better', he recalls, 'when Alex Mair (Group Vice-President) stepped out of the meeting and told me not to worry: everything would be fine. Once I got the call to take the podium, I took a deep breath and went for it. You don't want to make a mistake before the likes of Roger Smith, but fortunately everything went fine.'

The presentation included all facets of the proposed VN program, with a detailed analysis of the state of the market, the impact of the latest government car industry plans, alternative designs for the forthcoming Commodore, engineering concepts, targets and proposed dates. The key factors not ready at the time were the precise additional body width and the recommended power train. The presentation said that the extra width would be at least 28 mm and that various local power trains were being studied. Ray said that, initially, the engine would be imported from Japan but a local engine would be introduced during the model life.

He concluded by recommending that the 1988 Commodore should be defined as a wider Opel V-car adapted to 1986 Holden VL carry-over components. The next speaker, the Corporation's financial analyst, Pat Campbell, reviewed the budgetary implications. Ten minutes of questions followed, then Roger Smith looked around the table for possible objections. There were none, so he nodded that the Holden VN project was approved.

Chuck Chapman and Ray Grigg then left the room and heartily shook hands and made for the airport.

'I was so tired by then, I was asleep before the plane reached the runway', Ray recalls.

A few days later the formal notes of the meeting were faxed to Melbourne and the new Holden was officially on its way. On 18 March 1985, Chuck Chapman wrote to Mr Waters advising that the increase in body width had been finalised at 38 mm and that some styling changes had been made in response to criticism received at the model clinic.

Holden's new model program was now up and running, but there was still room for refinement. In September that year, the Product Policy Committee agreed that the instrument panel should be redesigned and the original plan to offer an optional front bench seat should be reconsidered.

In Oct 1985, Ray Grigg was promoted to new responsibilities as Director of Quality Control; Roger Gibbs, who had been Manager of Product Planning, took his place. Roger took up the job at a time of near crisis for the VN program. On 4 Oct 1985, the full product policy group, with Chuck Chapman in the chair, agreed to make a radical departure from the Opel design. They decided in favour of having a local flush glass design in place of the Opel flush glass currently in the program. Several factors contributed to the decision. The original concept was costly, needing an additional investment of about $15 million and adding $56 to the price of each car. Of greater concern was the possibility of water and dust leaks because of the critical assembly methods required.

Discussions on an alternative design were held with the German supplier who had worked with Opel on its system. However Holden body engineers came up with their own design which preserved the flush glass appearance but proved more suitable for Australian operating conditions.

This design added a 1 mm thick frame to the window and the program was accomplished to everyone's satisfaction in the remarkable time of 24 months in order to meet the first pilot build of vehicles. After tests, the new system was judged to be far superior to the European concept for Australian conditions.

On 8 Nov 1985, the product group agreed to drop the bench seat option from the program because of the limited demand. Market forecasts put potential sales at less than 2000 units a year, a volume which could not support the substantial changes needed to the transmission shaft, steering column and handbrake location.

THE VN ENGINE

In May 1984, Senator John Button, on behalf of the Australian federal government, unveiled a new plan which he claimed would make the local motor industry more competitive with overseas companies by 1992. A basic tenet of the plan was that the five local car-makers should share major components and models and thus benefit from increased volumes.

After studying the plan in detail, Holden's concluded it would make sense to reintroduce a local six-cylinder engine so as to maximise its use of export credits to import fully built-up vehicles duty-free. Export credits are offsets which allow a company to import components or complete cars without paying the usual duty, in return for exporting Australian-made goods of equal value.

Holden's had several options. One was to update the aging 3.3-litre EFI Holden 'six' which was slated to be replaced by Nissan's more modern 3-litre design in 1986. The thought was to make the 3.3 suitable for unleaded fuel and develop more power by converting it to a cam-in-head design with a cross-flow cylinder head. The capacity would be increased to 3.4 litres and hydraulic engine mountings and low-friction piston rings fitted. A redesigned crankshaft with improved torsional stiffness would improve the noise and vibration characteristics.

The study showed that these changes would cost $61 million in capital funds and would produce an engine with minimum scope for further upgrading. However, the cost study served as a valuable base line from which to judge other engine proposals.

Another possibility was to introduce a 3-litre, six-cylinder version of the existing Family II four-cylinder engine fitted to Camira and slated for use in the 1987 Holden Astra and Nissan Pulsar. The company also approached Nissan with a view to the joint-venture manufacture of Nissan's straight six power plant in Melbourne. The joint-venture study continued for 12 months without resolution and was dropped.

In parallel with it was the promising idea of creating a 3.8-litre V-6 from the existing Holden V-8. Work started on this concept in October 1984 and it seemed probable that the V-6 could be in production one year earlier than a revised version of the straight six. (Four experimental V-6s were built from Holden's V-8 before the project was dropped in favour of the more modern engine eventually used.)

At this point, the company still had not received confirmation from Nissan whether or not a 3.3-litre version of its straight six would become available. Nissan had, however, expressed reservations about designing an engine solely for Australia and the project was becoming increasingly unlikely. By September 1985, it was clear that, whatever the decision, an enlarged Nissan engine would not be ready for VN's launch. Negotiations ceased soon afterwards.

Meanwhile, several departments were keeping tabs on overseas engines which might be available for VN. Geoffrey Chamberlain, Alistair McKinnon and Alan Jones were among several Holden's people exploring the world's shopping list for suitable engines. Although they knew that GM had several very modern designs on the way, they were wary of getting excited about any of them before final Corporate budgetary approval had been given. Experience showed that only one third of all promising GM engine concepts actually reached production. Roger Gibbs happened to be

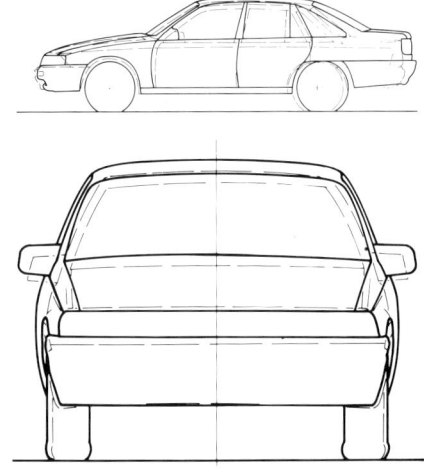

Greater body width and increased passenger room compared with the previous Commodore was considered essential. The broken lines represent the VL, the heavy lines the larger VN.

31

in Detroit when news arrived that final approval had been given to a V-6 being developed for BOC (Buick-Oldsmobile-Cadillac). This unit was just the right size for Australia but, unfortunately, it seemed improbable that it could be ready in time for the VN launch.

The alternative was to announce the new car with the existing Nissan 3-litre engine and follow with an updated version a year or so later when the BOC V-6 was ready. This idea did not sit well with the marketing people who argued strongly that a bigger engine was needed from the word go. Their reasoning was sound. The initial reaction to an all-new car is crucial to its long-term success. Accepting this reasoning, the Product Strategy Committee decided to pull out all stops to get the new V-6 ready as quickly as possible.

The 3.8-litre BOC engine became a serious prospect for VN in February 1986 when Holden engineers completed an in-depth review of the engine. To expedite possible production in Melbourne, Holden's sent key manufacturing and engineering people to Detroit to work with their BOC counterparts. In March 1986, financial and materials people went as well. Things were looking good by April, but Chuck Chapman insisted that he could make no commmitment to use the V-6 until it had been evaluated in an actual vehicle.

Finally, on 18 June 1986, Chuck (a skilled professional engineer) and Don Wylie (by now Director of Engineering and Design) went to GM's proving ground in Detroit to drive a Buick fitted with the new V-6 engine. To provide a realistic comparison, a Nissan-engined VL was flown to Detroit and tested back-to-back with the V-6. Chuck and Don were delighted with the BOC unit and agreed that it offered significant customer benefits.

One month later, the V-6 was confirmed in the local program with production scheduled to start in March 1989. This meant that the initial VNs would have to use Nissan engines and that the V-6 Commodore would follow as a major revision. One factor which made it very difficult to bring the engine forward was the reduced lead time available for matching the engine with the GM Turbohydramatic 700 automatic transmission needed to handle the high torque output. Extraordinary assistance would be needed from the Hydramatic Division who were already in the middle of an extremely busy program for another GM affiliate.

Despite the engineering problems, the marketing department again argued strongly against the proposal to launch VN with the 3-litre engine. Although a detailed study was made, there seemed no way that the engineering program could be advanced in time using the present staff and equipment. March 1989 was again confirmed as the launch date for the V-6 model.

Marketing went directly to Chuck Chapman with a plea that a full-scale attempt be made to advance the V-6 program. He agreed, and all departments urgently reviewed their targets. Engineering found that the development program could be shortened only by using electronic CAD/CAM technology and computer graphics to accelerate the design and production of test components. The additional work cost an extra $3.26 million but was judged to be worthwhile.

Chuck Chapman meanwhile had obtained a commitment from the parent company that maximum assistance would be given to ensure that Holden achieved the new deadline. To be safe, however, the company started a parallel development of VN prototypes fitted with both Nissan straight six and BOC V-6 engines.

Finally, on 24 June 1987, a gruelling test program at Holden's proving grounds at Lang Lang, Victoria, convinced the directors that the the V-6 was everything they had expected and that production models would be ready on time for the VN launch. Instructions were given to cease work on the Nissan-engined prototypes.

The first Holden V-6 model ever was about to become a reality. It would be a car that was truly Holden, offering an engineering and interior package unlike any other GM car in the world and a body which, although developed from another, would be as distinctive in appearance as it was in dimensions.

Roger Gibbs

Like several other senior Holden people, Roger Gibbs comes from a Holden background. His father, Bill Gibbs, is a former GM-H managing director; his elder brother, Peter, is Manager of Direct Purchasing for power train and materials. Roger joined Holden's after graduating from Melbourne University in 1964 with first-class honours in mechanical engineering. After some years, he went to England and worked at Vauxhall Motors, mainly on chassis and transmission design. From there, he went to GM's Technical Centre in Detroit, a period he recalls as the most technologically interesting in his life. Among other things, he became involved in applying the newly developed Computer System Modelling Program to reach solutions of complex equations of motion, simulating the total power train and vehicle dynamics. As early as 1972 this system was used to determine why a particular vehicle suffered from clutch shudder and where the optimum solution lay.

After two years at the Technical Centre, Roger returned to Holden's transmission design section. With more experience under his belt, he went to Stanford University to undertake a Master of Science Degree management. He returned to Holden's as Assistant Experimental Engineer, subsequently became Electrical Engineer and then moved into the Planning Department just in time for the VN program. He is now Executive in Charge of Product Planning.

'In this job, I act as cook to stir the broth made up from all the experts in the company', he says.

'With any new model program, the finance men want the minimum level of investment, the marketing people look for every possible selling feature, the engineers want the latest in technology, the manufacturing group like to keep things simple and the materials management department is worried about the ability of vendors to supply our needs.

'Together they make up a fairly vocal and aggressive group; each has strong opinions and makes no apologies for them. These talented people must be welded together to make a working program.'

It must be seen to be big
... the design story

To a design team which thrives on excitement, the VN project was the biggest bonus of the 1980s.

Not since the HQ series of 1971 had Holden Design had the opportunity to shape a completely new family car and see it through to completion. And never had it been presented with the myriad of challenges involved in designing a world-class car for the 1990s.

The VN was just the project to inspire the people from the department where art, engineering and big business meet. To these people, morale is as important as in an army or Grand Final football team — and there is no fillip like a 'ground up' new car.

The demands placed upon car designers are varied and complex. Their handywork must project all the qualities expected by the buyer while meeting thousands of other factors determined by mechanical, safety, financial and marketing considerations. A new car has to be adaptable to varying levels of specification, future facelifts, new technology and mechanical changes. Most importantly, the public must see it as fresh and exciting. Those intangible, indefinable qualities that make a shape appealing to the eye are absolutely critical to the newcomer's success.

There are 25 people in Holden Design, using six studios, several computers, a wealth of electronic equipment and, of course, pencils and sketchpads. It is a young team and a small one at that, especially in view of the way the department is constantly juggling several projects at once, working at times ten years ahead.

Although surrounded by expensive technical aids, the Design people fully realise that their success depends on their ability to work harmoniously as a team and to originate fresh, original and saleable ideas.

The Executive in Charge of Design is Phil Zmood, one of the company's many young recruits of the 1960s. In the early 1980s when Phil was promoted to the top job (following the return of Leo Pruneau to the USA) it was a time of 'go, go, go', with the VL Commodore and the smaller JD Camira requiring immediate attention and the VN already in sight.

The design of the VL Commodore had been settled earlier but, in Phil's words, 'Management sprung on us the fact that the planned facelift was to be revised'.

'It was clear that it would be some time before we could bring out a totally new car', remembered Phil, 'but we had to overcome certain marketing issues, most notably the belief there had not been enough change since the first Commodore was released in late 1978'.

'We set about broadening the car's appeal with a larger, more aggressive appearance and a more spacious-looking interior. At the same time we

The VN front and rear design treatments were developed after hundreds of sketches had been made and many models built.

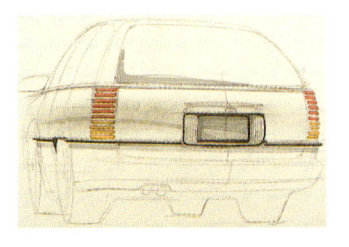

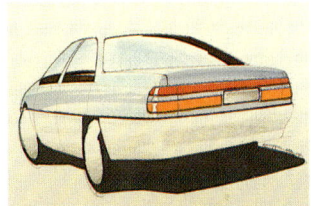

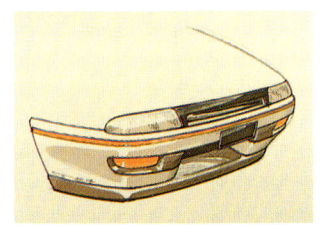

were busily studying the brief for a totally new replacement called 2158 or VN.'

The start of the VN project coincided with a new way of thinking at Holden's, one which would affect the final appearance of the VN and every aspect of its design.

The world car concept which shaped the original Commodore was no longer to be the guiding force. Hard-earned experience had shown that certain requirements of the Australian buyer — such as sufficient width for three people across the rear seat — would weather fuel crises and any other setbacks. And, in the designer's equivalent of the maxim that 'justice must be seen to be done', it is not enough to just make a car that is big. A car must be 'seen to be big'.

Holden's needed a car which was not only as spacious as the enormously successful HQ-HZ series but which would be perceived as such by the public. (By way of example, Holden's market research on the Astra 1.8 had shown that most people believe the sedan version to be an all-over bigger car than the hatchback. In fact, the wheelbase and interior room are identical.)

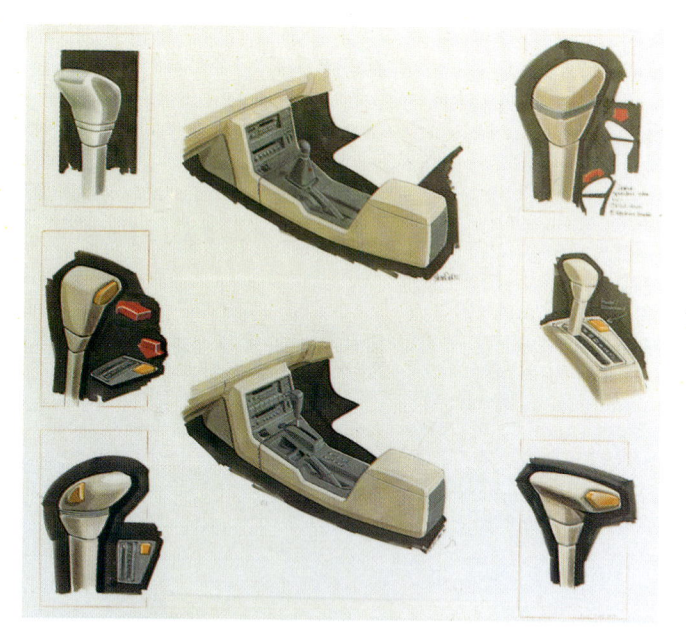

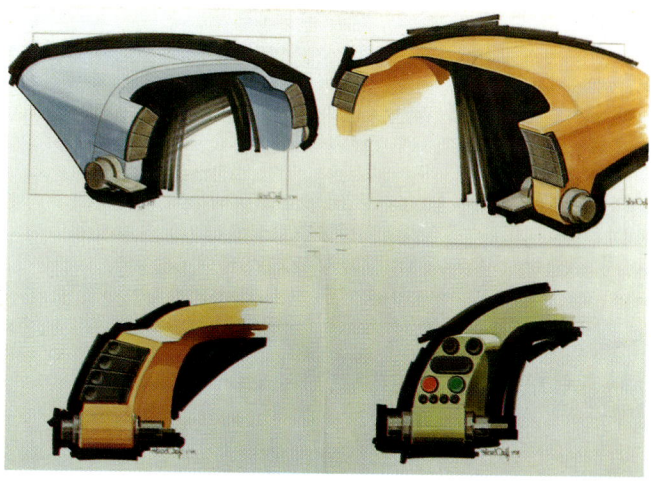

As with the exterior, every aspect of the VN interior was the subject of intense design work and a large number of evolutionary changes.

The changes in Holden's own set-up and in the new car market put a greater-than-ever emphasis on quality and efficiency. Although the VN was to be, to a certain extent, a sum of diverse parts, it needed a totally integrated form, executed with full regard for the people who had to engineer and build it.

The future of Holden's depended on the company's ability to compete against the world's best car-makers in the deregulated market of the 1990s. For Holden Design, the VN was the challenge of a lifetime...

Below Right:
The design team worked hard to 'soften' the rear appearance of the wagon while maintaining the required cargo capacity. Note the Camira-style tailgate/bumper arrangement on this early mock-up.

THE EXTERIOR

The VN started life in Design in the early 1980s, long before there was a formal request for work to begin. Such ideas as a J-car/Camira-based Commodore and a widened VL were floated and sketches and studies done. By constantly throwing ideas around, Holden Design produces a steady stream of innovations and builds upon a house style which permeates through all its work.

'When the firm request for VN was received in October 1983', Phil recalled, 'we gathered the design team, that is the key players from each discipline, discussed the brief, worked out a timetable and considered various concepts'.

The team members reviewed their sketches in the light of the latest information, sketched out some new ideas and made a selection to present to management as the suggested direction.

Their sketches were stylish, innovative and often extreme. What emerged from them was a clear trend toward soft aerodynamic shapes.

'The team was really firing by this point', says Phil. 'Everybody was working closely and giving their all. We were absolutely determined to break down any suggestion that Australian designers are staid.'

In his present executive position, the only sketches Phil gets time to do are quick thumbnail jobs, usually to suggest a new approach or direction.

Above left:
The first outdoor review of the emerging VN took place in June 1984. This raw clay mock-up, based on the early 'tape' drawings, is of the narrow car in Calais form, with semiconcealed headlights. Note the 'blister' above the front wheel arch and the rounded rear wheel cut-out. The decision had already been made to go for the 'straight-through' cut-out, as this accentuated the length, but the rounded opening was mocked up on one side of the car for review purposes.

Below:
Ted Schroeder, Phil Zmood and Joe Whitesell (left to right) inspect a clay model of the widened car at the outdoor design studio in July 1984. By this time, the basic profile was pretty well established. There were two schools of thought on the front indicator placement but it was eventually decided that the wraparound bumper-mounted units were too vulnerable and too expensive.

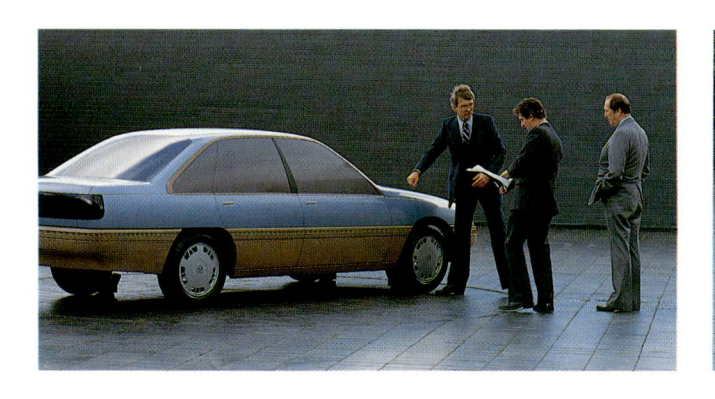

37

Above left:
One of a designer's many short cuts is seen here. Only half of this early front treatment has been completed but a mirror gives the full effect. By this time the front was close to its final appearance but the bonnet was still too high.

Above right:
In 1984 the Audi 100 was the only car on the Australian market with a resemblence to the VN's 'aero' character. Here the VN is placed next to an Audi for a management review. The Audi was a radical departure from the designs Australians were used to, so it is not surprising that some Holden executives were nervous about taking the theme still further.

He operates as something between a manager and catalyst. Often his task is not to spur on the design team, but to exercise restraint after 'letting them go'.

'When everybody lets their creative ideas out', Phil says, 'we often need to pull them back to get an appropriate commercial design'.

As the early VN sketching progressed, engineering package drawings were being done and the modelling team prepared armatures (metal and wooden frames) for full-size clay models.

Engineering package drawings are layout diagrams, used to make sure the new body will wrap around the planned mechanical components and provide the desired interior space. Once the known points are plotted, tape drawings are made.

These drawings, which are full-size, two-dimensional profiles, use thin black tape for their outlines and are 'fleshed out' with coloured spray paint. They show the proposed exterior design as seen from the front, side and rear. Changes to a line or curve are easily made and the designers can evaluate different ideas in actual size. Tape drawings are the last stage before a full-scale clay model is made.

By this stage, GM Corporation in the USA and Opel in Germany had been developing new-generation family cars for about a year. Both designs were available to the Australian company if required.

'In terms of the body', said Phil, 'we decided to pick the best of what we had designed and, where specific high-cost technology was concerned, marry it with that available from overseas. The decision to use the flush glass, six-window Opel sedan as the base and carry over certain Holden features, components and design characteristics gave us the best of both worlds at a reasonable cost'.

After Phil and other Holden Design executives had inspected GM's overseas programs, a clay version of the Opel body was produced for review purposes. The first tape drawings officially presented to management consisted of a car with an Opel-based shell, a VL floor pan and a front with semiconcealed headlights.

These drawings were largely the work of Peter Nankervis, who was later to shape much of VN's interior. Although many details in these drawings were not used in the final product, Peter said they 'showed pretty much the way Design was going'.

'We were aiming at an aerodynamic form which was distinctive and had a functional elegance. We were also shifting the emphasis down onto the bumpers and grille, rather like in the old bigger Ferraris.'

The VL Calais-style front used in this proposal was one of dozens of ideas considered but never taken up. Sometimes it is Design which rejects an idea, sometimes Management. If an idea gets further than this, there could still be objections from Finance, Marketing, Manufacturing or the parent company.

Nevertheless, for the VN project, Holden Design was given more autonomy than ever before, something Phil puts down to corporate confidence in the team's ability to produce what is appropriate for the unique local market.

In the case of the semiconcealed headlight front, Phil says both Design and local management decided against that direction.

'We thought it looked a little contrived. We needed an integrated design which only carried over characteristics from previous models where appropriate.'

Although several other front design proposals were considered, the rear profile of the car did not change much after the first tape drawings. The decision to produce a wider car than the Opel had Design staff experimenting with various additional widths. Even with an extra 38 mm spliced into the middle, there were problems.

'From the rear, the full-size model looked about the same width as a Camira!' said Phil. 'The problem was that we were going from crisp edge design to a soft aerodynamic form.'

Phil says that 'knocking the edges' off a shape can make it look smaller.

'Take the the HQ Holden and XA Falcon of the early 1970s. The Holden is rounded but the Ford is squarish. Although dimensionally they are about the same, the Ford looks like a much bigger car.'

Producing a soft shape with the desired 'big car' appearance was one of the biggest challenges of the whole program. Design staff embarked on re-shaping the fenders, bonnet, facias (integral bumpers), quarter panels and boot lid but the car still didn't look as wide as the marketing brief requested. As a result, the team worked long and hard on detailing. Wrap-

Above left:
The proposed VN in early 1985. Although the rear shape did not change significantly, the graphic bands, which became so important in increasing the perceived width, were still being worked out.

Above right:
The VN was lined up against the Falcon on many occasions to compare the perceived sizes.

Below left:
A Calais proposal is 'di-noced' (covered in a plastic coating to give a painted appearance) by Modelling Manager Peter Churchill in April 1985.

Below right:
One of the many front proposals for the Calais incorporated an integrated bonnet/grille assembly and inset driving lights. To the annoyance of the security-conscious people in Holden Design, a blurry photo of this front end appeared in some motoring magazines in early 1987. Magazine artists grafted this grille to an Opel Omega/Senator-style body and decided they had established precisely what the VN would look like. Design staff had the last laugh.

39

Holden Design staff and their Berlina and Calais proposals in May 1985.

around graphic bands incorporating the tail-light and headlight assemblies became a major factor in reconciling the apparent size with the real dimensions.

'When you stand from the front or back', explains Phil, 'you read to where the graphic band finishes, not to the dead corner of the car. So your eye goes right around and gives a perception of a much wider car'.

This emphasis on the horizontal aspects of the car was in contrast to the European style adopted by Opel, which tended to follow the Mercedes tradition of focusing on vertical elements.

'We did everything possible to give a sleek, rounded breadth to the car', says Phil.

The new body was also required to have an appearance which would be considered modern and attractive by a wide cross-section of Australians from 1988 until well into the 1990s.

'Australian preferences still owe something to the US-styled cars that were popular in the 1960s', says Phil. 'But now they are more conditioned to European and Japanese-designed cars. We had to incorporate all these aspects with ruggedness, Aussie ingenuity and Holden flavour.'

'We needed a good simple shell which could evolve over the years, one which lent itself to evolution, not tacked on facelifts. In essence, we needed a total design to meet present and future requirements.'

Built on a longer wheelbase, the wagon became even more distinctively Australian than the sedan.

The European perception of wagons — they are considered more commercial vehicles than family cars — usually means the 'black box' area is the major consideration. When the squarish Opel back was grafted onto the widened, lengthened Holden, the 'black box' area was enormous but the design pleased nobody. Management authorised a rethink.

Below and opposite:
Before full-scale wind-tunnel testing was performed, a detailed scale model was tested at the Royal Melbourne Institute of Technology. The mini-VN had an accurately shaped undertray, with suspension, exhaust system and all mechanical components reproduced in wood. Past experience showed this technique can produce accurate results.

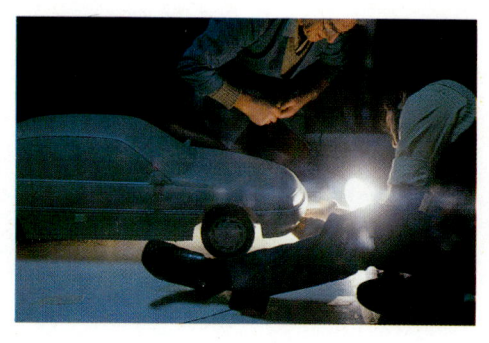

'There were no clinics needed', said Phil. 'Everyone agreed we should change the form to a softer, more integrated rear. We restyled it completely; we still have a massive cargo area but we also have a total vehicle rather than a sedan with a box on the back.'

From the early stages of design, the task of giving the emerging VN a third dimension went to Peter Churchill, Holden Design's Modelling Manager. The modelling staff first produced an armature then 'clayed it up' to represent the Opel design, which was then in its infancy. Then they started again and, as directed, modified everything except the doors and roofline.

During the 1980s, Holden Design has been using some of the world's most sophisticated computer equipment. Among other things, it enables them to 'copy' a model onto a floppy disc. A full-size model is scanned by a three-dimensional coordinate measuring machine which runs along the sides of the clay model on a massive steel bedplate. Equipped with electronic arms which measure points along each surface, the coordinate machine can scan a body panel and measure up to 120 points in three dimensions every minute and instantly convert the information into a digital form which the computer understands.

As other GM studios use the same system, Holden's is able to take a disc from another division and produce an exact facsimile in clay. With the VN, Holden's became the first GM division (and perhaps the first car-maker in the world) to do this. The method used to perform this reverse procedure was to start with a slightly oversize clay mock-up. The electronic arms were equipped with small drills (rather than the usual point-takers) and these made thousands of small, shallow holes in the clay model as directed by the information on the disc. When modellers scraped the clay back to the base of these holes, the team had a precise representation of the model produced overseas.

Using digital information, Design team members can use computer graphic facilities to view the actual lines and alter these on-screen. When on-screen editing is finished, and a 'prove-out model' is required to visually verify the results, the drilling method is again used. The system has a third advantage: when a model is finished, one side can be used as a master and this can be reversed electronically and drilled back onto the other side to make sure the model is symmetrical.

This 'digitising' technology replaces the slow and laborious post-and-beam scribing method of point-taking which once had technicians sliding 'arms' up and down poles manually and making thousands of separate manual readings. Digitising is also used to help design interior components.

Extremely difficult to design, wheels are most important to the final appearance. Here are some of the many VN proposals.

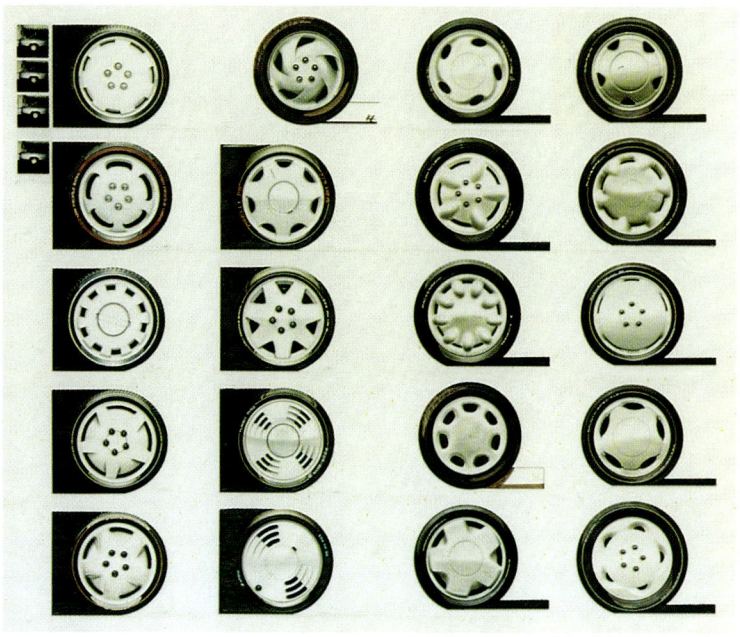

When a car is being produced in clay for the first time, the work is extremely painstaking. The VN took three months including 'Di-nocing', which involves applying a plastic coating to give the clay the appearance of painted metal. A general rule is that the squarer the shape, the easier the work.

'The VN was very much a modeller's challenge', says Peter Churchill.

'Being a much softer shape meant there were no intersections or sharp lines to work with. When something is crisp and sharp, you can work to an intersection then knock the radius off, but here you've got tapering radii and highlights running all the way. Every time you move one line, you have to change everything.'

The clay model is still an unwieldy object with a tendency to break up, though less so than in the old days.

'We try to keep the weight to about one to one-and-a-half tonnes', says Peter. 'You start with the tape drawings and usually allow for about 25 mm of clay all over. On some past models, we've had 100 mm of clay or more in some parts, such as when they decide to change the angle of the screen. You can be talking about a three to four tonne weight in such situations. Fortunately, we now get more precise design directions and work around a much tighter package.'

The modelling team does more than work to a plan when it builds a 'clay'. It transforms a two-dimensional idea into a three-dimensional shape and that is not a matter of following a recipe. Experience and gut-feel play a big part.

The modelling staff numbers ten, about half the number employed a decade ago.

'We work harder now', says Peter, 'but we also work smarter. There was a great deal of cross-reference with the VN; the modelling people examined the very early sketches and everybody in Design considered the production and engineering implications'.

When the development work was done on the VN 'clay', the next stage was to make a full-size fibreglass model. In the case of a facelift, the Modelling team could make the new panels out of fibreglass and bolt them to the previous model. This time, however, four people spent six months working on the full fibreglass model of the sedan, which had been moulded from the clay one.

Working the details into clay models is an exacting and time-consuming task.

42

The fibreglass model is lighter and considerably more durable. Most of all it has real windows, rather than painted ones, and a mock interior (behind non-opening doors). The 'see through' quality makes a big difference in styling clinics and management reviews. The fibreglass model was designed to be easily modified to demonstrate the appearance of SL, Berlina and Calais variants.

In addition to the European and Australian elements incorporated in the VN design, there is also a touch of America. Ted Schroeder, then Assistant Chief Designer at Buick, was brought to Holden's specifically to assist with the new project. Ted was responsible for much of the detail work after the basic shape was decided.

In the words of Peter Nankervis: 'Ted brought a lot of ideas from the USA with him, including a strong feel for soft form. He complemented the team perfectly'.

Though understandably biased, the people at Holden Design believe they have the best looking GM 'V' car yet seen. They say the extra width makes it more attractive and gives the appearance of extra stability. Because of the increased width, they have been able to dispense with the usual body-side blisters for the wheel arches, providing visual and aerodynamic advantages.

Summing up the exterior design Phil says:

'The front of the vehicle is a soft form aerodynamic statement with a traditional Holden family image.

Above left:
In October 1985 the proud team from Holden Design joined their creation at the Fishermans Bend open-air turntable. This was the final Berlina 'clay' and work on a lighter, more durable fibreglass model was about to begin.

Above right:
This 'fast-window' proposal for the wagon C-pillar would have made it possible to use the sedan rear door. Unfortunately, other problems arose, so an upright pillar was used.

Below left:
Building the full-size fibreglass model in late 1985. It was cast from the clay model.

Below right:
The use of CAD (computer-aided design) techniques in the modelling area.

Top:
The Calais front was one of the last exterior details to be settled, with the design team opting for a simple, fresh approach rather than the ornate treatment often associated with level-three models. This fibreglass model was modified to Calais specifications in early 1987.
Above:
This clay model of the sedan was mocked up as a proposed sports derivative in early 1987 for review purposes.

Following completion, the Berlina fibreglass model was transported to Lang Lang for an open-air review.

'The airflow is efficiently guided over and around the low and slim headlight/grille configuration and the majority of the engine cooling is channelled through the bumper opening.

'The steeply sloping windscreen and rear window give good visibility. The flush glazing reduces drag and allowed us to achieve the total shape we were striving for. The wide rear end is integral in appearance and contains a large boot with ample room for luggage even with an LP gas cylinder inside.'

Aerodynamics were an important factor in the design but not to the point of sacrificing other attributes. Stability and quietness at all speeds were considered more important than achieving a sensational coefficient of drag (Cd) figure.

'We have achieved a respectable Cd figure of 0.34 for the level one and level two models and an impressive 0.32 for the sports derivative', says Phil.

'The Opel, which is less wide, returns a slightly better Cd figure but we are extremely happy with our results.'

In the early stages of the Holden's design, wind-tunnel testing was done with scale models at the Royal Melbourne Institute of Technology (RMIT). Later a prototype was sent to GM in Warren, Michigan, for full-scale wind-tunnel testing.

As with all Holdens since the 1982 JB Camira, the VN makes substantial use of polypropylene. For 'soft form', polypropylene is one of a designer's best friends.

'It allows the use of a lot of shapes that would be too heavy and costly in steel, yet in applications like bumper bars it is just as strong', says Phil.

'There are other advantages. With the polypropylene integrated front valance panel and bumper approach, about two thirds of the front is bumper panel. This provides lots of scope for model differentiation, by using paint and tape and mouldings.'

Wheels too are important in establishing the identity of each model, says Phil.

'Attractive wheels are complicated and difficult to design because of the tight engineering parameters. We have worked hard to give our wheels a simple, soft organic look which relates to the form of the car, while still making them distinctive for each model line.'

There is a hint of concern about the reaction to the rear wheel cut-out, however. Most wheel openings seen in Australia are elliptical or rounded. In the early in-house styling clinics, the straight-through aero skirting was, in Phil's words, 'one of the things that some oldtimers in the company found hard to accept'.

'In the past', says Phil, 'some Holden people have been extremely conservative and not attuned to the fact that design sells products. But now there is more enthusiasm for the car end of the business than ever before. Everybody — in finance, marketing, manufacturing and so on — now realises the way to profitability is through having the right product, not by saving money and producing something that nobody wants'.

THE INSIDE STORY

Michael Simcoe is perhaps the only person in Holden Design who resembles the popular conception of an artist.

But his Dali moustache, small triangular beard and jewelled earrings are complemented by a sound professional knowledge and a flair for interior design that is commented on by everyone in the department. A self-confessed car nut, Mike is one of several graduates of the RMIT Industrial Design course who now work at Fishermans Bend. But before becoming Design Manager at Holden's he gained much of his experience working in England on helicopters.

After producing the early tape drawing 'themes' for the VN sedan and wagon exteriors, Mike moved to interiors and, given free rein, shaped a series of full-size foam mock-ups of instrument panels. Although these were too 'way out' for production, the object was to establish a design direction. As things turned out, some of the basic themes were retained.

This was 1983 and the interior was following the same direction as the outside: soft 'organic' shapes. At this point Mike had only the package dimensions to work with and, as Engineering started to consolidate its design objectives, more restrictions came into play.

A major consideration was the knowledge that they were to have a high belt-line in front of the driver and front passenger. Mike worked to get the visual weight out of the top of the instrument panel but the real crunch came when the slide-in dash-panel module was adopted.

'This forced the visual weight back up high, because of the need to accommodate the large structural steel bar running across the car to the bottom of the A-pillars', Mike recalled. 'Another problem was the air-conditioning unit which had to be totally within the interior, not half inside the engine bay as in the VL.'

These factors prevented the instrument panel being as far from the occupants as Design had wished. A wraparound dash-to-doors theme was developed by Design but this was dropped from the program due to potential manufacturing problems.

'In spite of all these difficulties and tight financial constraints', Mike says, 'we still ended up achieving a soft, contemporary theme with maximum visual spaciousness and an airy environment'.

Design produced a binnacle rather than cockpit style of instrument panel; that is, one with the instruments and controls grouped around the steering wheel rather than wrapped around to join an integral centre console. This was done for fashion and ergonomic reasons, as well as for additional spaciousness.

A series of futuristic instrument panels, modelled in foam in 1984, helped set the direction for the interior.

Like so many individuals working on large projects, designers face many small defeats. Design staff put an enormous amount of work into detailing and integrating a fully electronic instrument panel. This concept was pursued almost to the end, when Holden's management decided that it couldn't get the reliability figures it was chasing as part of the Total Quality Control (TQC) philosophy. The analogue instruments eventually decided on are of conventional European style with big, easy-to-read dials designed at Holden's.

'All the lettering and symbols had to be easily understood', said Mike. 'We have been conscious of the fact that the population is getting older, just as we are conscious of Australians getting bigger in stature. We worked very hard to make sure no detail was missed.'

The switchgear also provided disappointments which Mike says caused everybody 'a great deal of pain over the years'. He worked very hard on a switchgear system with controls in the steering wheel centre. This was seriously considered, but eventually rejected for cost reasons.

Nevertheless, switchgear improvements are numerous. Unprecedented lengths have been gone to in ensuring that the ergonomics are first-rate. This bordered on paranoia at times, and fine-tuning of switches continued until late in 1987.

Very early in the piece, ergonomic experts from the Industrial Design Council were brought in to study the instrument and control layouts and report to Holden Design. In addition, Design cornered every possible person from Holden's (and supplier organisations) and sat them in the interior 'buck' to get their comments and impressions. To this end, all the controls on the buck were made operational — a first for Holden's.

Using a continuation of the VL binnacle theme, the VN incorporates a far more 'user-friendly' positioning and grouping of the controls. One criterion was to have switches on the binnacle for the controls which are common to all models (thus reducing the number of 'blanks'), another was to avoid small 'fiddly' switchgear. For the first time in a Commodore, the heater and fan controls are on the correct side for a right-hand drive car.

In spite of being able to handle more functions, the instrument panel layout is visually more simple and the controls are easier to use.

'When all the whizz-bang technology turned up', Mike says, 'many people threw it into cars without studying how it could be best used'.

'I believe ergonomics and aerodynamics are now major considerations for buyers. This is good, because our work results in a marketing edge as well as a better car.'

Mike is most enthusiastic about the overall result.

'We've worked exceptionally hard on this project in full cooperation with all the other departments. The result is a total product. So it is not just the appearance, it is the whole car — how it will hold people, how it will move people — that makes VN so good.

'In Design we were sure that if we put together the right package and injected some European flair and an aerodynamic feel, we would have a very desirable car.'

Similar comments are expressed by fellow designer Peter Nankervis.

'Early on, some people thought the VN was going to be too unusual. It didn't fit the form recognised as being a large car — it didn't read like a big box. Yet, with the VN, we have a car which is very different yet clean and simple with a lot of form and shape.'

Peter Nankervis, another RMIT design student, is a veteran of 30 years at Holden's. Even in a place full of automotive enthusiasts, he stands out. Asked exactly how much cars dominate his life, he replied 'What else is there?'.

Like Mike Simcoe, Peter moved to interiors after being very involved in setting the design direction for the exterior. The 'interior' team worked on Saturdays, Sundays and programmed days off for about six months to get the program on schedule.

'Probably the biggest bugbear', says Peter, 'was the door trim design'.

The intricacies of the door are such that Holden's usual method of trimming the inside — cutting a masonite board and attaching the trim and armrest to it — is unsuitable. Opel's door trim system was complicated and expensive, so Holden Design was set the task of finding another approach.

'Having convinced management that we need moulded door trims', said Peter, 'we were told to do it economically. It took a long time, but our system is simple in construction, conforms with cost requirements and blends well with the interior'.

The air-conditioning was an added problem as its bulk greatly limited the positioning of the sound system. The auto-gear lever was eventually moved off-centre so the sound system would be more accessible.

Audio considerations led to another decision. Moulded headlinings are being used by Holden's for the first time (replacing the former cut-and-sewn approach) and several different coverings were tested. The planned 'base' version of the headlining, which had a low-cost vinyl covering, was rejected because it bounced too much sound around. Lightweight knitted materials are now used throughout.

'The seats were another hassle', says Peter. 'We started planning for an industry seat [i.e. one that was to be used by all Australian manufacturers] but, for reasons beyond our control, things didn't work out. We started working with a picture of seat frames that didn't exist and so lost a lot of time.

'However, the exercise resulted in many components being shared so it did improve economies of scale.'

Work on the seats was still going on in the second half of 1987, long after most design matters had been locked up. The last thing to be completed was the Calais seat, which incorporates decorative 'gatherings' on the squab facings.

Peter was extremely conscious of the need for innovation and teamwork to overcome the tight budget restraints.

'In spite of the fact we had a brief to produce an interior package better than that of any previous Holden and superior to those expected from the competition, the VN cost objective was the same as for the VL or better', he said.

'All aspects of the design had to appear to be, and actually be, an improvement, yet everything was quantified down to five cents.'

Such quantifying is done in The Design Objective Manual, which individually lists every component with its estimated cost. The Manual also stipulated the interior was to have more headroom and better provision for

Left:
Another foam instrument panel styled in 1984.

Right:
Early 1985 brought a firming-up of the interior design. This example has a fully electronic instrument cluster.

Row below:
In October 1985, the interior team was well on the way to finalising its part of the design but plenty of detail work still lay ahead. Left to right: David Ferguson, Peter Nankervis, Jim Colias, Rik Orell, Michael Chester, Jack Mendes and Michael Simcoe.

Bottom left:
'Our concern about ergonomics at times bordered on paranoia', said Phil Zmood. All controls on the buck were operational and photographic studies were made of the hand movements between the controls.

Bottom right:
The interior buck of the automatic Berlina in mid-1986.

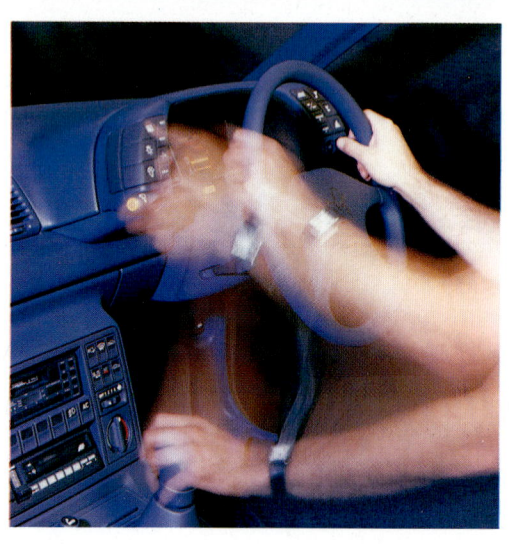

entry and exit than VL. It had to be wide enough for five Australian adults to sit with complete comfort. A large, easy-to-load luggage area was essential. Peter says these and all other objectives were achieved in full.

Attention to detail was also reflected in the use of colour, the domain of John Hart. In some ways, John is the odd man out in Holden Design. His specialist training has come more from a practical than a formal level. He doesn't have petrol in his veins; he prefers the throb of a jazz band to that of an engine.

In 30 years of working for the company, he has become the final arbiter on colour. It is a more important and complicated area than most people realise.

For example, the 700 visible parts on the interior of the VN have to harmonise with each other and with the exterior paint schemes. And that is not just in daylight. Twilight does strange things to colour perceptions.

John needs more than a good eye for colour. He has expertise in the manufacture of cloths, plastics and other materials. They all react differently where things like gloss levels are concerned and they take dyes and pigments differently.

Knowing what is popular or, more importantly, what is about to become popular is also John's business. He scours the world's fashion trends to see what is in and what is not.

'We have found that two or three years after colours are popular in clothing, they tend to drift into furnishings and architecture. After another two years or so, they come into the automotive field. Of course, you can't grab all the colours that are in vogue, not all will work in cars.'

The reasons are varied. Some colours, like greens, tend to polarise people. Glare and reflections have to be considered. High chromes (hues with a lot of strong colours) are good in some applications but are not ideal if you have to stare at them for hours on a long trip.

Technical considerations are also foremost. Coloured polypropylene, for example, is fashionable but, because of the high temperatures at which it is shaped, it is not usually suitable for the same dyes used for nylons or knits.

'Colour matching can be extremely hard work', said John. To illustrate his point, he took two pieces of carpet, both of which looked blue. He adjusted the equipment in the light studio and lit the samples with 'daylights', designed to simulate the midday sun.

'A perfect match, you'd say, wouldn't you?' he suggested. 'But we rejected these and I'll show you why.'

John then hit the switch and produced a redder light, which simulated the late afternoon. The carpet on the left turned grey, the carpet on the right went green.

'Many parts appear to match but as soon as you shift them from one light source to another, they change colour. This is especially true if you haven't used the same pigments or if the pigments you have chosen react differently.'

Fluorescents also can affect the apparent colour and John likes to look at major components under striplights and in sunlight as well as in the studio. In past days, all colour matching was done by eye in normal sunlight. Nowadays, the constant light source studio is one way Holden's tackles the difficult problem. Another is the Colour Analysis Computer, which gives an instrumental value to each colour. The required colour readout can be given to those vendors who have similar equipment and the computer allows John to electronically check samples sent by vendors.

As for the exterior, 13 colours are offered with the VN range, but no more than eight with any one model. This limited array of colours provides cost and stock inventory advantages but the major reason for the decision emerged after extensive meetings with paint suppliers and technicians from Holden's paint shop. The TQC concept demands that if something can't be brought up to the required standard, it should not be made available irrespective of marketing or other considerations. That was the case with some colours.

With fewer colours to choose from than in the past, the designers have to work harder at achieving differentiation.

The new Commodore offers a choice of three interior colour schemes. Once Holden offered up to eight choices but various restraints (including demands from dealers who were having stock problems coping with hundreds of combinations) have seen the list restricted to two old favourites, Palomino and Grey, and one 'fashion colour' called Mulberry. Light and dark variants of the same colour are included in each scheme.

Some colours are easier to work with than others. Lighter colours have less pigment in them, so a slight shift in formulation can drastically change the effect. Mulberry, being a dark colour, proved a breeze but there were all sorts of hassles trying to get a perfect match in carpets.

Interestingly, one trick of the interior design trade involves the use of colour to affect the apparent size. The VL featured light colours as this made it appear bigger inside. The VN, which Holden's consider large enough, was 'darkened up a bit' to give it a richer appearance.

Another 'trick' relating to colour played no part in the VN project.

Traditionally when the Design department builds its full-size model to 'show off' to management, it colours it silver and does everything else possible to flatter the shape. Historically, it has also displayed the top-line model mock-ups first.

'Building the level three car can be misleading as it is not the volume seller', says Phil Zmood.

'This time we consulted with the [then] Managing Director, Chuck Chapman, and agreed it would be better to build the middle range car first, then the low range, and finish with the level three car. And in each case we used a middle-value blue colouring rather than silver.

'We believe the level one car should be a good looking vehicle', he added. 'We don't want to force people up to the next level by presenting something ordinary as the base car. We want to offer them a good car to start with, and encourage them up the line by offering something even better.'

THE OTHER SIDE OF DESIGN

The Design department is often considered the glamorous end of car production, but it is as tightly run as everything else. As with virtually any car designed for production, the first question might be 'How good does it look?' but the next is 'How much will it cost?'. There are dozens of other questions asked when the pretty sketches are produced, including 'Can it be manufactured?', 'Can it be marketed?' and 'Is the appearance likely to hamper the performance of any mechanical part?'.

With the VN project, the person responsible for much of the liaison between Design and other groups — including Management, Finance, Marketing, Engineering, Manufacture and outside vendors — was Norm Thurling, now Manager of Technical and Administrative Services.

While the design was progressing, Norm and his staff conducted investigative studies on the feasibility of manufacture, vendor requirements and legal aspects such as compliance with Australian Design Rules. The team was also responsible for providing support to the design and modelling personnel.

There were countless deadlines to be met for the sake of other departments because any delay in the early stages can be magnified many times later on. The result of the initial consultations is written down in what is affectionately (and sometimes despairingly) known as 'The Bible'. It is officially the Master Timing Document and this, together with the Program Schedule and Status Report, is the blueprint that the people in Design work to.

Design met its deadlines in almost all cases, albeit with no time up its sleeve, but missed out by four months on the seats and door trims, partly because of factors beyond its control.

'The VN was the first time this department has successfully planned every aspect of a program of this magnitude and substantially adhered to it', says Norm.

The ability to plan so precisely lies with new technology. If management says it wants a new front on a car, Design can estimate how long it will take. For the last four years, everybody in the department has been using the computer to record how much time they have spent on each facet of their work. Now, by identifying the areas of change in a new design and totting up the hours (while allowing for variations peculiar to a new project), an accurate picture can be built up of the requirements in time, manpower and money.

Phil Zmood remembers that, when he first came to Holden's, 'it was a time when there was very little understanding of that type of management and planning. You just kept working until it was done. If management wanted a whole new car in a week, you got in as many people as needed'.

Phil is not the only one in Holden Design who can remember times when they would work two days straight without going home and few would claim they deliver their best work at four in the morning. Careful planning has now changed the way Design goes about its business. People still work after dark, but what they call 'kooky hours' are out.

Norm Thurling and his staff have estimates for every job likely to be undertaken. These estimates are interesting and, at times, staggering. A front-end integral bumper bar/valance panel, for example, requires 1480 hours. This comprises 120 hours for the sketching and design direction, 480 hours for modelling in clay, 760 hours for technical design and 120 hours for fabrication and painting of a fibreglass model.

Even things like badges require a great number of man-hours. With detailed criteria covering size, graphic identity and placement, the designers found themselves not only doing countless drawings and inspecting models, but performing many other tests. In the case of badges, it was agreed they should all be identifiable from a distance of 30 paces.

Norm has to tread the line between design and management. Himself a trained and experienced design engineer, with a track record which covers GM activities in the UK, Europe and South Africa, he was one of several who stood up strongly against the proposal for an exact rendition of the exterior and interior Opel design. He knew there would be tight financial restrictions on tooling parts exclusively for Australia but still believed the Holden Design proposal could work.

He participated in identifying the costs involved in having all-new fenders, hoods, facias (integral bumpers), quarter panels and decklids and Holden Design presented them to management and received permission to proceed.

'Some areas were a bit of a fight', he admits. 'And unfortunately costs forced us to compromise our original interior concept. But we still think we have produced the best Holden yet.'

The manufacturing requirements of the new car were investigated while it was still in clay. This is done by a team taking sketches and data of a component, such as a headlight, and presenting it to whoever is expected to manufacture it. In the case of the headlights, the maker was an outside vendor, Hella, and Holden's had a tall order. It wanted a multipocket headlamp system with the least possible height — 100 mm — to stay in keeping with the car's wide frontal appearance.

In areas like this, one continually finds conflicts. There is no point achieving the desired look if the component does not deliver the required performance. Often there are protracted negotiations between Design and Engineering until a compromise is reached or Engineering finds a way to make the design work. Even then, there can be budget problems, either in development, tooling or unit cost. In the case of the headlights, Design got the 100 mm high headlights and there was no loss of performance.

Close cooperation between the Design, Engineering and Manufacturing departments took place from the time the shape of the VN started to emerge. Much of the quality of the final product, including the fit and finish of panels and components, is related to the initial design.

'The VN design', says Norm, 'was breaking new ground with its flush glazing and low-profile mouldings around windscreens and openings generally. The methods of construction were a challenge for the designers.'

'In the past we have been building to basically Fisher standards [Fisher Body Division is part of GM Corporation], which involved leaving gaps and margins to allow for substantial build tolerances. This time, we were able to tighten the car up to European and Japanese standards which is very rewarding for us and means a better appearance for the end product.'

With the VN design, there was an effort not only to take full advantage of tighter tolerances (and avoid the pitfalls which tighter tolerances can bring) but to minimise the 'patch up' detailing required after each car is built. This patching up — which can include blacking out window frames, touching up painted panels etc. — was greatly reduced by techniques which included the strategic use of mouldings and overlapping panels.

Much technical work is done within Holden Design. For example, the 'raw data' taken from models by the digital coordinate measuring machine has to be 'sweetened', that is, put through the computer to ensure that all surfaces mesh mathematically. The software used for this, called CGS (Corporate Graphics System), was developed by GM Corporation specifically for the development of exterior surfaces, instrument facias, door trims and other panels. Installed at Holden's in mid-1984, it allows accuracy of about .05 mm in panel shaping. Previously the French Catia system was used for bodywork and this could be up to .33 mm out.

At least three processes, including manual drafting, are eliminated using CGS and, aside from the obvious advantage of a reduced lead time, the chances of errors creeping in are reduced.

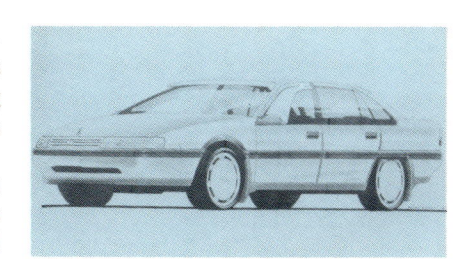

The Design department computers are also used for such things as package layouts and Australian Design Rules (ADRs) requirement checks. The numerous ADRs cover such things as the field of vision of the interior and exterior rear-view mirrors and the visibility of instruments and gauges. Many can be checked on-screen by Design.

Norm Thurling sees a great challenge in making cars in Australia, where people expect the latest technology in spite of the relatively low volumes.

'I believe a car designed and developed in Australia could be sold anywhere around the world. Our engineering standards are high, our standards of vehicle performance are high, and so are our safety standards and test requirements.'

Of course, none of these advantages amount to much if a car is not thought to be attractive and, consequently, fails to sell. Early in the program, some people within the company expressed doubts about the radical departure from previous Holdens that the VN presented. The Design staff stood firm and insisted they were on the right track. The first styling clinic in October 1984, however, didn't serve to raise anybody's confidence. The participants considered the car's back to be too high, the rear view unattractive and the whole thing just 'too way out'.

Phil Zmood was not unduly worried and the second styling clinic supported his view.

'It was about 18 months after the first clinic', he recalled, 'and people had become more conditioned to the aero-style cars coming out of Europe. So in the second clinic, the VN came out a lot better and confirmed that we were on the right track. We had made some changes since the first clinic but no major ones'.

'We had wrapped the lights around the back more, lowered the decklid very slightly and made the linework emphasise the horizontal bands front and rear to give the perception of a wider car.'

Phil says having the more realistic fibreglass model at the second clinic was also a big help. At the first clinic, Design had blanked in the windows of the real cars to give them similar appearance to the clay VN, but the newcomer was still at a disadvantage.

All through the VN program, Holden Design had regular design review meetings, both indoors and outside, and everyone filled out critique sheets. After the second clinic, it was agreed there was still some fine-tuning to be done.

One source of argument centred on the front turn-signals. The cheapest solution was to use orange plastic lenses. These are well accepted, but the Design team wanted to use a more expensive smoky white lens to emphasise the graphic band across the front.

Phil is the arbiter on what points the Design team should argue for most strongly.

'We have to be realistic and find a balance between design, cost and manufacturing elements and also look at the competition. Often we have to compromise so, on many small issues, I have to disappoint the team. If it's a big issue we will pursue it to the end.'

Phil decided the lenses presented such an issue. Aside from affecting the aesthetic appeal, Phil argued that an orange block on each side made the car look narrower. And every bit of detail work they had done was aimed at increasing the perceived width. He won.

The basic exterior of the VN was locked up in April 1986, although some interior detailing work continued until late 1987. By 1988, the people in Design had already started considering the brief for the car to take the company into the 21st century.

After a Design is locked up, there are only two reasons for changes to be made, summed up in the expression: 'Can't build, Can't sell'. This can be a period of nail-biting, wondering how the public will take to the shape and where the market will go in the year or more after lock-up. Even after assessing every possible thing in the early design stage, it is still necessary 'to take a punt' on which direction to go. This is where experience and gut-feel come in.

In the lead-up to release, members of the team, including Phil, were becoming increasingly convinced they had designed a car that was going to create a sensation.

'Some people here would have preferred us to have been more conservative with the VN', said Phil at the time the design was finalised. 'But I believe that at Holden's we have traditionally been the Design leader in Australia and that is one of our great strengths. I am certain we have gone the right way with this design.'

'I have endeavoured to bring out contributions from everybody', he added. 'When you're a small team you have to use all available resources. The VN was conceived with commitment and dedication beyond the normal working relationships I know in Australia and that is reflected in the product. It is really an extension of the personalities of the guys who worked on it.'

Phil has very definite ideas on what designers need and the Australian public wants.

'A good car designer needs a combination of an art, business and engineering mind. Most importantly, he needs to talk cars and breathe cars and live cars.'

A designer, he says, also has to know the market extremely well.

'Australians demand change. Each new model needs to be different and zappy or there is a tendency for buyers to move onto the next brand. Australians also demand that a car be contemporary in appearance and that it look strong and not effeminate.'

Phil concedes that the original Commodore, the VB, looked 'a bit timid' in the eyes of the male buyers.

'We traditionally aim our full-sized Holdens at the family man, from the blue collar through to the executive. In the 50s and 60s, he aspired to American-style cars like the Monaro. Now he is conditioned to softer shapes but still demands a car that looks rugged.

'All the lessons we have learned over the years, and over successive Holden models, are put in memory boxes around here.'

Phil says many buyers want a car that looks like a Holden. Much detail work including the placement of lines and badges, the shape of the headlights and grille, the styling of wheels and so on, was aimed at making sure the VN is a recognisable member of the Holden family.

'Most buyers could not describe in words what makes a car look like a Holden but they can recognise certain traits immediately. The "Holden look" comes unconsciously to us, I guess, but we are very aware of it.'

Phil says that styling, although important, 'is essentially the marketing facet of design. A design must be meaningful to be successful, not just a shape which looks glamorous'.

Each time Phil goes out on an Australian road, he is surrounded by his handywork, reflected in over 20 years of Holden cars. He sees the designs he is most happy with, the designs that made the biggest impression on the public and, just occasionally, he sees a line here and there which he would change given a second chance.

He'll be very happy to be surrounded by VNs.

'I am sure the reaction from the general public will be one of great excitement. Our design intent for the exterior and interior of this car was to blend all the needs and desires of local buyers into a package which was absolutely state-of-the-art in appearance and function. The VN is dynamic in form yet pure and up to the moment.

'For these reasons, it should have even more impact on the market than the original VB Commodore, or even the HQ.'

While the public is reacting to the VN, Holden Design will be well advanced on the next project and the project after that.

'The VN sets the pattern for even brighter and better things in the future', says Phil.

'We have a professional, internationally trained team which can do anything.'

INTERNATIONAL AWARD

Design for two-seater open sports car which was awarded first prize in London at a recent Automobile Manufacturers' competition. Designer P. Zmood, Industrial Design Student R.M.I.T.

The award to a local industrial design student of first prize in a British Automobile Manufacturers'

Phil Zmood

For Phil Zmood, Holden's Executive In Charge Of Design, the VN has been the most challenging project of an impressive career. Melbourne-born Phil, who owes his unusual surname to Russian parentage, started drawing when he was about ten. One day he decided to show his parents what the family's 1953 Ford would look like if he had styled it.

That exercise was the start of an automotive obsession which led to reams and reams of drawings, subscriptions to all the car magazines and 'How do I become a designer?' letters to all the editors. Eventually Phil settled for a course in Industrial Design at the Royal Melbourne Institute of Technology.

An issue of *Modern Motor* in the early 1960s brought news that the Institute of British Carriage and Automobile Manufacturers was launching an annual competition for young car designers. Entries flooded in from around the world and, in 1963, a Zmood-designed rotary sports car was declared the winner.

The *Melbourne Age* ran the story of our new whiz-kid; a short time later a phone call invited Phil to meet Joe Schemansky, GM-H's Design Director. Within a short while, Phil was not only working for 'The General' but had been selected to go to Detroit Design Studios to study GM design and business techniques. He returned to Australia to become Assistant Chief Designer around the time of the HQ project. Soon afterwards, he was appointed Chief Designer of the Torana small car range.

The later 1970s saw Phil in Germany working for Opel, by 1983 he was back in Australia as Executive in Charge of Design. The irony was that his new position left him less time for his favourite activity — drawing cars. Nevertheless, the VN Commodore project was just starting and it was to be completely his baby.

Technology orchestrated
... engineering for Australia

'It's hard to please everyone', says Tony Hyde, Holden's Manager of Mechanical Engineering.

'Some customers prefer a soft ride because they mainly use the car around town. Others want the ultimate in roadholding. We had a VL owner living in a New South Wales country town who complained that the rear end of his car had hopped sideways when he drove over a narrow, timber-surfaced bridge. I asked him at what speed this had happened and he replied 150 km/h. That sort of criticism is difficult to handle!

'But with VN, we have gone to extraordinary lengths to produce a vehicle which should please virtually everyone likely to buy it. It has, after all, taken nearly eight years to design and develop.'

As early as mid-1980, the then Assistant Chief Engineer Don Wylie and body engineer Jack Gow sat down with Director of Engineering Joe Whitesell, and informally kicked around ideas for the next all-new Commodore.

'We agreed that whatever happened, Holden's should return to the original Kingswood size', says Don Wylie. 'We did not want any compromise here.'

The first official discussions with Opel on the subject were held in February 1983 when Joe Whitesell, Phil Zmood and Don Wylie went to Germany to review the proposed Omega design. By then, Holden engineers and planners had produced a comprehensive manual setting out their design objectives, reliability and durability testing standards and the relevant Australian Design Rules relating to the 1988 Commodore. The manual was passed to Opel with the request that the specifications be incorporated to the greatest possible extent in the new program.

Some of the key players in the VN project gather at Lang Lang. Those in the foreground include (left to right): John Bagshaw, Roger Gibbs, Adrian Harris, Tony Hyde, Phil Zmood, Don Wylie, Ray Grigg and Ray Borrett.

CONTROL TEAMS

While Opel worked on the basic design, Holden's set about planning a radically different way to approach its side of the project. Past practice has been for the design, mechanical and body engineers to create a new model with little reference to the people expected to manufacture it. Not surprisingly, there were occasions when the production technicians took one look at a drawing and threw up their hands in horror. The component in question could not be readily made with the available equipment or techniques. Costly and time-consuming modifications were then necessary.

Additional pressure came from GM's Chief Executive Officer, Roger Smith. In the early 1980s, he became increasingly concerned about the inroads Japanese car-makers were making in North America. He issued a directive that all GM companies were to set a new standard of world quality as their priority target.

Back in Australia, Joe Whitesell summoned the engineering team and said that Holden's must urgently find new ways to design quality into all its cars. One way was to simultaneously design both the vehicle and the means of manufacturing it. Laurie Sparke, a veteran of 22 years in Holden's engineering, was given the task of planning details of a new approach, an idea the company called SE for Simultaneous Engineering.

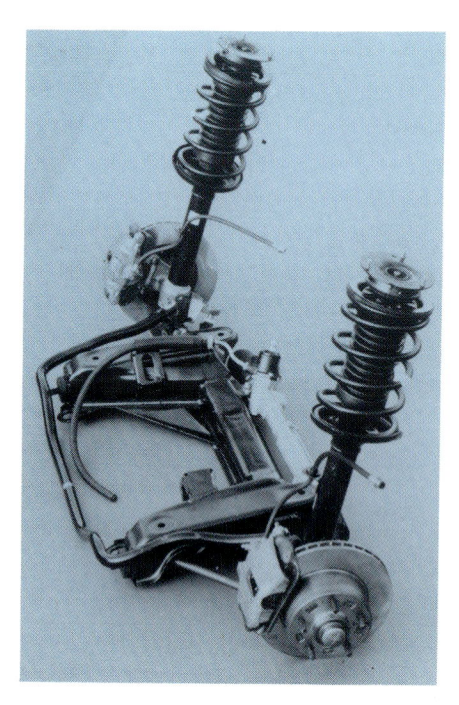

It was adopted for the very start of Project VN. Holden's also appointed a Program Manager (initially Rob McEniry, later Doug Cleary) to coordinate the numerous facets of design and production and ensure all objectives were met in full.

To effect the SE concept, Holden's established 31 control teams, with representatives from manufacturing, design, quality control, planning, engineering, body design, marketing, service and supplier groups. Spearheaded by product engineers, these multidiscipline groups concentrated on all aspects of preparing the car for the market. They jointly set the design objectives, reviewed them at critical stages and checked the actual design against the objectives. During the coming months, the same teams were to monitor progress and design changes. Even after the design was finalised, they stayed together to maintain a clear focus on the products that the customers received.

This concept of combining the skills of a variety of specialists originated in Japan where it is known as 'orchestrated technology'. Along with another Japanese innovation — the just-in-time (JIT) assembly technique — it became a keystone of the VN project.

When the Holden multidiscipline teams first assembled, VN was intended to have the same Nissan 3-litre engine and power train used in the VL. Holden's also planned to continue the Nissan 2-litre, six-cylinder engine for sale in New Zealand and other markets where small-engined cars have a marketing advantage. By mid-1987, two far-reaching decisions had been made. One was to use a Holden-built V-6 as the standard engine in Australian VNs, the other was to fit the Family II four-cylinder unit for some export markets. This engine is basically the same unit built by Holden's for the Opel Omega and some Vauxhall models.

Although several options were still under review, the Engineering department was confident that the most successful mechanical features of the VL Commodore would continue in the VN. It told Opel it expected to use local components, such as a five-link rear suspension, rack-and-pinion steering, brake master cylinder, propeller shaft and the existing front steering knuckle and wet strut suspension. These components had already been proven in the toughest of local conditions and would help Holden's meet the Australian government's local content regulations. Complete dust-sealing and a high level of performance from the air-conditioning and ventilation systems were specified.

Although Joe Whitesell and Don Wylie were highly impressed by the Omega design, they realised that changes were needed to suit the local market. They also recommended that Opel consider some features appearing around the world, such as an anti-thief magnetic key system, automatic window closing, synthesised voice instruments, air purifier, audible reverse signal and a removable waste box. Holden engineers expressed a keen interest in Opel's five-speed transmission and independent rear suspension and studied them in depth. Later it was decided to improve the existing VL suspension and fit a local Borg Warner manual transmission. The sonar device did not eventuate but the VN Calais has a sophisticated Cobra security system which immobilises the car electronically and locks the doors.

As the VN started to take shape, Don Wylie was asked to make an engineering presentation to Group Vice-President J.F. Waters to keep the parent company informed. The work involved in the presentation helped crystalise the design, at least in a formal sense.

On 31 October 1984, Don told Mr Waters that the 88V was the first Holden program directed from concept toward achieving world class quality and engineering. VN would be roomier than its predecessor and would have a similar performance, fuel economy, handling and ride quality. The appearance would be new and contemporary and the aerodynamic shape much improved.

He said there would be two body styles: a four-door, six-window sedan available with three levels of equipment and a five-door station wagon sold with two equipment levels. The sedan would have a 2731 mm wheelbase (63 mm more than the original Commodore design) and the body would also be wider. The wagon wheelbase would be extended to 2822 mm.

Strong progress was being made in all areas of design, he said. The necessary technical information was being progressively received from Opel in the form of magnetic tapes and discs and hardline drawings. A schedule had been established whereby the major body panel drawings would be signed-off by March 1985 so that work could commence on the tooling. Don told Mr Waters that numerous body items, including the door frames, were unchanged from Opel's design, but 17 body items would be unique to Holden. They included the windscreen, front bumper, decklid, fenders and instrument panel.

The timing schedule envisaged approval by the Corporation by April 1985, body samples being built by June 1987 with pilot vehicles coming off the production line in Elizabeth, South Australia, by February 1988. Don Wylie concluded the presentation by saying that an essential part of the program was to adopt a variety of new manufacturing concepts developed by Opel which would enable Holden's to achieve greater productivity and higher quality standards.

In October 1985, Mr Waters received a progress review which confirmed that the 114 kW Nissan engine would be the standard power plant, with a 147 kW turbo variant and a high-torque 122 kW, 4.9-litre Holden V-8 offered as an option. Japanese-produced transmissions would be fitted to the Nissan engines and a Borg Warner Gear T5 five-speed manual or a GM Turbohydramatic (THM 700) auto to the V-8. Don Wylie told Mr Waters that they had hoped to use an Australian-made Borg Warner four-speed auto transmission but that the unit would not be ready in time for the VN launch.

Behind the presentation was one of the most dedicated engineering departments in the country. It comprises 500 engineers, technicians, test drivers, draftsmen, modellers and support staff. They are divided into eight main groups handling design and styling, body engineering, mechanical engineering, electrical engineering, current product engineering, executive engineering, experimental engineering and the Central Laboratory. Executive Engineering covers technical specifications, manpower and budget control, whilst experimental engineering includes experimental manufacturing and assembly, development, reliability, vehicle and component testing, a laboratory and the proving grounds at Lang Lang, Victoria. The engineering facilities are split between Fishermans Bend and Lang Lang, 90 km to the south-east. There is also a Quality of Work Life coordinator who has direct access to Don Wylie.

During the development of the VN, the Engineering department became increasingly integrated into international electronic data transfer systems so that all engineering activities could be coordinated electronically with other GM divisions.

Although not as large as it was during the 1960s, Holden's Engineering department has retained the skill, capacity and ability to engineer a complete car, says Don Wylie. The new Commodore was not wholly designed at Holden's because the huge cost of duplicating work already being done by other GM divisions could not be justified.

Don Wylie says that during the VN conceptual stage, he and Joe Whitesell gave serious thought to using front-wheel drive and, at one time, considered creating an enlarged version of the Camira. After some studies, they concluded that for a car of Commodore's size and weight, conventional rear-wheel drive offered more customer benefits. He believes that it will still take a few years before the engineering limitations of front-wheel drive, as applied to large cars, will be eliminated. By that time, he says, full-time four-wheel drive may be common on family cars.

How does Don Wylie see the VN project?

'It's the first really smooth car we have designed. With flush glass and other aerodynamic features, we've tried to get rid of the crevices which create wind noise and increase air drag. The mechanical components are orthodox but very modern. Most important of all, we've pulled out all stops to make sure the VN is built with world class quality and absolute reliability so that owners can take a real pride in their car.'

SUSPENSION

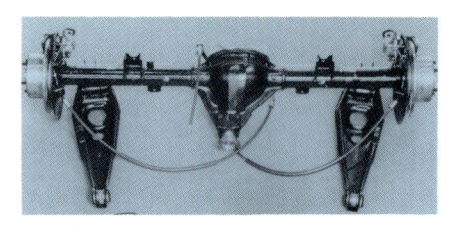

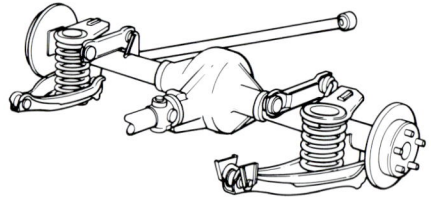

Holden's introduced Radial Tuned Suspension during the 1970s and has since extended the concept to all passenger models. 'Radial Tuned' means that the suspension springs, suspension bushes and shock absorber settings are chosen to match the profile, stiffness and other characteristics of radial ply tyres. RTS was used on the original Commodore and progressive changes have been made over the years. The same basic concept has been retained in the VN design.

During the initial design stages, Holden engineers had seriously considered using Opel's independent rear suspension but they faced a torque capacity problem when the optional V-8 engine is fitted. (The largest capacity Opel engine is a 3-litre 'six'.) The VN sedan has the same wheelbase as Opel but a different floor pan. The rear suspension retains the VL's five-link design with an increased track to suit the wider body. The front suspension has VL's oil-cooled MacPherson struts modified by fine-tuning. These 'wet struts' give a much longer life than conventional shock absorbers when subject to rough road usage. VN's front lower control arm ball joints are prelubricated and permanently sealed. The front system also has a pendulum-type roll bar mounting.

The big difference between the VL and VN is that the new car has a better balance between high-speed handling and low-speed riding comfort. Great care has been taken to ensure no abrupt change in handling characteristics takes place between power-on and power-off cornering conditions. Unlike some 'slippery cars', the VN also has a high resistance to side wind disturbance and problems associated with passing semitrailer trucks. Because of several refinements, VN has a slightly stiffer suspension than its immediate predecessor and its road characteristics are closer to VK than VL, say Holden development engineers.

The front track has not been widened but the front variable rate springs have been replaced by a linear rate type. According to Tony Hyde, whose group has done much of the suspension development work, the new springs give improved stiffness in both roll and ride situations. One effect, he says, is to 'calm down the front end' on a jittery road surface.

The rear suspension retains variable rate springs as fitted to VL but they are slightly stiffer. A lot of work has been done on compression and rebound in the struts and shock absorbers by testing different valve settings. The torsion anti-roll bars are slightly smaller in diameter at the front and rear.

'I'm confident that VN's suspension is a major step forward', says Tony Hyde.

'Some of our engineers — Bill Hooper for example — are superb drivers. They agree that VN's handling is much superior to VL's. It's got good riding comfort and is very controllable on difficult road surfaces.'

Special suspension packs for police work and country use have also been developed.

As Manager of the Mechanical Engineering Department, Tony Hyde carries much of the responsibility for the detail design. In 1966, he gained a Diploma of Engineering from Caulfield Technical College (now Chisholm Institute of Technology) and joined Holden's two years later as a technical report writer. He graduated to prototype testing and became a design engineer and later a development engineer. During a two-year working stint at Pontiac, Michigan (and simultaneously studying at the General Motors Institute), he concentrated on some specialised areas of vehicle dynamics. With this experience under his belt, Tony returned to Holden's to manage the vehicle test group at the Lang Lang proving grounds. He moved from here to become a suspension and brake design specialist.

Tony Hyde was associated with the design of the JB Camira when working at Opel as Holden's resident engineer. He returned to Fishermans Bend at the end of 1980 and joined Peter Hanenberger, the noted suspension specialist who had helped develop Holden's first Radial Tuned Suspension system in 1976-77. Tony was promoted to Technical Service Manager, then joined the VN program in 1985 as Chassis Engineer.

Tony said that as soon as V-6 engines became available and their exact weight known, a series of suspension reviews were done at Lang Lang. They involved VN and VL models being driven back-to-back with a series of competitive cars such as Falcon and Skyline. Several drivers, including Don Wylie and Holden people from outside the Engineering department, drove all cars and reported their findings.

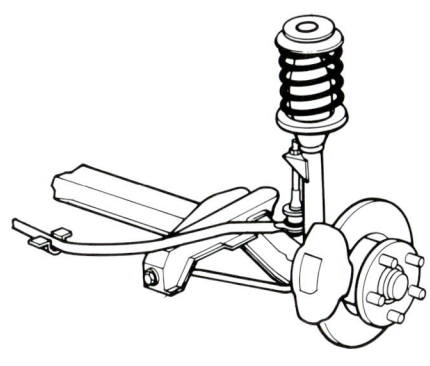

CAD-CAM (computer-aided design and manufacture) techniques helped to speed the development and improve the design quality of VN components. The system can be linked to overseas design sources via satellite.

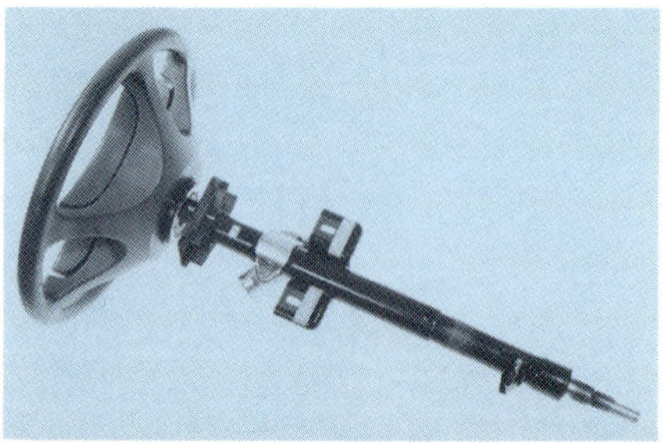

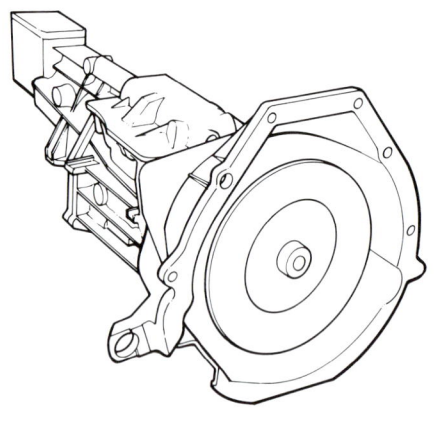

STEERING

The Opel uses a recirculating ball steering system but Holden engineers prefer the rack-and-pinion system used since the VB Commodore. The VN steering column is made by Tubemakers Australia but is interchangeable with the Opel unit. The manual steering, which is virtually a delete option for fleet use and expected to be ordered by less than 10 per cent of buyers, is a compact variable ratio system. It gives precise response and allows rapid directional changes thanks to a steering ratio which varies from 19.7 to 1 in the centre position to 23.3 to 1 on full lock.

Both the manual and power systems are made by Kirby. The power steering is also a variable ratio design and will be standard in the Executive and other high-specification models. Basically the same system used on VL, it has a different hydraulic pump and hosing to suit the V-6 engine. Regulated by engine speed, the power steering has a centre ratio of 17.2 to 1 and a full lock ratio of 11.8 to 1.

The turning circle is 10.4 metres, which is slightly larger than the VL figure because of the increased wheelbase.

Above:
Incoming Managing Director John Bagshaw gets an engineering briefing on VN. Left to right, Don Wylie, John Bagshaw, Brian DuCasse, Phil Zmood and Roger Gibbs. An Opel Senator is at hand for comparison.

TRANSMISSION

Borg Warner's Australian-made T5 five-speed manual transmission is used on both V-6 and V-8 models. This is new for Australia and is not the transmission offered on Commodores built before the VL. The THM 700 four-speed automatic unit was developed by GM and is currently fitted to Corvette and Camaro models in the USA. Highly respected overseas, the 700 originally derived its name because it could handle torque up to 700 newton metres. That's to say, with a 2 to 1 torque converter ratio, the transmission could be put behind an engine developing 350 Nm. However, the torque capacity has since been increased to cater for higher torque engines. Commodore V-8 models have a 298 mm torque converter, V-6s have 245 mm units.

The conventionally designed hydraulic transmission is noted for its smooth shift qualities. It features a fuel-saving, lock-up torque converter clutch and allows the driver to select the lower gears when desirable. The THM 700 has a numerically high first gear ratio, allowing rapid getaways from a standing start. The unit is equipped with a protective circuit in case the transmission oil should overheat in extreme operating conditions such as excess torque converter slippage in the lower gears.

BRAKES AND WHEELS

All VN models have four-wheel, power-assisted, disc brakes with dual hydraulic circuits. The system is based on the VL design which had been extensively upgraded to accommodate the higher performance of the turbo model. The changes included an increase in front disc diameter and the use of a Corvette-type caliper body with heavy finning to dissipate heat. The pad backing-plate thickness was increased to cope with high energy conditions. Don Wylie says the system has done such an outstanding job for VL that nothing would be gained by changing it for VN. The only modifications required were a re-routing of the pipes to suit the increased wheelbase and rear track. The performance objectives were set at a minimum of 40 000 km pad life and 80 000 km disc life with normal operation.

A new alloy wheel design with one-piece casting has been produced exclusively for Calais. The previous VL Calais composite alloy wheel is offered as an option for other models.

The standard cars have 14-inch wheels (by convention, wheel sizes are not given in metric) and the smaller of two disc sizes (271 mm against 289 mm). The V-8 models have the larger diameter brakes and 15-inch wheels. All police vehicles are fitted with the bigger brakes, regardless of engine size.

AERODYNAMICS

Although VN has a larger frontal area than VL (2.144 square metres against 2.033), wind-tunnel tests show it has a Cd value of 0.34 compared with 0.42 for VL. According to John O'Connell, whose responsibilities cover aerodynamics, this represents a 15 per cent reduction in aerodynamic drag and is sufficient to give a 5 per cent improvement in top speed. Although aerodynamic considerations have only a small effect on fuel economy at urban speeds, they are most important on the highway. The slippery shape also reduces wind noise, he says.

Holden's uses the GM wind tunnel at Detroit for testing full-scale models and the Royal Melbourne Institute of Technology for the initial quarter-scale models. They find that the figures achieved with quarter-scale testing are very close to those for full-scale testing.

FRONT DOOR AT B-PILLAR

BODY SHELL

The traditional sedan body shell has two main torsional load-carrying members. One is behind the rear seat. The other, which is commonly called a firewall, is between the engine compartment and passenger compartment. Together, they provide the major torsional stiffness. Neither of these traditional load-carrying members is present in VN. The firewall has been replaced by the modular dash panel assembly, the rear panel was taken out to allow access to the boot. The required torsional stiffness was therefore obtained by redistributing the stresses and loads.

The basic body shell construction follows the Opel design apart from a heavier centre pillar to give greater strength for rough road work. According to Brian DuCasse, Manager of Body Engineering, the structure is extremely strong.

'The Commodore VL body was also exceptionally good in this respect', he says. 'This is evident from the way it performed in the marketplace. Our aim, with VN, was to match the rigidity of VL and we have done so.'

'The body design is so advanced that its overall weight is not significantly greater than VL's, despite the increased length and width.

'With our road conditions, one of the most critically stressed parts of a motor car is the rear seat back panel which is subject to stresses resulting from road surface inputs through the rear suspension.

'Based on previous experience, we decided that, for maximum strength and durability, it was better to have a rear seat back panel giving access to the boot, rather than a full fold-down seat. The width of the opening — 400 mm — should be adequate for most applications.'

Brian DuCasse says the doors on the sedan and wagon are distinctly different from Opel's.

'We started off with the full flush glass system developed for the Opel Omega but decided to change it. This was partly because of local manufacturing capabilities and environmental reasons (such as dust) but also because of our rough roads. We designed a flush, sliding glass system which is similar to Opel's except that we have added a sheet metal channel to the door frame in which the glass slides. The glass is still offset toward the outer surface of this channel to retain the flush appearance. In effect, we have produced a cross between the German concept and a conventional system.

'We are very pleased with the result. Not only have we overcome dust entry and rough road problems, but the windows themselves are easier to open and close than previous models. Wind noise is also significantly reduced.'

The body is designed to take semiconcealed windscreen wipers similar to Opel's, providing a more stylish appearance and less drag. Extensive use is made of precoated steel, such as Zincrometal, for doors and other areas which are vulnerable to corrosion. Virtually all body lead-loading has been eliminated to protect the health of the work force.

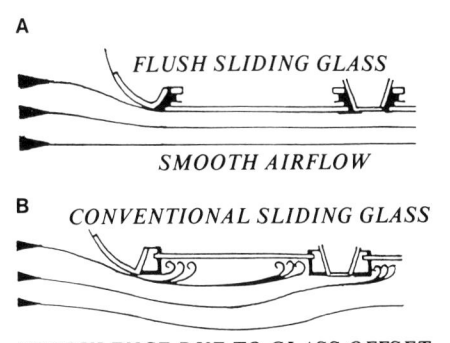

A *FLUSH SLIDING GLASS*

SMOOTH AIRFLOW

B *CONVENTIONAL SLIDING GLASS*

TURBULENCE DUE TO GLASS OFFSET

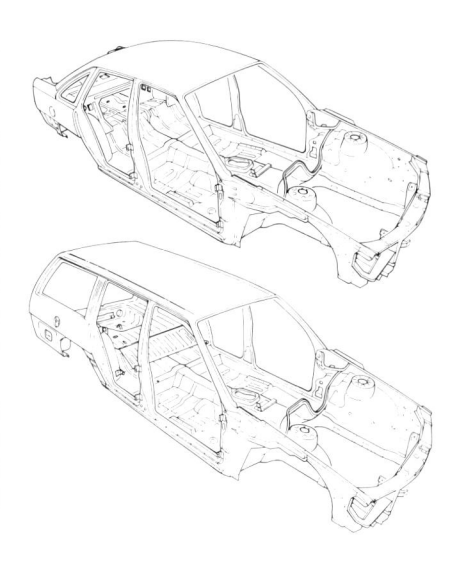

61

COCKPIT MODULE

A major difference to previous practice is that the body shell does not have a conventional firewall. Instead, a separate cockpit module fits into a groove across the body at firewall level and is rigidly fixed there by a special adhesive.

'The modular concept is an attempt to build a large piece of the motor car off-line', says Terry Carroll, design project engineer.

'The cockpit module is a substantial structure and includes the instrument panel and air-conditioning system. We also have to consider the steering column, part of the brake system and the wiring harness.

'I doubt that there's any part of a car which is more complex than the dash panel and instrument area and this is why numerous design groups are involved in putting it together.

'Opel pioneered the idea of building it off-line because it is perhaps the most difficult part of the car to control in a quality sense. Traditionally, the assembly operator installs many of the components when lying on his back. Often, he has to drag hoses through the door and do a difficult job in a very cramped space.

'With the cockpit module concept, the operator works at a sensible height and can easily see everything that is being done. The module is on a fixture and is rotated when work is done on the underside. Of course, the finished job is much more easily inspected and tested off-line.

'The module is a metal structure made from four or five panels and includes what is usually called the cowl, which carries all the major systems. It incorporates the structural area we call the dash panel but others refer to as the firewall. When all parts are assembled, the module is glued into the main body using a silicone adhesive. The reason for using an adhesive, rather than bolts or spot-welding, is that it gives a completely leak-proof structure which also enhances the overall body rigidity.

'The module is a more costly approach than the conventional system but enables us to build a better car. It can be serviced in the usual way without any drawbacks.

'Our unit is not the same as Opel's although the principle is. Our car is wider and the air-conditioning, which forms a large part of the structure, is totally our own design. We've built the ducting right into the module to reduce the number of parts and to eliminate squeaks and rattles. Another reason for redesigning Opel's work was to maximise interior room and provide an enhanced feeling of spaciousness. However, we use the same instrument envelope as Opel and could take their instruments and, with some minor modifications, put them straight in', he said.

The Holden uses instruments which make electrical contact when plugged into the panel, thus eliminating additional connections. The idea was developed for Gemini and proved so successful it was designed into the VN. The VN also uses an electronically sensed analogue speedometer to eliminate the need for a cable. The instruments are made by VDO Australia.

The part of the module which can be seen by the occupants is made from conventional foam and plastic fixed to a plastic base. Electromechanical analogue instruments, based on the Opel cluster with local graphics, are used on all VNs with specific graphics for each model. The Calais has a unique local instrument cluster with four analogue displays and liquid crystal displays for the integral trip computer.

ELECTRICAL SYSTEM AND ACCESSORIES

The entirely new VN electrical system provides a great improvement on any previous Holden. Adrian Harris, Manager — Electrical Engineering, says that exhaustive testing of the system as a whole and of the individual components will ensure a fault-free, functional vehicle.

For example, all components and associated wiring have been subjected to a deliberate short circuit to the vehicle body and to the battery positive.

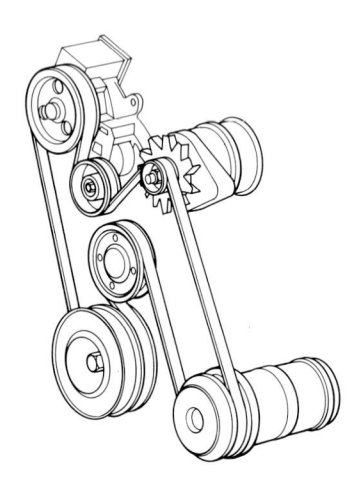

The lessons learned will greatly reduce the risk of a failure which could force the occupants to walk home.

The cars have also been tested for electromagnetic compatibility (EMC) which ensures that all electric components will work harmoniously with each other and the outside world.

The one-piece main wiring harness is mounted, and tested, in the cockpit module prior to the vehicle being assembled. Neat, plug-in encapsulated fusible links allow easy serviceability. Also new is the thin-wall insulation to reduce the harness weight and bundle size whilst maintaining colour matching between the harness assemblies. Identification labels eliminate possible mistakes during servicing. The number of components connected to each fuse has been reduced, there being 19 fuses, one circuit breaker and five fusible links. This multiplicity of protective devices enables the optimum fuse size to be chosen to match the component's expected power demand.

Holden's design team has gone to considerable lengths to eliminate unnecessary movements by the driver. Seven important control switches can be reached without the driver's eyes leaving the road or the hands taken from the steering wheel.

Adrian Harris says the company has been careful to use high-technology to maximise driver benefit. For example, research shows that digital displays are most suitable for trip-related information. So, for the Calais, electrically driven analogue indicators are used for the speedometer, tachometer, fuel gauge and engine temperature gauge, but the trip computer has digital displays. It provides nine useful items of driver information, with a three-window display to allow the main functions to be grouped clearly and logically. Three readings can be taken at a time without pressing a button to go from one to the other.

The first instrument group provides the data frequently checked while driving: overspeed alarm setting, instantaneous fuel consumption and distance-to-empty. The second group provides the less frequently checked data: average speed, average fuel consumption and odometer reading. The third group provides the trip totals: elapsed time, total fuel used and distance travelled.

The small liquid crystal displays have excellent reliability and are not washed out by strong sunlight. The new unit incorporates a calibration system which enables an owner or serviceman to calibrate the trip computer to give 100 per cent accuracy.

The analogue gauges in all models are complemented by a comprehensive array of warning lamps, covering functions as diverse as a vehicle speed warning and a reminder that the cruise control is engaged.

The analogue instrument clusters in the Executive, Berlina and S have large, easy-to-read dials for the speedometer, tachometer (S only), fuel and engine temperature gauges. Information such as low oil pressure or alternator failure is indicated by warning lamps which give an immediate and clear indication if something goes wrong.

An electronic speedometer drive is used in place of the conventional cable drive, giving reduced noise, better reliability and a steadier needle.

The low-profile headlamps provide even light distribution with a sharp cut-off pattern for low beam and improved high beam penetration. The total high beam output is 230 watts. Improved lamp sealing and terminal connections enhance the overall reliability.

The heating, ventilation and air-conditioning systems provide a 30 per cent improvement in occupant cooling and a 25 per cent increase in total air flow through the passenger compartment. The air-conditioning unit has 24 per cent more cooling capacity and the compressor pumping capacity, when the engine is idling, has been increased by 25 per cent for improved cooling in stop-start driving conditions. The clutch which drives the compressor deactivates automatically at high engine speed to prolong compressor life and at full throttle to ensure that the driver has full power for rapid overtaking.

To ensure that comfortable conditions are achieved in the minimum of time after entering a VN, distribution and balance of air flow from the

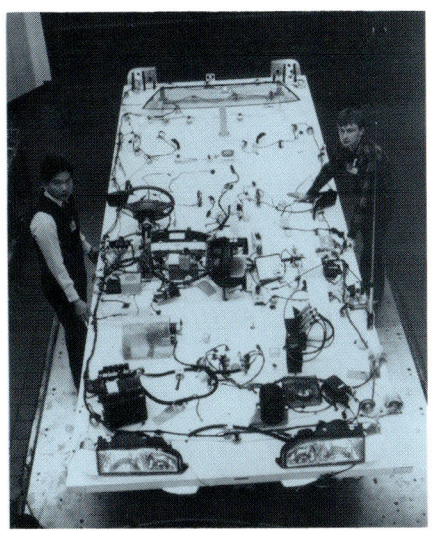

An extraordinary amount of development work was done to ensure that all electric and electronic components work in harmony with each other and with the outside world.

vents have been carefully tailored to provide optimum draught-free circulation within the cabin. Rear console vents ensure the back passengers enjoy travelling comfort on a par with those in the front. The heating and air-conditioning systems have been tested under extreme climatic conditions in Australia, Japan and the USA.

The semiconcealed windscreen wipers are designed to stay in contact with the glass at high speed and cover a 10 per cent larger glass area than the VL wipers. The revised motor has a 'park on upwipe' action which will increase the life of the wiper blades by 25 per cent, says Adrian Harris.

Electric windows are standard on Calais, optional on other models, and have an 'automatic down' function for the driver's side. The window can also be 'inched' down if required. All windows can be operated up to 45 seconds after the ignition has been switched off, provided that none of the doors has been opened in the meanwhile. The interior lights remain on for ten seconds after the doors have been closed, or until the ignition has been switched on.

The completely new electric door-locking system, which is also standard on Calais, has an electronic control unit and an anti-thief feature. The latter enables all doors to be mechanically deadlocked by turning the key a further 30 degrees on the driver's door barrel. The anti-theft alarm fitted to Calais is similar to the VL unit and has a 'radio key' for press-button operation of the electric locks and for activating the alarm.

The cruise control unit has been redesigned to ensure a more stable cruising speed and greater reliability. Another innovation is the Calais 'phase lock loop digital tuned' audio system with a person identification number (PIN) for extra security. Special theft-deterring head screws are used to mount the audio system in all models.

UNDERBODY

John O'Connell, who led the team designing the floor pan, says the underbody is essentially a carry-over from VL, suitably lengthened and widened to suit the increased body dimensions. The front floor is completely new and the tunnel was changed to provide clearance for the slightly larger THM 700 transmission. The structure taking the rear suspension load was stiffened to take the extra torque reaching the axle.

SEATS AND TRIM

All seat pads are made from moulded urethane. The front seats are redesigned carry-overs from VL and have height adjustment mechanisms and recliners which are infinitely variable between their limits of tilt. The seats in Berlina, Calais and Executive models have variable lumbar support control as well as fore-and-aft rake, cushion up-and-down, side wings and adjustable head restraints. The rear seat has been widened for both the sedan and wagon. In the case of the sedan, it incorporates a fold-down section which also serves as a small table and creates a 400 mm wide access panel to the cargo space, allowing skis and other long items to be carried. The wagon's rear seat can be folded flat.

Holden's has paid considerably more attention to seating comfort than ever before. Where the company once relied on subjective feedback from a small number of people, the designers now measure many more comfort criteria and compare them with feedback from a much larger group.

The most important part of a seat is the pad, its profile and hardness. The work in this area is five or six times more intensive than in the past and has resulted in what the company claims are the most comfortable seats it has ever produced.

According to one Design Engineer, seats which are ideal on a long trip usually appear to be rather firm when first sat on.

'We face a juggling act between getting what you might call good showroom reaction and satisfactory comfort when the seats are used for hours on end.

'For the Calais, we have a soft overlay which provides an initial feeling of comfort but, when you sit on it, the same firm pad is underneath to provide long-lasting comfort.'

The moulded trim for the wagon's rear compartment uses a triflex substrate (or base) made from resin, cotton and fibre, with a carpeted top surface. There are noise suppression advantages and a soft feel, giving a friendly environment.

Holden's has traditionally used a cut-and-sewn headlining but VN has a noise-suppressing moulded headlining made from a composite material (wood fibre and resin) covered with moulded foam and fabric. There's a smooth contour throughout the car, instead of the more usual series of seams and fabric stretching between the roof bows.

BADGEWARE AND BRIGHT METAL

The VN badges are made from injection-moulded plastic with a thin metal foil stretched across the top. During manufacture, a heated element ensures that the foil locally melts the face of the badge where raised letters are needed. The badge is fixed to the body with double-sided adhesive tape which is so durable it could actually outlast the car. In the event of body damage, the tape can be removed by means of a solvent and a new badge fixed in place.

These days car-makers use three types of bright metal for decorative purposes. Stainless steel does not have the very bright surface associated with chrome plating but is popular with European and Japanese manufacturers. The Europeans also like aluminium. Holden's, however, has kept bright metal to a minimum on VN. The fairly dark finish known as 'component grey' is a powder coat on an aluminium moulding and is used for the drip gutter and along the belt-line. The resulting product is more durable than the alternative technique of using wet paint over an aluminium moulding. The Australian vendor, Silcraft, installed special facilities to achieve the required standard of powder coating.

NOISE, VIBRATION AND HARSHNESS

'If you can hear it, that's noise. Feel it and it's vibration. But if you can both feel and hear it, that's harshness', explains Mike Hammer when defining his role in tackling NVH.

NVH is the automotive term for Noise-Vibration-Harshness, a problem which has been present in motor vehicles from the earliest days but one which engineers have tackled with increasing success in recent years.

'Noise comes from three main sources', says Mike, an electrical engineer by training.

'There's wind noise, road noise and noise generated within the vehicle itself and commonly called mechanical noise. To some extent, these basic noise sources mask each other. As you reduce one, you tend to highlight another. For example, when you cut down mechanical noises, the passengers become more aware of the wind or road sounds. You tackle that problem and a deficiency shows up elsewhere.

'It's not possible to have a completely quiet and vibration-free car but we've a team of engineers and a fully equipped NVH laboratory and special facilities at Lang Lang, devoted to that end.

'Road noise is the noise generated by the tyres and relates to the tread and sidewall stiffness. We test it by using a vehicle with minimum sound insulation and plot the tyre noise generated over a variety of road surfaces. Of course we work closely with the tyre manufacturers and select tyres which give the best combination of good handling, low noise level and long tread life.

'To measure vibration, we use a piezoelectric accelerometer, a quartz-based instrument which measures the rate at which a component accelerates from a stationary position. Basically, this is similar to a ceramic record-player cartridge without the needle. We glue one or more to the item under test. The vibration is measured in terms of frequency and this is produced as an electric signal which goes through a preamplifier similar to a record-player. From here, we produce a tape which we can analyse and retain for comparative purposes.

'We also use the tape to determine the actual frequency and how it relates to the engine or another rotating component. A problem in a gear for example will occur at a frequency relating to the gear speed and the engine speed.

'We not only track down noise and vibration and reduce it at the source. Where necessary, we create barriers which prevent the problems from reaching the vehicle occupants. For example, we do static tests by removing the engine and placing a loudspeaker under the bonnet. We can then accurately measure the amount of sound which penetrates into the passenger compartment. It takes only a pinhole to allow a significant amount of engine noise through the sound barriers.

'The VN body is inherently quieter than VL because of its shape. In the mechanical area, we have used hydraulic engine mounts at the front of the V-6 and they are a major step forward in reducing harshness. All engines create radiated noise, that is, noise generated by the engine in the air and transmitted through the vehicle's structure and instrument panel. The hydraulic engine mounts have been very effective in cutting down problems in this area. In addition, we have rubber installed over the floor to improve isolation.

'Of course a vehicle has to be designed on good NVH principles in the first place. Our job is to make sure that the many parts of the car come together in such a way that noise, vibration and combinations of both are kept to a minimum.

'There's no doubt that customers will find the VN is significantly quieter than any previous Holden.'

SAFETY ENGINEERING

A barrier test is a process in which a complete vehicle is deliberately crashed at a controlled speed (usually 50 km/h) into an immovable concrete wall. The extent of the body panel deformation and the intrusion of components into the passenger compartment indicate the likely effect a serious crash would have on the occupants. A 50 km/h collision into a concrete barrier is of course equivalent to a much higher speed in most accident situations because a vehicle is unlikely to run into anything as unyielding as solid concrete.

The Australian Design Rules demand that cars provide a high level of passenger protection during a collision and this means that the steering column and other components must not be pushed into the passenger cabin beyond a stipulated distance. The objectives are achieved by requiring all body panels to deform in such a way as to absorb as much of the impact energy as possible and so provide a cushioning effect. Dummies may be strapped in the test vehicle and then examined after a barrier test to determine the type and extent of 'injuries' they have sustained. Rear-end and angle collisions are also performed on prototype vehicles and the effect of these impacts is examined before approval is given for the production and sale of a new vehicle.

Holden's had its initial barrier tests conducted in Detroit, Michigan, during the early 1960s and, in 1968, installed facilities at the Lang Lang test track. The Holden HK series became the first car subjected to a barrier test in Australia. Many of its safety features, including an energy-absorbing steering column, were five years ahead of government regulations.

The Lang Lang facilities have been progressively improved over the years and now rank amongst the finest available anywhere in the world. Specialist engineers take about one week to prepare a vehicle for crash testing. A large number of instruments are needed to record the crash data and the vehicle needs to be accurately measured and marked so that every possible distortion can be measured. The analysis of the crash data can take up to several weeks and the lessons learned from it are incorporated in the final design.

Holden engineers tow the car into the barrier at the required speed, using a winch mounted behind the barrier and powered by a V-8 engine. It rotates a pair of drums carrying a cable which pulls the test vehicle toward the concrete block. As the vehicle approaches the barrier, high-speed colour cameras whirr into action and record all aspects of the collision and subsequent deformation of the body. The cameras can run at speeds up to 1500 frames per second and are triggered by a light cell placed across the approach path. They roll for about eight seconds at high camera speed, providing time to show the undamaged vehicle in motion, the impact, subsequent rebound and the deformed vehicle at rest. Provision is made to abort the test if something should go wrong once the vehicle is in motion. Provided the abort system is activated in time, the test vehicle stops before reaching the barrier.

There was once an incident in which the Holden test engineer stood by the barrier, with an emergency button in his hand, watching his first live barrier test. Unfortunately, he became so excited as the car rumbled down the track that he unintentionally squeezed the button. By this time, the test car was travelling too quickly to stop and crashed into the barrier at half speed. This was enough to destroy the car without providing useful data. As a result, engineers now have two panic buttons and must operate them simultaneously.

In addition to the usual front-end barrier crash, Holden's VN was subject to a number of collisions during which it was hit from the rear by a moving barrier. It was also subject to dynamic side impact testing. Neither rear nor dynamic side tests are required by current safety legislation but Holden's has conducted them for a number of years in the interest of passenger safety.

Numerous structural tests were made to ensure the integrity of all aspects of the body, including the front and rear seats and seat belt anchorages. Highly specialised checks were needed for the head restraints, strength of the door side-intrusion bars and the wheels. The door locks and hinges were tested to see how they would react in an impact. A particularly interesting test was to simulate a blow-out by blowing a hole in the tyre

A VN is made ready for the all-important crash barrier test and towed into the solid concrete at an impact speed of 50 km/h. High-speed photography records every moment of the impact. Evenly spaced marks allow the extent of the damage to be assessed. The intrusion of the steering column and other components into the passenger compartment is accurately measured. Possible injuries to the vehicle occupants in a head-on road collision are gauged by means of fully dressed male, female and child dummies fitted with a variety of load-measuring devices.

sidewall when the vehicle was travelling at 100 km/h. The driver was able to brake to a halt without the tyre leaving the rim, thus assisting driver control.

'The VN is a very high-tech vehicle in all respects, including its safety standards', says Frank Pound, Holden's Vehicle Safety Engineer.

'The passenger compartment has been designed, engineered and manufactured to create what industry people call a 'friendly interior'. This protects the occupants if the vehicle should be involved in a collision or rollover.

'The exterior has been designed to minimise the possibility of injury to a pedestrian or cyclist who comes into contact with it. Undoubtedly, VN is a world leader in minimising injuries during an accident', he says.

'Our tests indicate that the entire range surpasses the requirements of all Australian Design Rules existing now and, in some cases, those planned for the 1990s.'

Don Wylie

Don Wylie, Director of Engineering and Design, comes from a family with a four-generation association with Holden's. His grandfather, Bert Wylie, started the family tradition. After leaving his native Adelaide in the early 1920s, he went to Detroit and learned a new trade as a pattern-maker working on steel bodies for Ford. Three years later, he came home and was snapped up by Holden's Motor Body Builders, then Australia's fastest growing body builder.

Bert had two sons, Bill and Tom, who joined Holden's as trainee body draftsmen. During the Great Depression of the 1930s, the company struggled to survive and work was spasmodic. When more stable conditions returned, Tom stayed with Holden's and was later in charge of body tooling programs. He played a major part in crafting the original 1948 Holden body and worked on all subsequent Holden models until his retirement in 1968. Bill, meanwhile, had started a small metal fabricating business called W.H. Wylie & Company and later obtained the manufacturing rights to Monroe products. Over a period of some years, he built Wylie-Monroe into Australia's largest manufacturer of shock absorbers. He stayed with the firm until Chrysler Australia bought a controlling interest in September 1968.

Don Wylie — Tom's son — had shown a leaning to the sciences at school and it seemed natural that he should join Holden's plant at Woodville, near Adelaide. He did so in December 1948 as an engineering cadet. During a development period lasting some years, he received extensive training, including two years of study in Detroit and now has several qualifications including a degree in electronics. He is also a Fellow of the Institution of Engineers, Australia.

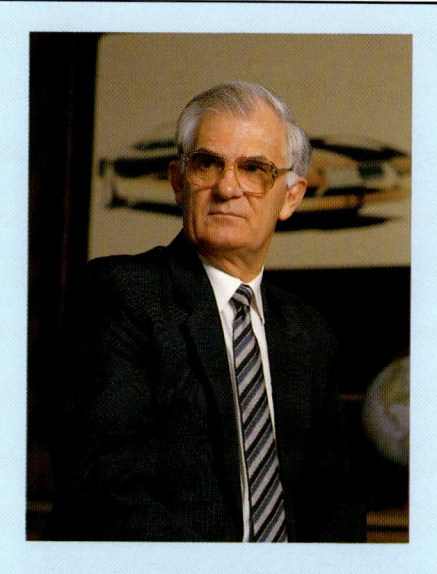

In 1978, following a wide variety of technical assignments, Don was apppointed Assistant Chief Engineer working under Joe Whitesell. He became Director of Engineering and Design in 1986. In keeping with the family tradition, Don's son David also works for Holden's.

Compressing the years
... durability, reliability and road testing

Deep within Holden's Engineering department in Fishermans Bend an early VN sedan prototype sits within an insulated wooden box.

Four hydraulic rams continuously push out the doors and big springs whip them back into place with a resounding crash. A belt lifts the bonnet and allows it to drop. The boot lid is constantly opened and slammed closed. At the same time, an electronic control activates the central locking by sending a signal at the precise moment the doors and boot slam shut. Even the flap for the petrol filler cap snaps open and closed, contributing to the almost unbearable noise.

By the time this testing schedule ends, the bonnet and boot will have dropped more than 15 000 times. Each door will have crashed into its frame on 60 000 occasions, with the windows alternating between being up, down and in between.

This 'slam rig' forms part of a vast network of over 200 machines which test the quality, reliability, durability and performance of every aspect of new Holdens.

The VN has been subjected to more such tests than any of its predecessors and possibly more than any other car built in this country. Laboratory testing is nothing new to Holden's but, with the VN program, it has assumed an even greater importance.

'This time around', says Fred Jamison, Manager of Experimental and Reliability, 'we have put much more emphasis on rig testing in the early stages of development'.

'Rig testing is traditionally a problem-solver used when a car failed', he says. 'You would look to see why they failed then test the revised parts on the bench.'

Now Holden's is testing a large number of components on the bench before they are put into a car, in an effort to identify problems at the earliest possible stage.

The slam rig.

'Problems are found all through the development period', says Fred, 'and the closer to the start of production these are detected, the less chance there is of fixing them before it is too late'.

'Laboratory testing compresses years of customer service into days, so it enables defective parts to be quickly identified, redesigned and retested, saving valuable development time. By the time the first test vehicle reaches the proving ground, the performance of many parts is already known.'

Fred says the proving ground was an extremely important factor in the VN program.

'Durability testing involves an extremely complex array of tests to recognise all types of customer usage. These have to be conducted on-road as well as off-road so that activities such as rough road driving, heavy load carrying, towing, and city, suburban and highway operating can be taken into account.'

Accelerated bench testing is primarily done for durability but provides much statistical information to assist the reliability engineers. In explaining the difference between reliability and durability, Fred says:

'When we talk about reliability, we mean random or chance failures of components or systems which are of basically sound design. Durability is a

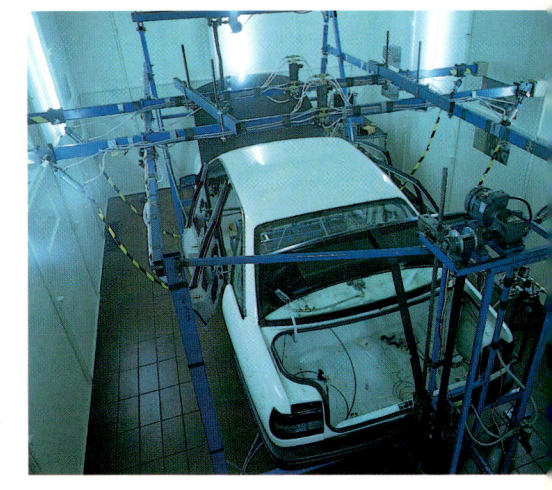

*Above and opposite page:
Hundreds of separate testing operations are performed in Holden's Fishermans Bend test laboratories, with components, shells and entire cars being twisted, heated and vibrated.*

measure of the ability to perform an intended function without requiring an overhaul or rebuild due to wear.

'The fundamental durability of our cars is what it should be', he adds, 'and the VN is everything the traditional Holden owner has come to expect. But the new approach means we have significantly shortened the development time while improving rather than compromising the product'.

For reliability studies, rig testing is often done at 'real time' rather than in an accelerated manner.

Some tests at the Fishermans Bend laboratory last for minutes, some for hours, some for weeks. On no two days are exactly the same tests conducted.

During a typical day in the early prototype testing, 100 or more machines are twisting, thumping and shaking components and assemblies. At shoulder height there are two VN body shells — both fitted with windscreens and cockpit modules — clamped firmly on each side and being twisted from each wheel arch by hydraulic rams. The rams do not provide a consistent torsional load but are working on cycles recorded on software to simulate on-road conditions in a greatly accelerated manner.

To measure their testing, engineers establish a 'design life' (sometimes called a 'bogey') which is a number of test cycles representing the required on-road usage. For the VN body structure the VL body test results were used as the basemark and engineers found the first VN body shells were falling short. The problem centred around cracks in the opening in the rear seat back panel. This problem also showed up with early prototype testing at the proving ground, so additional strengthening was built in. In its revised form, the VN shell is required to take the severe (and noisy) twisting and wrenching non-stop for about 1.6 million cycles.

This takes two weeks to accomplish and is the equivalent of speeding down potholed roads for years without a break.

Near the twisting body shells, a fatigue test on a cross-member is underway. Hydraulic rams are again used to simulate the kind of loads experienced on very rough roads. Holden cross-members are notoriously hardy devices. This one has done three times its design life.

'In recent years', says Fred, 'we have tended to test components until they fail, rather than stop a test when the desired number of cycles has been reached. We learn a lot more by looking at how things fail and at the range of test cycles at which failures for a certain component occur'.

Nearby a fuel tank, half filled with water, is being thumped up and down in an extremely violent manner. It also remained undamaged well past its design life, but the test goes on.

Another rig is designed to check the engine mounts and cross-members by simulating the dynamic loads which the engine applies to the mounting system. Someone joked that the rig had failed after two million cycles but the parts were fine!

The hydraulic engine mounts are subject to other harsh tests, with continuous thumping up and down controlled by a computer. Previously, much of this type of testing was done with big shaking machines but the operators lacked precise control over the load settings. Another once-used testing technique was to perform static tests, such as jacking up one side of the car with the other clamped down. The deflection under strain would then be measured.

The VN exhaust system and bumper bar receive a tough workout by being furiously vibrated. The nut and bolt assemblies connecting the various parts of the polypropylene bumper bar/valance panel assembly have been tightened with a torque wrench; at certain stages they will be removed with a torque wrench and the effect of the shaking measured.

A throttle control assembly is continuously operated on another bench. None of the springs, linkages, bushes or other parts has failed after five million open-and-close cycles. Elsewhere, complete examples of the V-6 and V-8 engines are put through a demanding cycle for hundreds of hours on end. Afterwards they are stripped down, examined and evaluated.

In the centre of the main laboratory room, next to a strange looking vehicle on a hoist (about which no questions were entertained!), a complete

VN body shell is set up, fitted with wheels, drive train and most other parts except the doors. A series of tests are taking place to seek out changes in brake pedal travel and fatigue in the brake pedal stand. This is done by repeatedly hitting the brake pedal with a 'foot' driven by compressed air. The pressure applied is 400 newtons (about twice the pedal pressure of a normal emergency stop). The brake light, master cylinder and cruise control cut-out are also being tested in the same operation. Later the 'foot' will be moved to operate the clutch.

This same VN has its front wheels clamped in a straight-ahead position. Every so often, a compressed air-driven 'arm' turns the steering wheel to the right or left or pushes it down. This turning tests the ability of the steering system to withstand regularly being 'parked in' against the kerb. The pushing tests the steering wheel and column's capacity to cope with the strain when a weighty driver uses the wheel for leverage when getting into the seat. The VN steering system has done six times its design life.

In the same machinery-crowded VN shell, the automatic transmission lever is being brutally pushed through its gear selection movements to ensure it can take regular rough treatment. A torque loading is applied to the tailshaft.

'This test program', says Fred, 'simulates the effects of hundreds of thousands of real actuations'.

Another VN body shell — with doors but no front or rear panels — contains four electric motors which constantly open and close all windows simultaneously. The engineers are not looking just for failures. They determine the wear on seals, changes in winding effort and other factors. Electric windows are tested nearby and readings taken of the current needed to operate them. It is important that the speed of winding does not decrease as research shows that, if an electric window takes too long to wind, it lowers the perceived quality.

As in most workshops, the Fishermans Bend laboratory has music blaring. In this case, it comes from a radio/cassette sound system which is being shaken like a maraca. The test cycle simulates forces which range from the mild effects of normal city driving to the type of punishment suffered in a Wynn's Safari.

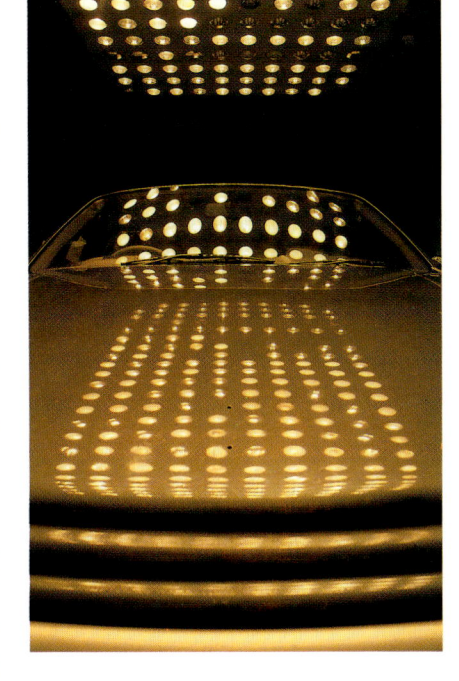

Holden's Materials Test Laboratory undertakes a wide range of technical services, including corrosion protection, failure investigation and material analyses.

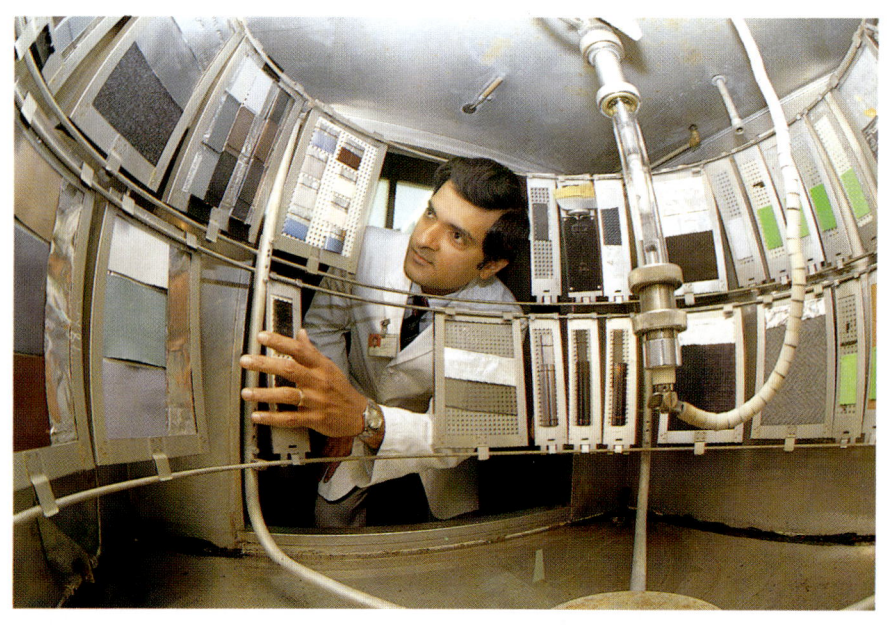

There are many other tests. Axles are twisted at a measured force which translates to maximum V-8 torque with one wheel locked. The force is supplied by having a weight on a lever lifted and dropped. A brake dynamometer runs the brakes until they are red-hot. In what is known as the 'squirm test', a padded weight is forced down on a seat squab and twisted 25 000 times.

Shock absorber testing, done in two massive rigs carrying eight units at a time, was once a major operation. This is now mostly done on Holden's behalf by suppliers.

One surprisingly involved operation is the new testing program for hubcaps. One cycle involves hubcapped wheels being repeatedly lifted and dropped from varying heights. After this the hubcaps are taken off the wheel and replaced 20 times. Then the cycle starts again. Hubcapped wheels are also vibrated through a range of frequencies, subjected to G forces the equivalent of hitting a curb at 80 km/h, and alternatively frozen and heated.

These many and varied tests help ensure that Holden cars achieve the desired levels of durability, but there are also many safety-related checks that the company must do to ensure that the vehicle complies with all Australian Design Rules (ADRs).

In one such test, a steel ball representing a human head is fired at what are known as the 'head impact areas' of an instrument panel. Head restraint and seat backs are subjected to measured pull-loads to determine their ability to withstand the impact resulting from a severe collision.

In a bare VN shell, the seat rails, seat belt anchorages and child restraint anchorages are tested. Wooden 'body blocks' are strapped to the seats (with strengthened belts) and pulled by massive cables until the strain deforms the floor. The VN's seat belts are required to conform with numerous criteria regulating the buckle position and the minimum length of the webbing.

In an operation known as 'the side door crush', a hydraulic ram pushes in a door from outside to test the intrusion bars. Elsewhere, water is sprayed on the windscreen and the wiper speeds and pattern measured. Clay-like Fuller's Earth is sprayed on the glass and the wipers must be able to remove it cleanly from critical areas. They must also function under extremes of temperatures; Holden's are required to perform 8000 wiper activations under four temperature conditions to satisfy the ADR authorities. The testing connected with the wipers alone takes five to six weeks.

The demisting system is also subject to a variety of checks. An environmental wind-tunnel (which can produce temperatures from below freezing to above 40 degrees Celsius) is used to freeze a car. A steam generator simulates the effect of a car filled with passengers and the demisting system is required to clear the screen in a specified time. The wind-tunnel also incorporates a chassis dynamometer and is used for air-conditioning and engine cooling development. It can simulate the effects of towing a gross maximum load across a desert or performing high-speed work at minus 7 degrees Celsius.

Not only have the heating, ventilation and air-conditioning systems been extensively tested in the laboratory, they have been evaluated in the field in the USA and Japan, and in such Australian places as Darwin, Katherine, Cairns, Townsville, Bourke, Mount Hotham and Bright.

Dust-sealing and water-sealing tests are also performed in the laboratory by blasting the car after a vacuum has been introduced to the passenger compartment. It tends to suck the dust or water against the seals and reveals any flaws or leaks.

During the last few years, the enormous amount of electrical and electronic equipment commonly fitted to cars has introduced a number of potential problems.

Inside a special chamber, the entire electrical system of the VN (which is completely new in design) is laid out on a big board and wired as per vehicle installation. This enables the electrical team to diagnose faults and perform special tests. One new check, introduced for VN, is bulk current injection in which a progressively greater current is injected into the harness to see what tolerance each part can stand. All components and associated wiring are subjected to a short circuit against the vehicle body and to the effects of reversing the battery leads.

Much testing revolves around the relatively new area of electromagnetic compatibility (EMC). This is essentially the art of making sure outside radiated signals do not interfere with the operation of the car and that the car itself does not transmit interference to its own systems or to external appliances such as radios and television sets.

'With the VN', says Fred Jamison, 'the electrical noises of each component have been measured, traced and analysed to ensure all components can perform in harmony under all conditions'.

Emissions radiated from the car are measured at first on the bench and later outdoors. Considerable work was also done to ensure that two-way radios and cellular phones are not subject to interference generated within the vehicle.

Holden's has developed its own electromagnetic field test capabilities to check that all components can operate in hostile electronic environmental conditions. Two-way radios and other transmitting stations likely to be used in or near the car can affect the engine management computers or cruise control unless the right steps are taken.

Previously, all Holden's EMC testing was done in the USA.

'Shipping vehicles to the States', says Fred, 'is expensive and time-consuming and, if a fault is found, you're a long way away when it comes to fixing it'.

The laboratory's electrical department also does a lot of work related to ADRs, including checking of designs and auditing of production samples. Spark plugs, temperature sensors, coils — in fact anything which could affect emissions — must conform exactly to design specifications over a car's working life. And, of course, dust and water testing of electrical components and instruments is essential.

Although testing starts at the Engineering department's laboratories before a single car is driven, Holden's is moving one step further ahead. More and more mathematical and computerised testing is being done at the design stage before the first component is even built. After a new component has been drawn, many factors, including stress checking, can be done by computer.

'Computer stress testing gives us the best possible chance of finding and fixing potential problems early on', says Fred. 'But naturally the computer doesn't tell the whole story.'

If everything checks out on the computer, trial parts are made and tested on the bench or in a car to prove the concept. They are then refined and given a full durability work-out on a test rig.

When everything is put together, total vehicle testing is done, also in an accelerated manner. For this Holden's makes use of two of the finest proving grounds known to the industry: Lang Lang and Australia.

RELIABILITY

Ray Borrett, Holden's Reliability Engineering Manager, was remarkably frank in explaining the changes in Holden's attitude toward matters of quality.

'At the start of 1985 we looked at new model programs and realised that if we were to achieve the quality and reliability needed for 1988, we had to change the way we did business', he said.

'In terms of reliability, the 1988 models had to be five times better than the 1984-85 VK Commodore.'

To achieve this ambitious goal, it was decided that Holden's needed a completely new approach to reliability planning and a much more efficient design and development cycle.

'In establishing the VN criteria, we examined the available data, including the Roger's Report, which is a survey of all cars on sale in the USA. This report looks at various facets of a car during its first 12 000 miles [19 200 km] and beyond.

'Toyota came first in the reliability stakes in the 1985-86 Roger's Report and we decided that we must be at least as good as Toyota would be by the time VN was launched. We took their reliability number — that is, the number of times each car is taken to a dealer for repair during and after the warranty period — and determined the improvement on this figure that would be needed by 1988.'

Using these calculations, a target was set for VN reliability during the first 20 000 km. Effectively, this target demanded one fifth as many failures — that is problems requiring repair — per car during the warranty period as had been the case in 1985. Similar targets were set for 80 000 and 160 000 km.

Although basically a sound and long-lasting design, the VK Commodore was subject to a relatively large number of minor but annoying faults. These had caused Holden's considerable expense in warranty claims and had lowered the public perception of the Commodore. The rescue operation mounted at Holden's had shown dramatic effects by the time the VL was on the market and the first-rate reliability of that car contributed to Commodore regaining its position as Australia's number one choice among private buyers.

Having established an ambitious reliability goal for the VN, the next step was to meet the overall targets with a product comprising thousands of separate components.

'We addressed the problem with a team approach', says Ray. 'In keeping with the VN's simultaneous engineering plan, we broke the car into 32 major assemblies, or operating systems, and set up what we call a New Design Control Team (NDCT) to take responsibility for each. Each NDCT was led by the design engineer for the part in question; the teams comprised designers, suppliers, reliability engineers, production people and others involved in the design, development and manufacture of components.'

The reliability program had to cover the design stage (utilising prototypes) and the manufacturing stage, utilising pilot cars. Each NDCT monitored its system from the initial design through to production.

'In effect', says Ray, 'everyone was contributing to the design to make it the most reliable, durable, highest quality part'.

'Having established the NDCTs, we analysed past warranty claims. With carry-over components we knew where we stood, with new assemblies we examined the complexity of the design and other factors. Then we apportioned the overall target to give each NDCT its own goal to achieve.'

For example, the wiper/washer assembly was given failure targets of .005, .031 and .108 for 20 000, 80 000 and 160 000 km; the manual and automatic transmissions were assigned .038, .078 and .155.

Each NDCT individually faced the same problem as Ray Borrett: meeting an overall target with an assembly containing multiple parts and (usually) required to perform multiple functions. The solution was for the NDCT to divide its target and tackle each part separately. With the door system, the NDCT broke the system into door trim, winder mechanism, window regulator and so on, working out a target for each. The next stage was to develop a test program to statistically prove that the targets for the total assembly had been met. This was done by taking a large sample of a particular operating system and rig testing each one until failure.

'We analysed how long each lasted and why it had failed', says Ray. 'If there was a problem, the part was redesigned before it was even tested in a car.'

Reliability testing must be accurate. To ensure that Australian driving conditions were faithfully simulated by the reliability tests done at Lang Lang, the tests had to correlate with field experience, as shown in warranty claims. As a result, a 30 000 km Reliability Audit Schedule was developed. A sample of VL cars was run on this schedule at Lang Lang (with some cars completing it three and four times) and the results were weighed against warranty claims. A complex definition of what constituted a failure was necessary to allow direct comparisons.

The VL had already demonstrated superior reliability to any previous Holden and the audit, which spawned a phenomenal number of reports and graphs, produced very similar results to the field experience.

An early VN prototype, in disguise, is put through its paces at GM's Desert Proving Ground, Arizona. The trailer exerts a measured load which can be adjusted.

'The VL Reliability Audit Schedule was invaluable for the VN program', says Ray. 'We took six early pilot VNs and ran them on this schedule, some more than once, and were confident we had accurately located failures that would otherwise have shown up in the field.'

Ray says that, because of the sound basic design of the VN, early quality failures — what engineers call 'infant mortality' — were down to a very low level. During the second phase, random failures occurred for a variety of reasons, as always with a totally new design. It was coping with the chance failures in the second phase which presented the major challenge for the reliability engineers. (The third phase is the durability or wearing out phase.)

There are two distinct types of failure, known to engineers as the 'trivial many' and 'significant few'. The NDCT teams aimed at knocking out the latter in the early design stages, but the 'trivial many' could not be tackled until late in the program.

'After studying all warranty data and similar research from GM in the USA', says Ray, 'we determined that 70 per cent of field failures have an

The Australian test crew with the VN in Arizona. The VL Commodore to the left is powered by a V-6 engine — a fact given away only by a slight bulge in the bonnet.

In September 1987, Holden's directors and senior executives spent a day at Lang Lang, inspecting and driving VN prototypes and competitors' models. Chuck Chapman (dark suit), who was Managing Director through much of the VN project, insisted on plenty of 'hands-on' involvement from senior Holden's people.

occurrence rate of less than 1 per cent. That makes them very difficult to find yet, if left unchecked, these 'trivial many' cause a great deal of financial pain and customer dissatisfaction'.

It was decided that the only way to beat the trivial low-frequency faults was to run a large sample of cars.

'With the VN', says Ray, 'an unprecedented decision was made to take all the pre-production pilot cars, some 150 of them, and run them on a short-term test of normal usage simulation.' [Note: After the prototype stage, there are three basic types of pilot: 'off-line', which are built using simulated production techniques, 'on-line', which are built on the real production line but at a slow speed and 'pre-production cars' produced on the line at full speed in small batches. Each pilot phase incorporates improvements resulting from the testing of its predecessor.]

'The technique with our low-frequency fault test schedule was to provide each car with the normal dealer predelivery preparation, have it driven 2000 km then check it over and debrief the driver. Each car took about a week to complete its schedule; we started with five cars at one time and ended up with 70 toward the end.'

Ray's team estimated this program alone uncovered about 85 per cent of low-frequency faults. As well as the short-term test, ten cars were run a distance of 100 000 km or more. Four were also driven around Australia, completing 20 000 km under all types of conditions.

'Of course all the testing would have been of little use', Ray says, 'unless we had devised a comprehensive program for cause analysis and rectification/redesign. By detecting potential problems earlier, we were able to maximise time for the development and testing of redesigned components and assemblies'.

He says the VN represents an integrated, well-planned approach to quality engineering.

'The result is that we have a car as good as those from the rest of the world or better.'

Ray Borrett and Fred Jamison agree that the biggest gains made in the developing of the VN were brought about by the SE concept. In Fred's words:

'Simultaneous engineering brought many benefits. In the case of the prototypes, we obtained a large proportion of prototype components from the production areas and had the cars basically assembled and painted at the Elizabeth plant. This caused us more hassles than if we had done it all here in Engineering, as is traditionally the case, but it forced everybody to become involved in the design much earlier than previously. In this way, we were able to conquer many difficulties early in the program and conduct our testing on more representative vehicles.'

LANG LANG

Late in 1987, Holden's directors found time for a 'vacation'.

In what might otherwise be called a busman's holiday, the car-men turned up at Holden's Lang Lang proving ground complex where they were given suitcases, maps, music cassettes, jelly beans and other things that one might take on a trip.

The directors jumped into waiting VN Commodores and went for a 'holiday' drive. Nothing was overlooked. One section of track had a firehose spraying on it to simulate rainy conditions and make the drivers use the wipers and other controls. A variety of road surfaces encouraged them to vary speed and overtake other vehicles as they would in normal driving conditions.

When this program had finished, the directors were asked to drive an array of competitors' models to provide a comparison.

Debriefing consisted not only of 'Were you comfortable in the VN?' and 'How did our car fare against the competition?'. The directors were asked if there was somewhere convenient to put the maps, cassettes and sweets,

76

whether they could hear the stereo properly in the back, how easy was it to load and climb in, and whether they could easily reach all the controls.

This was one of countless tests used to ensure everything about the still-secret VN matched the design intentions. Such tests have to be conducted in as much secrecy as possible and that is one of the many benefits of Holden's Lang Lang complex.

Lang Lang is an 877 hectare proving ground/research and development facility located some 90 km south-east of Melbourne. It is the 'sister' of the Fishermans Bend experimental engineering facility but, in contrast to the noisy activity of the mechanical testing laboratory, Lang Lang is a paradise of open spaces, greenery and wildlife.

Staffed by specialists using some of the world's most advanced equipment for testing and evaluating cars, Lang Lang provides an environment where practically anything of a mechanical nature can be undertaken in safety and security.

The manager of the Lang Lang facility during the bulk of the VN project was Tony Brougham, a former Reliability Manager who exchanged jobs with the current Reliability Manager, Ray Borrett, in 1983.

'The testing at Lang Lang is an essential back-up to the rig tests', says Tony.

'A complete car is the only device that tests all the systems working together. The customers provide the ultimate test, so at Lang Lang we attempt to simulate customer usage in an accelerated and controlled form.'

Tony's 90-strong team works around the clock at least five days a week. At hand is a network of 41 km of dirt and sealed roads, divided basically into 'durability' areas and 'road' areas.

The durability sections are strewn with cattle grids, corrugations, gravel, dust and dirt, steep hills, bumps, thumps and stretches of jagged and uneven rocks set in concrete. These areas have not been created by chance. Cars fitted with load sensors were driven over representative Australian roads and load histograms produced of the frequency, amplitude, and vertical, horizontal and lateral force loadings produced by the uneven surfaces. The outback roads were duplicated at Lang Lang and the same information used by the Fishermans Bend laboratory to ensure that their testing procedures correlated with real road conditions.

Lang Lang's 'road' areas include a circular 4.7 kilometre banked circuit for continuous high-speed durability testing, fuel economy checks, performance evaluation and brake development. Some ADR tests, N&V (noise and vibration) evaluation and other work is also done in this facility.

The sealed roads built within the banked area include a taxing 'ride and handling circuit', an enormous skidpan, an 'M-tar' section (which duplicates icy conditions for testing handling, brake balance and other factors), a 'noise' road and hills with grades up to 35 per cent. Other facilities include a heat-soak area where a car can be 'garaged' after intense driving and tested for hot fuel handling, engine cooling and air-conditioning efficiency.

The VN test program had its beginnings in early 1985 when durability, reliability and quality goals for the new model were set. Actual durability and corrosion testing of VN cars started in late 1986 and reached full intensity by September 1987. This involved 19 prototype and 150 pilot vehicles.

Rough track testing was increased five-fold compared with previous Holdens. One of the first prototypes built was dedicated to continuous rough track work, undergoing frequent modifications and retesting until engineers were confident of the body structure integrity.

The prototype was still going strong by the time the pilot testing program was in full swing. Test driver Chris Daniels was one of a team who helped put a record number of rough track kilometres on this vehicle.

Lang Lang's rough track is reached by driving through several kilometres of smooth, tree-lined roads. At the end of these, Chris inserts his ear plugs and pencils in the time and odometer reading. He then gives the car the sort of treatment which would horrify any owner.

The first part of the track consists of bitumen strewn with every irregularity found in Australian roads, including joints, lumps, depressions and

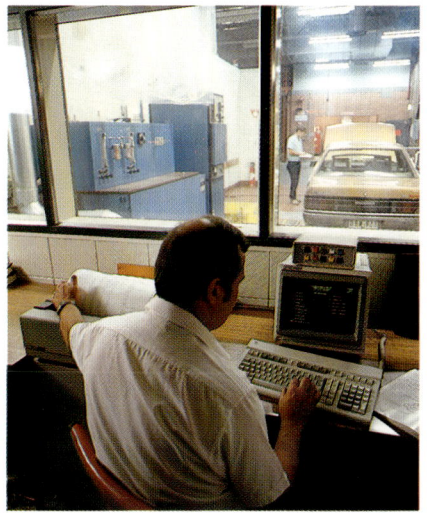

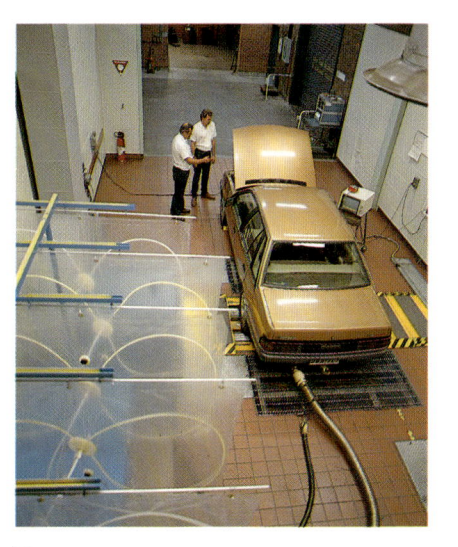

Top:
The massive Lang Lang complex — with its laboratories and sealed roads in the foreground and its durability sections winding through the picturesque Victorian countryside.

Above:
The sophisticated emissions laboratory at Lang Lang, Victoria.

varying textures. Following this section is a series of concrete corrugations which takes the car up a rise and over a crested left-handed bend where it shakes violently.

Like most prototypes, Chris's car is white because metallic fretting shows up best on a white surface. Chris keeps it at exactly 40 km/h to achieve the correct load inputs. 40 km/h is a speed which on any other road might be considered slow. Here, it is pretty close to the limit.

The corrugations continue over another hill, then the car faces a selection of extremely sharp rocks which look like they could instantly shred a tyre to pieces. They don't do so, but the car bounces all over the surface. The rocks eventually become spaced further apart, causing the road noise to markedly change tone. Then the driver reaches a surface of uneven bricks, known as Belgian Blocks. As the car's interior is incomplete — with no glovebox, headlining, back seat, insulation, carpet or rear door trims — every noise is accentuated as it twists and thumps over the surface.

A couple of long wave bumps and several corners have been built into the Belgian Block section.

Chris deviates to the water bath at regular intervals and drives through with the windscreen wipers racing. One reason for doing this is to cool the shock absorbers. Because of the abnormal treatment they receive in this accelerated test, the shock absorbers become cooked if not given a chance to cool.

Chris notes that a wallaby has sat at the side of the track for nearly half an hour, dining on leaves. This is a fairly unusual sight during the daytime but at night wallabies, wombats and kangaroos are out in great numbers. Unfortunately, machine and marsupial cannot always be kept apart. Only a week or so earlier a Holden Astra had collected a roo at dusk. Both car and creature were written off.

As Tony Brougham puts it, 'You plan everything, you take every reasonable precaution and still the unexpected occurs'.

The banked circuit is in almost constant use. Test driver Colin McKenna has probably completed more than 100 000 laps during his eight years at Lang Lang. Like most test drivers, he is at the wheel for eight hours just about every shift, usually broken up into two-hour stints on four different tracks.

On this stint, Colin is testing the VN V-6 sedan at a constant 165 km/h, but some variants are booted around at higher speeds (the 1988 VL Group A, for example, was tested at a constant 180 km/h). To equalise loads and maximise driver safety, the circular track has its lanes banked for various speeds. The outside lane, for example, is sloped to balance competing forces at 160 km/h. At that speed, the car will hold its line with no hands on the wheel. At lesser speeds, an unsteered car will move toward the centre of the track. At greater speeds (and high-speed testing is sometimes done at more than 200 km/h) a car in the outside lane requires a small amount of steering input from the driver.

At 165 km/h in the VN, the sensation of speed is all but cancelled out by the smoothness and banking of the track. Only the blur of the close fence on the right-hand side tells the driver that the car is moving rapidly. The lines which separate the lanes on the track are continuous rather than broken to stop the drivers being mesmerised by flashing white dashes at night.

Colin loves driving and says 'any new product is exciting' but especially the VN 'and a few other cars I can't talk about'.

Ken Hitchmough, another test driver, is equally enthusiastic.

'The VN is the best prototype we've driven in terms of build quality. In all the kilometres we've done, there have been virtually no mechanical incidents. I believe this is the greatest Holden yet built. It is certainly the best handling one I've ever had on dirt.'

While Colin McKenna has been punting around the banking, Ken has been driving a mixed road program which includes three cycles of what is called 'Module 5', alternating with one cycle of 'Module 4'. The former, mainly on dirt, includes three dead stops, a handbrake 'park' on a hill, a couple of reversing manoeuvres, some wide-open throttle sections and a

Above left:
Even at 40 km/h the driver and car are shaken furiously by these Belgian Blocks.

Opposite and above:
Lang Lang's durability sections incorporate every road surface found in Australia.

Opposite page top two:
The rough-road track as seen from above and a driver's view of the loop.

Opposite page bottom three:
Each lane of the Lang Lang banked track is rated for a certain speed. At 160 km/h in the outside lane, the car will stay in place without any steering input. The 'fifth-wheel' fitted to this wagon is designed to collect data for an onboard test computer.

A V-6-powered VL is put through the 'rock cycle' test.

share of steep hills. The latter is a five kilometre drive on sealed and unsealed roads and incorporates a section covered with ball-bearing-like stones.

Some modules include a 'Hardware Schedule' which may involve the driver stopping the car and activating the headlights, indicators, fan and radio for a stipulated number of times, then winding and unwinding the windows and opening and closing the doors, boot and bonnet.

The many other test programs include a brutal and noisy 'rock cycle' test for automatic models, which is done on the skidpan. Working to a set program (much of which involves having the right foot firmly on the floor and the left hand constantly shifting the transmission lever), the driver quickly rips a brand-new set of rear tyres to pieces. But the test has its purpose.

'It is the ultimate shock test for the drive components', says Tony Brougham.

Brake, towing and stability tests are also done at the complex. Engineers add to their experimental work by gaining a 'hands on' feel for stability in crosswinds, wind noise, wiper lift-off, ventilation system effectiveness and other factors.

The test drivers average about 500 kilometres per shift. Together, they notched up 1.54 million kilometres of VN testing prior to the car going on sale.

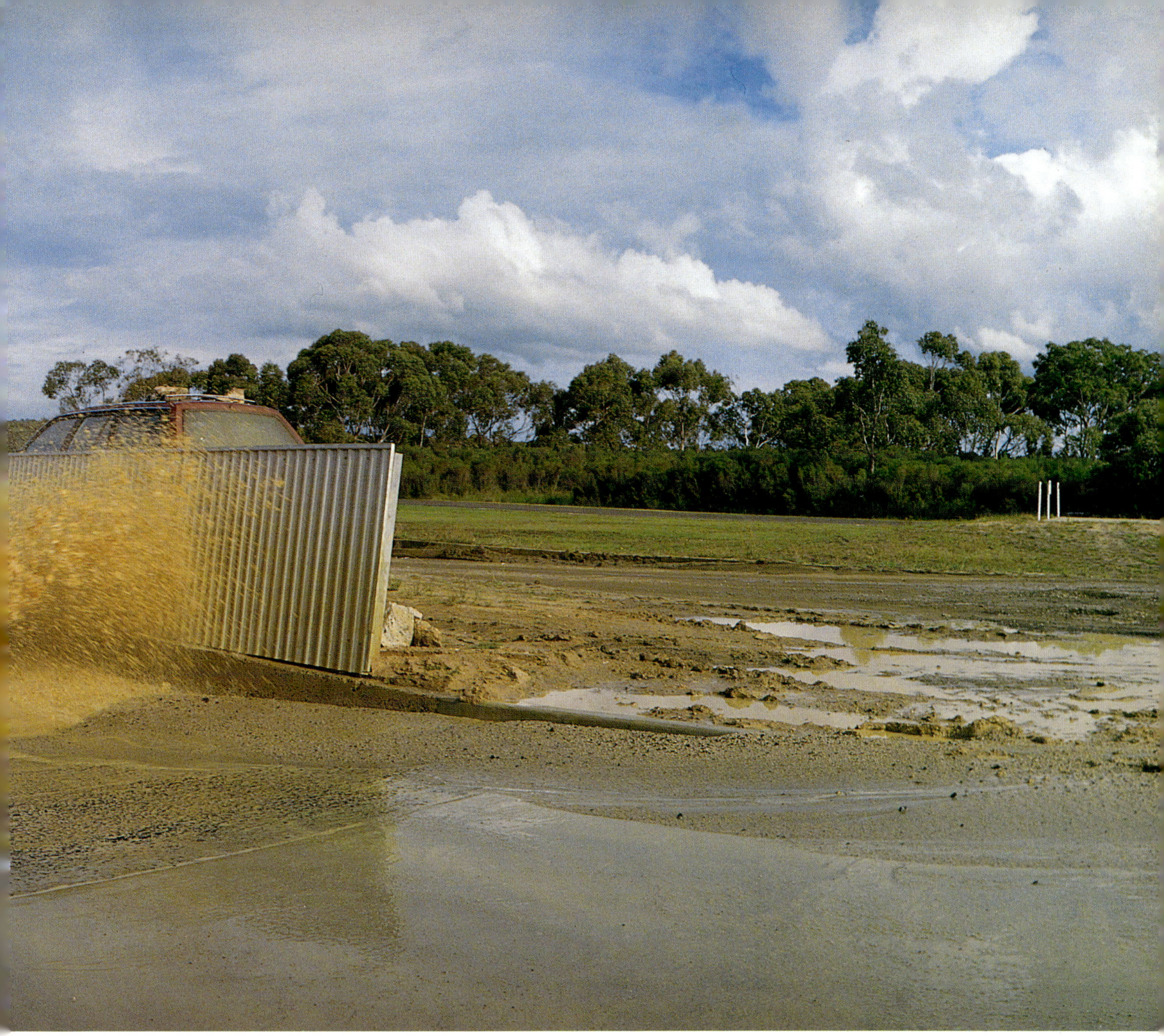

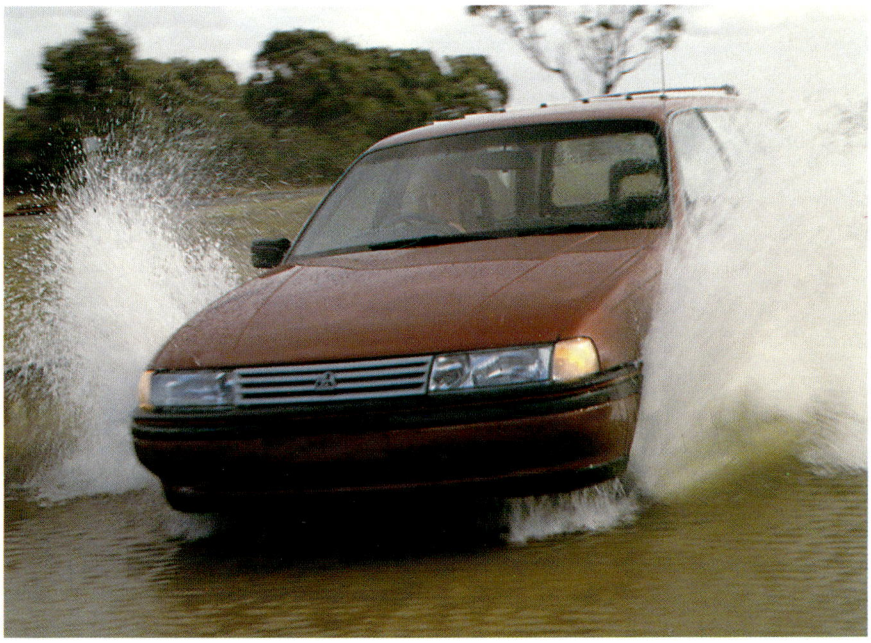

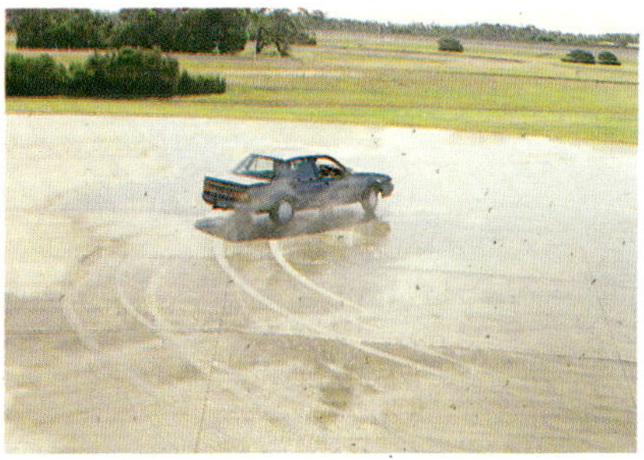

The high-G sled is an indoor facility which allows impact testing to be carried out in all weather and without destroying a car.

Winding 'country roads' within the Lang Lang complex. The way the trees have been cut back to increase visibility and run-off areas is typical of the staff's commitment to safety.

Driving is only half the story at Lang Lang; a great deal of scientific testing takes place at the same time. Lang Lang operates several approved NATA (National Association of Testing Authorities) laboratories and performs its own Australian Design Rule checking. Several million dollars worth of state-of-the-art emission testing equipment is installed there.

Modelled on the world's most advanced emissions laboratory at General Motors Corporation in Milford, USA, the computerised Lang Lang facility was completed in time for the VN program. The mainframe has the ability to talk directly to the Milford computer in the event of problems and to take advantage of upgradings in the US software.

The critical temperature control required for emission testing means that Holden's facility has an extremely sophisticated air-conditioning system. Lang Lang's on-site weather station, which has been providing ambient data for tests since the 1960s, is extremely useful in this regard.

Within the emissions complex is a Sealed House for Environmental Determination (SHED). As the name implies, this is a small enclosure where a vehicle is measured for total emissions, including those from the paint, tyres, fuel system and upholstery. One part of the test procedure is to heat the fuel tank to increase the vapour pressure (as on a hot day) and measure any hydrocarbons which escape. The second part involves measuring the hydrocarbons emitted from the engine after a hot driving cycle.

Dynamometers are used for fuel consumption testing (under Australian Standards guidelines) and, in a nearby workshop, 'accelerometers' are fitted to various points of the car to record the noise and vibration readings.

As part of the simultaneous engineering plan, NVH engineers have been examining the car at the design, development and manufacturing stages.

In the case of noise levels, no device has been perfected to test this during the design stage, so the work is done when the car is as close as possible to being representative of a production vehicle. The obvious complication is that noise problems cannot be found until very late in the program so, invariably, they lead to frantic rectification operations.

Lang Lang has a 90 tonne static impact barrier into which cars are towed. The impact is filmed from various angles at shutter speeds of up to 1500 frames per second to determine the reaction of the car and its dummies. Lang Lang has male, female and child dummies, fully dressed and fitted with a variety of load-measuring devices.

An 1800 kg mobile barrier is used to ram a car from behind to test its rear-end integrity (including the fuel tank). A massive pendulum, sited near the impact barrier sled, allows a variety of impact tests to be done with the weight and force varied accordingly. Polypropylene bumpers can be frozen, fitted to a car and struck against the pendulum to test for low-temperature brittleness.

Lang Lang has a high-G sled on which seats or whole car bodies can be mounted to check the effects of an impact.

'Collisions can be simulated indoors', says Tony Brougham, 'and such factors as windscreen retention, seat belt effectiveness and general occupant safety under crash conditions can be measured without weather problems or the enormous expense of barrier testing. The sled operates on compressed gas and everything is filmed so the effects of the sudden change in velocity can be studied in detail'.

Lang Lang has three workshops to service and prepare the test cars as well as other resident machines (such as graders and trucks). Here they also rebuild prototypes, as they need to be constantly updated as the design progresses.

Corrosion testing is another facet which has taken a big leap forward with VN. Completely new vehicle corrosion test booths equipped with extremely accurate temperature and relative humidity controls were commissioned in mid-1986, based on those at Milford.

'Corrosion testing is difficult', says Tony, 'because corrosion is a natural phenomenon which is very difficult to accelerate. A vehicle which is fully representative of the final car must be used which means that testing cannot begin until well into the final design stage'.

'The new facilities used to test the VN provided an immense improvement. Salt spray facilities have been upgraded to more closely control the droplet size to ensure penetration; tests on previous production models have shown very good correlation between our accelerated test and that seen in the field after years of exposure.'

Tony says the corrosion test schedule has been painstakingly designed to simulate 20 years of actual customer usage.

'We have sufficient space to test our competitors' cars at the same time as our own', he adds. 'We don't test blindly to find out who makes the best cars but to evaluate comparative performances and see if other technology, for example new paint systems, would provide worthwhile advantages.'

'With our research', he adds, 'we are constantly looking at the cost and the results, to ensure maximum value for investment. Tests must be meaningful if they are to genuinely improve the car'.

Tony says a lot of statistical work is involved in tying all the tests together. All reports from the drivers, whether subjective or objective are assessed by the foreman and inspected by engineers when necessary. The reports are typed into a database and regularly tabulated and reviewed.

'No failures go unnoticed', he says. 'If we have, for example, multiple alternator bracket failures, we know what distance each vehicle had travelled when the bracket failed. This data can be used to assist in the redesign and, later, to determine the life improvement achieved.'

Tony says the atmosphere at the proving ground is more quality orientated than ever before.

'Programs of the past have aimed to produce a quality product but now our sights are set on producing a level of quality that is equivalent to any other manufacturer in the world.

'I believe that with the systems we have in place, together with the enthusiasm and effort from the proving ground personnel and the whole chain, our ambitious objective will unquestionably be met.'

DASHING THROUGH OUTER GULARGAMBONE – ROAD TESTING THE VN

Above:
Unloading a disguised VN sedan for secret on-road testing.

Below:
Don Wylie (centre) discussing suspension settings with Tony Hyde (right), Bill Hooper (left) and Simon Cassin (obscured).

September 1987, Peak Hill (western New South Wales):

The young constable was sure he had them now. He stormed his Commodore Turbo up behind the massive transporter at the precise moment another police car arrived from Dubbo.

A third bluetop happened to be passing and it joined the fray, completing a classic pincer movement.

Peter Harker, at the wheel of the transporter, had written 'Happy Day Transport Company' on the doors but this did not fool western NSW's finest. They had the good oil, straight from the bush telegraph.

Several men had been seen dismantling a car next to the transporter at the side of a lonely road. A local farmer had seen another entire car — and a disguised one at that — disappear into the back. And it was thought that two other carloads of men were involved in this well-organised racket.

When Peter Harker stepped down from the cabin of the transporter, an explanation was demanded. A look of disappointment overtook the policemen as the story unfolded.

Already sensing that this operation would not affect the number of stripes on his sleeve, the young constable asked for the back of the transporter to be opened. He took a quick look inside. He wasn't interested in using his authority to get a good view of two examples of the 1988 Commodore.

'Testing new cars, eh? Well, that's a first for Peak Hill', he sighed as he jumped into his car.

This visit to western NSW was one of at least two dozen open road test runs in the two years leading to the launch of the VN Commodore. The purpose of this trip was to make a final check on the suspension system.

At the same time the suspension men were doing their thing, another group was pounding VNs through the Arizona desert in the USA. In addition, dozens of other testing procedures were taking place, on the road and off, in the wilderness and in the laboratory, here and occasionally overseas.

The suspension trip in NSW was a five-day affair but some test evaluations, such as those for air-conditioning systems, can take six weeks or more.

Unlike some areas of car development, suspension testing is still done subjectively. The test engineer has to have all senses working flat out as he tries the vehicle on as many surfaces as possible at a wide variety of speeds. Wet, dry, laden, unladen — every combination must be examined.

The team of five involved in the September 1987 trip included suspension engineer, Colin Sichlau, and Bill Hooper, who was in charge of overseeing the VN chassis development work. For the last night and day of the trip the Director of Engineering, Don Wylie, and the Mechanical Engineering Manager, Tony Hyde, flew in to examine the suspension under a variety of road conditions and, hopefully, approve it as the final VN set-up.

Bill Hooper was group leader for the one-week expedition, a situation that didn't change when Don Wylie and Tony Hyde arrived. Moving hats, in Don's estimation, is not in the interest of test-trip efficiency. Bill was responsible for organisation, planning the route and making major decisions. The team left Fishermans Bend on a Monday, driving two VL Commodores to use for comparison. After meeting the transporter at West Wyalong, NSW, the group found a side road out of town and unloaded.

The test cars were fitted with a proposed suspension set-up similar to the FE2 'sports' package offered on VL. In its VN application, this set-up had delivered everything expected of it in all tests to date. It had sailed through the initial checks at Lang Lang, had been impressive when taken around The Gurdies (a range of hills south of Lang Lang) and had completed a two-hour drive through suburban Melbourne early one morning.

'Some of the roughest driving takes place at slow speeds around the suburbs', explained Bill Hooper. 'It can make you aware of harshness in the vehicle as much as a dirt road.'

The Gurdies have sections that are test favourites with Holden engineers, but do not provide the range of surfaces likely to be encountered on a long-distance drive.

In spite of passing the tests at Lang Lang, The Gurdies and in the suburbs, a small amount of driving on country roads was enough to convince the team that the proposed suspension was too harsh on rough bitumen, especially at the front.

The two nights of driving which followed were punctuated by strut and spring changes to the sedan. On the second day at Peak Hill, a front suspension change in a dead-end dirt road was seen by a farmer, who slowed his ute, drew the wrong conclusion, and called the police.

The VN wagon had been kept basically unchanged to provide a comparison. By Wednesday, however, the team decided they had got it right, so the wagon's suspension was rebuilt in line with the sedan set-up.

The changes being made at this point were variations on spring rates and damper settings. The official deadline for major suspension reworkings had passed but the Holden engineers believed that only fine-tuning remained.

On the Wednesday night, Don Wylie and Tony Hyde flew into Moree to meet the team and check progress first-hand. They were picked up at the airport at around 9.00 pm and whisked (by VL) to a location about 15 km out of town. The transporter was unloaded at the side of a dirt road and the prototypes driven out. The cars were not overdisguised, as this could serve to attract more attention, but they were stripped of grilles and badges and fitted with some strategically placed tape to confuse the shape.

The sedan was white, the wagon metallic brown. The latter could have been mistaken for a VL in a half-hearted night-time glance but, even in disguise, the rear end of the sedan was very distinctive.

The convoy took off, with VL front and rear, and travelled at speed down the almost empty Newell Highway. A poorly illuminated patch rolled before the VN wagon; Holden's had drawn the line at $1200 apiece for prototype sealed headlights. With these virtually handbuilt vehicles already costing in excess of $250 000 each, the company had decided to equip the wagon with protective plastic covers over the globes. The results were adequate but a long way short of the production standards.

Aside from the makeshift headlights, the lack of a lock for the petrol filler and a couple of other small details, this was an authentic VN. There were slight differences between the sedan and wagon, however. The wagon had one of the first prototype engines, still fitted with the original exhaust system (which was superseded by the quieter version fitted to the sedan). The wagon was a five-speed manual model, the sedan had the four-speed auto transmission.

Travelling in the back of the wagon gave a feeling of spaciousness unrivalled by any past Holden. It was smooth and insulated from road noise, although plenty of squeaking noises came from the handbuilt plastic pieces which, at this early stage, did not fit perfectly. The interior showed signs of hard use. No two panels were the same colour and various interior bits were taped together. By contrast, the exterior body panels looked nearly perfect.

Traits which stood out included the squareness of the rear door-window, the lipless window frames, the low front window sills (and corresponding large glass area) and the steep bonnet. This bonnet was responsible for an unusual problem during the early testing. The car seemed to be rolling much more in corners than expected, in spite of the suspension system's increased roll stiffness compared with the VL. As a result, engineers did tests which showed the 'fault' was an optical illusion caused by the steep, rounded bonnet. This was further confirmed when some Opel engineers recalled the same feeling during the early days of Omega testing.

The night drive from Moree was undertaken to get Tony and Don familiar with the recent modifications. They swapped cars at a halfway point and drove back. The serious evaluation, which involved filling rating sheets and driving comparative sections in both VL and VN models, would be done the next day in the first full session of daytime driving.

Tony flattened the accelerator. At various times during the hour-long night-drive, private roads were used and Tony could give the powerful car its head. He spent some time with the accelerator firmly against the floor, on the dirt, in the dark, in a car worth the price of more than a dozen 'off-the-shelf' Holdens. There were no kid gloves to be seen.

Tony seemed happy with the suspension and commented that he especially liked the steering. Everybody, he said, 'loves the performance of the engine'. The V-6, at this point still being developed, was more noisy than the VL's straight six, but the NVH team was already well on-track curing the problems. Funnily enough, a touch of extra engine noise is something the suspension team would not necessarily complain about.

'We received some complaints about the VL's handling', says Tony, 'but in most cases the reason was that people were driving much faster than before because the engine was so quiet and smooth. They thought the car didn't handle as well as the previous VK, but in fact they were trying to do the same things at much greater speeds. And, because the engine was so much more responsive, they were continually breaking traction on the loose stuff'.

Both Don and Tony agree that there were some problems with the VL rear end on rough surfaces at speed but they say the main problem was not the actual design. It was that the set-up didn't sufficiently allow for all possible production tolerance variations in the shock absorbers. This is something they are certain won't happen the second time around.

Lunch was taken beside the shrouded VN somewhere near Collarenebri and here Don explained how VN testing was a no-chance business.

'With an open road test trip every few weeks and constant driving at Lang Lang during the prototype and pilot stages, we will have knocked up more test kilometres than ever before. But just as importantly, our testing program started much earlier than in the past: long before a single VN was built.'

This suspension testing was being done in 'Phase Three' prototypes. More than 60 cars were built before the pilot cars came off the line. These included 31 pretest cars, which were widened and lengthened versions of the VL, fitted with the proposed VN mechanicals; 14 Phase One prototypes (VNs fitted with Nissan engines and GMC-built 3.8 V-6s) and 15 Phase Two prototypes (mainly fitted with US V-6s). Four Phase Threes — complete VNs, fitted with all interior and exterior appointments including the Holden-built V-6 — were produced from scratch and many earlier prototypes were lifted to the same specifications.

Early open road testing was done in 'pretest' cars. These do not provide many security hassles as it is not too disastrous if someone notices a bulging bonnet or a slightly too-long or too-wide rear section. Pretest VNs were driven far and wide, to the Northern Territory and to other favourite Holden test areas including the Flinders Ranges, near Adelaide. Here the Bunkers Hill Road provides an exceptional suspension/body rigidity test in the form of a series of long wave bumps. If a car is driven at a critical speed, it virtually flies between these bumps, getting the suspension totally out of phase and giving the car such a hard work-out that severe structural damage can result. Don says: 'If the body passes that one, it will do me!'

The names of the towns alone ensure western NSW is colourful country. This is the domain of Boggabri, Wee Waa, Come-by-Chance, Coombogolong and Gulargambone.

The sleepy town of Collarenebri gave way to red soil plains as the team headed south toward Walgett. Collarenebri was almost deserted with only one or two people in the main road troubling to look at the strange cars. On the way out, a group of Aborigines sitting at the front of a petrol station offered a relaxed wave.

Don Wylie was at the wheel of the wagon, looking through a $4000 prototype windscreen covered in insects and cracked down the middle. The road offered nearly everything a test team could want: corrugations, spoon drains, cattle grids, potholes and grader mounds plus dust, dust, dust and more dust. Plenty of kangaroos had fallen by the wayside.

Don drove at a wide variety of speeds, sometimes aiming at the best part of the road, sometimes the worst. He commented on the way the rear of the leading VL bounced around on the worst bumps and discussed the reactions of the VN with front-seat passenger Bill Hooper.

At various times both VN prototypes had been set up to represent Executive/Berlina and Calais packages. The important difference is that the Calais runs 15-inch wheels with 65 aspect ratio tyres, the Executive and Berlina have 14-inch wheels with 75 aspect ratio tyres. The lower profile of the Calais tyres ensures slightly better handling at the expense of rough road comfort. The Executive/Berlina, which is considered more likely to be used on the rough, is equipped with a more inpact-absorbing wheel-tyre package. Bill said the object was to get the Calais set-up working well under all conditions so that this translated into a ride comfort gain on the Executive and Berlina.

As the cars bulleted through an unusually green section of countryside, Colin Sichlau, driving the sedan, explained how four different suspension set-ups had previously been 'locked in' for VN. Suddenly the car in front started violently swerving across the road.

'What he is doing', Colin explained, 'is called a "fast step steering input". It is one of the most important priorities in Europe, where 180 to 200 km/h lane changes are representative of real driving conditions'.

Colin exhibited a couple of Opel-test-style lane changes, throwing the car violently into the right lane (of the otherwise deserted two-lane road) and back again at a very high speed. It was real 'leave your stomach behind' stuff and Colin found the car's limit on the way back. A quick and confident swing of the wheel and the car immediately straightened up.

Handbuilt prototype cars can cost anything up to $500 000 each but once the prototype stage has been passed, they are 'written off'. Some are used as testing mules, others are cut up or cannibalised for parts. Sometimes, on a Lang Lang Open Day, one will be 'run into the wall' to demonstrate crash barrier testing to the picnicking visitors!

With plenty of rallying and test-track experience (and no small measure of natural talent), Colin is recognised as the suspension team's 'hot-shot' driver. But a testing trip is by no means a high-speed bash down the worst roads that can be found. The needs and wishes of every buyer have to be considered.

'Elderly people want an isolated ride', says Colin. 'People who push on a bit prefer a harder suspension. It's the old story about trying to please everyone. With the standard springing, for example, we managed to please almost everybody. Some farmers loved it but the staff from a certain Queensland company kept ringing us up. We investigated and found they were loading their Commodores with five hefty farmers, a couple of spare jerry cans and several crates of tools. Their complaint was that the cars wouldn't do what they wanted on the dirt at 110 km/h. From that experience evolved the Country Pack.

'There's all sorts of things to consider in choosing a suspension system, including tyres', Colin said. 'Tyres are critical as they alone connect you with the road. If you changed the tyre specification, several aspects of ride or handling could immediately alter. One factor could suddenly drop from, say, a rating of nine out of ten to five out of ten. But even then it's not that simple. I find the best tyre in the dry is usually the worst in the wet.'

Colin had recently returned from a six-month assignment at Opel. He rated the standard Holden VN set-up at about eight out of ten for lane changing. The Opel was better in this regard, he said, but European suspension systems do not need to be also suitable for gravel roads.

It is on gravel roads that the VN prototypes shone. Even by Holden standards, which are generally very high in this department, the VN delivered a level of ride and handling which had thoroughly excited the suspension team.

In the words of Chassis Development Engineer Simon Cassin:

'The VN is a lot easier to drive than the VL on quicker roads, particularly the more difficult unsealed roads. You can relax a lot more. The VN is more stable, rides flatter and is more comfortable. These are the chief areas of gain over VL.'

Simon was certain this trip to western NSW was worthwhile.

'The major thing we've realised is that within our proving ground environment it is hard to assess the directional stability of cars.

'Until you get on a road where there are poles and trees on the side, you tend not to rate the lane change stability of cars. You are much more critical when you can't use the edges of the road.'

Seat Development Engineer David Owen was on the trip as part of the integral design approach that has permeated the VN program.

David says: 'There is a realisation that seats contribute greatly to the feel of the suspension and the effect on the driver and passenger. The seat's suspension must harmonise with the vehicle's suspension.'

There was much to be learned about the seats once the cars were out of the controlled environment of Lang Lang. Considerable testing had been done at the proving ground for comfort, durability and high G-force conditions, but this was the first on-road examination of the VN seat in a VN prototype. So far, all on-road VN seat testing had been done in the more narrow VL-bodied cars.

The prototype VN sedan was fitted with the Calais seats which David described as being a generation ahead of the VL-derived SL/Berlina seats. David was looking at the basic form and function of the seats. He made notes of his own then surveyed the impressions of the rest of the team. Getting 'additional bums on these seats' was a bonus because there was still time for minor changes.

Seat design is done on a 95 percentile male basis. With the VN major consideration was given to long-distance comfort, something which requires a harder pad. A good seat, David says, is one which you don't notice.

'We are trying to provide a seat with a correct ergonomic profile, good support and a bit of what we call "showroom feel", provided by putting a soft overlay on the hard pad. If people can get out of these seats without having thought about them while driving, we have done well.'

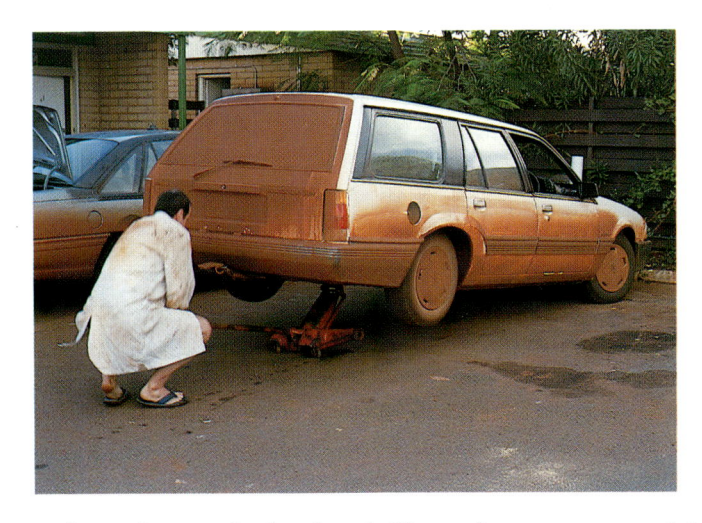

David placed himself, Don and Tony across the back seat of the wagon prototype to ensure it afforded true three-person comfort. After a long stint of driving, various swapping of places and much note taking, the three agreed the Berlina seats were 'exceptionally good in all respects'. Unfortunately, the same could not be said for the prototype Calais rear seat. The opinions of Don and Tony confirmed David's suspicion that some changes had to be made to the pads for optimum long-distance comfort with three persons.

Fortunately, the Calais front seats passed the mini-population survey with flying colours.

Testing is mainly hard work but it can have its lighter moments, even if they are not funny at the time. There was the occasion when two HX Holdens left Fishermans Bend, bound for long-distance durability testing in the Northern Territory. One ran into the back of the other in Swanston St, Melbourne, and the trip was aborted. The cars had travelled only a few kilometres.

More than once, an entire test team has been involved in a lengthy 'find-it-at-any-cost' exercise after a prototype hubcap has shot off into the bush. Once or twice a whole car has suffered a similar fate at the hands of an over-enthusiastic test pilot. Nevertheless, Holden's is proud of its safety record. In millions of kilometres of open road testing there has never been a serious accident.

On this trip there was no drama. No drivers had anxious moments and the only hubcap lost was a VL unit misplaced after a wheel change. Furthermore, Don Wylie and Tony Hyde were as enthusiastic as the test team about the performance of the new suspension set-up. All that remained was a trip to Lang Lang for extreme speed testing.

This final double-check uncovered a hitch. High-speed cornering tests showed that, even though the VN's body roll was exaggerated by an optical illusion, the car could still benefit from a reduction in roll angles. It was here that Colin Sichlau's recent six-month stint at Opel paid off. Colin had been experimenting with 'pendulum' front stabiliser bars in Germany and had continued this work in Australia for possible use in future Holden programs.

A pendulum stabiliser is a GM term for a direct-acting bar, mounted on the front strut tube. Although such a set-up was not previously considered appropriate for the VN (with its solid rear axle), Colin rigged up a system and was staggered by the difference it made. He said later:

'This proved to be just what the VN required. Without compromising any of the other attributes, it reduced the body roll and significantly improved the steering response.'

Don Wylie and Tony Hyde were equally impressed but it was very late for such a major change to be made. However, in late 1987, a presentation

Inspecting a 'pre-test' wagon during an extended test session in early 1988. This trip involved several prototypes and pretest cars. An example of the just-released EA Falcon was also taken for comparative purposes. The high-mileage pretest car shown here has a VL body, lengthened and widened to fit a VN floor pan. A V-6 lurks beneath the bonnet.

was made to try to sell the idea to the top management. Fingers were collectively crossed. Since the conference room was not the right place for improved handling to be demonstrated, Chuck Chapman and John Bagshaw reserved any decisions until they were able to compare the new and old at Lang Lang.

Tony Hyde later remarked: 'It is fortunate that Chuck and John are both so interested in the product side of the business. At Lang Lang they immediately recognised the benefits of the new stabiliser bar system and authorised it in spite of the late timing'.

'Although everybody had to work that bit harder to accommodate the change, the result is a Holden which handles better than ever under all conditions; a car that everybody in Engineering can be extremely proud of.'

At last the team was happy. The suspension system was locked in for the production VN.

Fred Jamison and Ray Borrett

Fred Jamison joined GM-H in 1958 as a cadet engineer and was sent to the USA a year later to study at the General Motors Institute.

After returning to Melbourne in 1961, he has played leading roles in transmission and chassis design, program control, mechanical design and is now Manager, Experimental and Reliability.

Fortunately Fred's favourite hobby, computers, also fills a major part of his work life.

'I was involved in some of the earliest use of computers within Holden's', he says, 'back when we used them to work out suspension geometry and gearings. And I have watched it grow all the way to CAD/CAM [Computer-Aided Design/Computer-Aided Manufacture]'.

In the same time he has witnessed the change from 'small' computers which filled whole rooms to 'big' computers which can sit on a desk top.

Of the VN, which has benefited from computer technology at every stage from design to production, he says: 'The appearance is fantastic, so is the performance and interior package. And I am sure the gains in quality and reliability will not go unnoticed'.

Probably no man in Holden's is more fanatical about motor sport than Ray Borrett, who started his automotive career working for driver/team manager Harry Firth in the early 1960s. After joining Holden's in 1974, he quickly became involved in motor sport. He was part of the team which developed one of the most famous racing Holdens of all — the Torana A9X. He also worked closely with Peter Brock and the Holden Dealer Team on the early racing Commodores.

Although now filling the more important (if less spectacular) role of Reliability Manager, he is a much-consulted consultant to Holden Motor Sport and Holden Special Vehicles. As is to be expected, he is keenly waiting to see the VN on the racetrack.

Vee power
... the new six and eight

IF AN ENGINE CAN PERFORM WELL IN AUSTRALIA, IT WILL PERFORM SUPERBLY ANYWHERE

Much of Australia is a virtual desert, punctuated by rocks as old as the planet itself. The continent is subject to weather as diverse as tropical downpours and soil-searing droughts. The temperature can soar in places to almost 50 degrees Celsius during the summer months but there are other areas which become so cold in winter they can be covered with snow for months on end. Driving conditions vary from an endless ribbon of isolated highway to the dense congestion in Sydney's peak-hour rush. Not suprisingly, the climate and traffic conditions create one of the best engine testing grounds in the world. Car-makers from around the world bring prototypes to Australia for this purpose.

Holden's engineers have a motto: 'If an engine can perform well in Australia, it will perform superbly anywhere'. The motto provides the philosophy behind the company's approach to design, development and testing its power units.

Holden's made its first engines during WW2, producing power plants for boats, planes and torpedoes (and thereby becoming the first company to mass-produce engines in Australia). The first car engine was built for the 48-215 model, the original Holden car launched in 1948. That 2.15-litre, six-cylinder unit, known as the 'grey motor' because it was sprayed that colour, was later enlarged and remained in production until 1963 when the 'red motor' was released. This completely new unit was originally available with a capacity of 2.45 or 2.96 litres and, over the years, grew to 3.3 litres. In 1969, the red motor was complemented by Australia's first locally designed V-8, launched with the HT range.

The 'red' six-cylinder design was reworked for the HQ in 1971 and revamped yet again for the 1978 Commodore VB. The trusty unit was fuel-injected in 1984 and production continued until 1986 when an imported Japanese-built 3-litre straight six was fitted to the VL Commodore. By that time, Holden had manufactured over four million six-cylinder engines, 390 000 V-8s and almost one million four-cylinder units.

In December 1986, GM-H announced a major restructure of its activities, replacing the existing General Motors-Holden's Ltd with two sister firms, Holden's Motor Company (HMC) and Holden's Engine Company (HEC). Chuck Chapman was named as Chairman of both companies and Peter Thomas became Managing Director of Holden's Engine Company. Separating the car-making and engine-making companies allowed each to focus on its main task with renewed vigour. The reconstruction also recognised the increasingly important role played by the engine division which, by then, had become Australia's largest exporter of manufactured goods. Engine sales amounted to $1.3 million per working day.

At the time, HEC was producing about 1050 engines daily and had plans to boost this to 1300 units thanks to major contracts received from Opel, Pontiac and Vauxhall. HEC employs 2600 people and has the capacity to build almost 450 000 engines a year. It comprises two business units. One has the task of designing, developing, manufacturing and selling

92

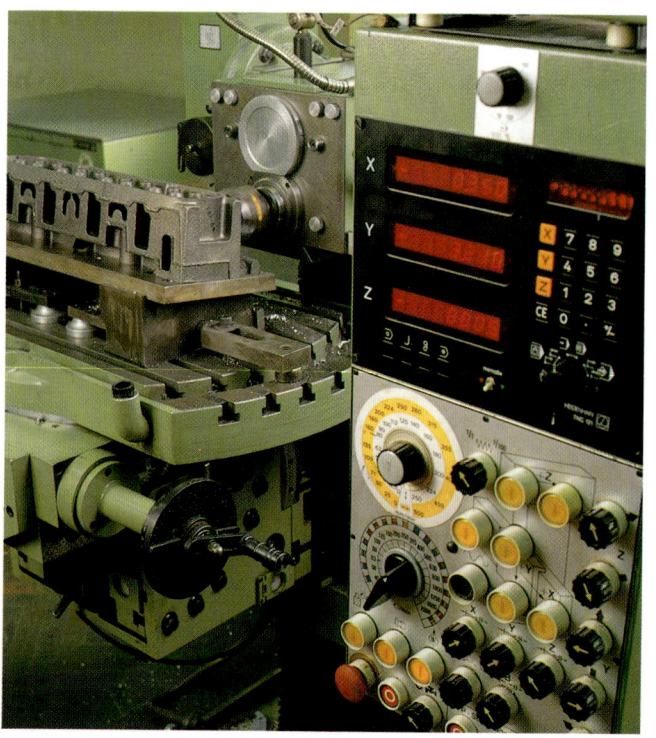

Opposite page top:
Holden's Engine Company (HEC) operates as a separate entity but shares the main Holden complex at Fishermans Bend near Melbourne. HEC produces the greatest range of vehicle engines and is Australia's largest exporter of manufactured goods.

Opposite page left:
Advanced CAD-CAM (computer-aided design and manufacture) techniques were used to develop the Australian versions of the engine components including the V-6 intake manifold.

Opposite page right:
One of HEC's CNC (Computer Numeric Control) machine tools shaping an experimental cylinder head for a Family II engine.

HEC's experimental engineering division is heavily involved in making prototype components for test and development purposes.

engines with special emphasis on export markets. The other operates the on-site foundry, producing and selling castings to Holden's sister companies and other customers around the world.

HEC's main product is the four-cylinder, overhead camshaft Family II engine built in a $300 million plant commissioned on 9 November 1981. By mid-1987, the same basic engine was being produced in 1.6-litre, 1.8-litre and 2-litre forms and the plant had topped the magic production mark of one million four-cylinder engines. By April 1988, HEC was able to announce that it had exported one million Family II engines.

This monumental achievement has not received the recognition it deserves. For example, during 1987 no less than 58 variations of the Family II engine were being produced for export. Each variation is subject to painstaking scrutiny to ensure that it complies with the customer's specifications and the environmental and legislative requirements for the country where it will be used.

Exhaust emissions standards can be particularly tough and, to help meet them, all 1988 Holden vehicles have electronic fuel-injection. This means that the fuel is injected into the intake manifold just before the intake valves so that it mixes with air before entering the combustion chambers. When combined with advanced engine management systems, fuel-injection allows good fuel efficiency with low exhaust emission levels.

With the four-cylinder and V-8 lines running smoothly, HEC was ready for a new challenge and relished the opportunity to put almost 40 years of experience into a completely new design for the VN Commodore.

V-6 POWER

The engine chosen for the VN is based on the 1988 BOC (Buick-Oldsmobile-Cadillac) 3.8-litre V-6, fully assembled and partially manufactured locally by HEC and some specialist Australian suppliers. The US unit itself has evolved from a 1962 design which quickly became a main

HEC is one of the few engine companies in the world with a fully integrated foundry on site. Here cylinder blocks and other castings are made.

Top:
Skilled foundry technicians work with the design engineers to produce working prototypes to test several options before a design is finalised for production.

Above:
This early prototype V-6 was installed in a 1986 VL for its on-road testing.

Opposite:
A prototype V-6 with port fuel-injection is tested under extreme load on one of HEC's nine dynamometers.

Opposite page:
A prototype V-6 is lowered into a prototype VN during development.

power plant for GM cars in North America. Although externally similar to the original V-6, the unit was completely redesigned for 1988 and very few of its components are interchangeable with their predecessors. It is the fifth generation of V-6s built by GM and, in transverse form, powers the current Buick Riviera, Electra and Le Sabre models, also the Oldsmobile Toranado, 98, Delta 88 and Pontiac Bonneville. The VN installation required the development in Australia of a longitudinal version.

Just as the 3-litre straight 'six' fitted to the VL Commodore was a quantum leap for Holden, company engineers regard the Holden V-6 as an equally significant step. It combines a high power-to-weight ratio with outstanding fuel economy and ease of servicing.

GM's BOC division made some major changes to the successful V-6 concept for 1988, turning it into one of the most advanced units of its type made anywhere. Compared with its immediate predecessor, there is, for example, 23 per cent less reciprocating mass thanks to a fundamental redesign of the cylinder block. GM engineers had pioneered the use of an offset crankshaft in 1978 to allow even firing of the 90 degree V-6. To achieve this, they had to split the crankhead, an idea which involved accepting some trade-offs. One was that the connecting rods were no longer centrally located within the cylinder bores, but were offset in relation to the piston pin centre. This in turn created further engineering compromises which, though acceptable, meant higher internal friction due to the need for increased piston ring tension.

For 1988, the cylinder block was lengthened and the left side of the block shifted forwards and the right side rearwards (relative to the block's centre line). The bore spacing was appropriately revised. The net effect was to place the connecting rods in the centre line of the bore and on the centre line of the pistons. A myriad of benefits resulted. Because the engine's reciprocating mass had been substantially reduced, it was possible to use considerably less piston ring tension than previously. Another advantage is that the intake ports could be redesigned to make the injectors spray the fuel in the optimum position for maximum atomisation and distribution.

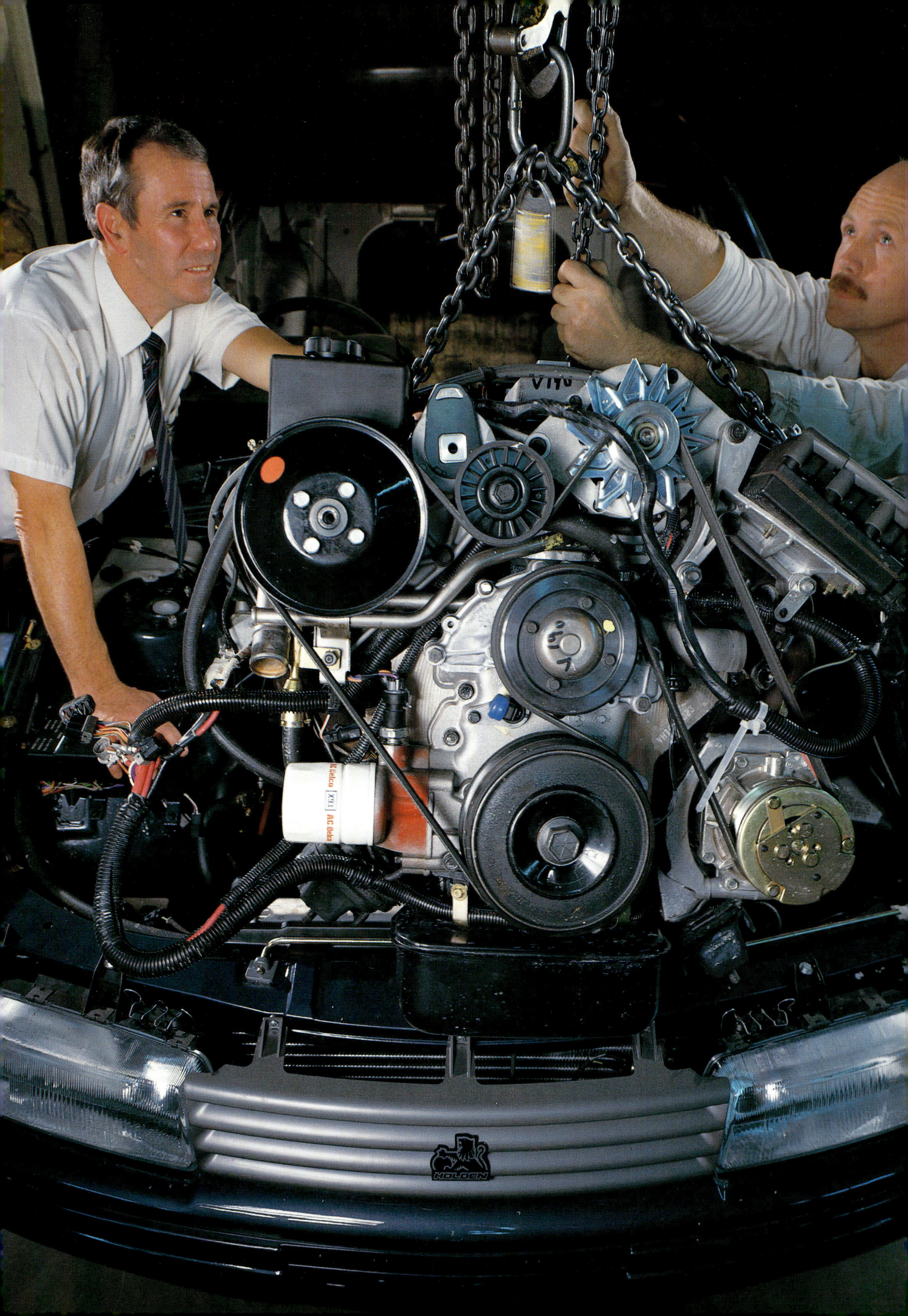
AC Delco
HOLDEN

The assembly line is designed to deliver at least 30 complete V-6 engines per hour.

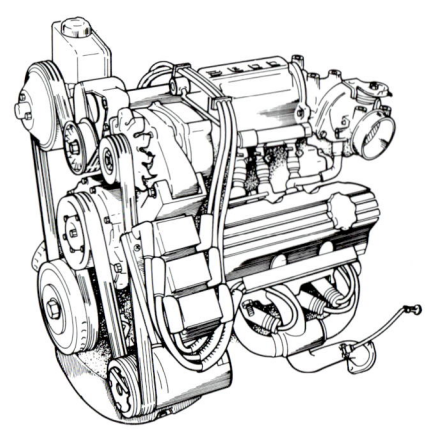

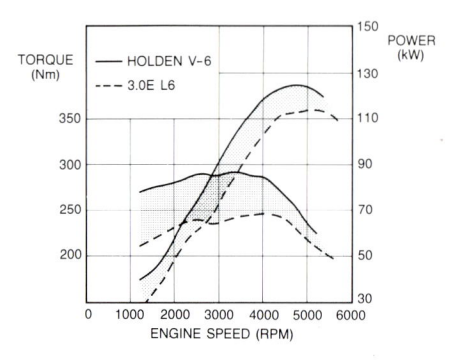

Another significant improvement was the introduction of a balance shaft which, in conjunction with hydraulic engine mounts, greatly enhanced smooth running over the entire range of engine speeds. Compared with its immediate US predecessor, the 1988 engine provides 10 per cent faster acceleration, improved top-gear flexibility and better fuel economy.

According to Alistair McKinnon, HEC's V-6 and V-8 Product Manager, the decision to adopt the American design and modify it for the VN Commodore means that Holden's can offer customers a significant cost advantage compared with the available alternatives as well as providing exceptional performance and ease of maintenance.

He says the Holden V-6 is a very compact and efficient package with a simple, straightforward design. It weighs 5 kg less than the straight six it replaces but is superior over the entire operating range.

'Owners will notice especially the rapid response at low and mid-range speeds because the torque output just above idle speed is almost equal to that developed by the previous engine at 4000 rpm', he says.

'It's the flexible, "torquey" type of engine that Australians have always loved.'

Senior Project Engineer Peter Vawdrey agrees.

'It's a fabulous highway car and excellent for towing. It cruises effortlessly with minimum movement on the accelerator pedal when negotiating hills. The customers will find it an exceptionally easy car to drive.'

As engineered for Australia, the new V-6 develops 125 kW at 4800 rpm and 292 Nm torque at 3600 rpm and has an unusually flat torque curve. The extra torque allows the VN to run a more direct or 'taller' axle ratio of 3.08, compared with 3.45 for VL. This ratio is used for manual and automatic cars.

Holden engineers were becoming concerned about the growing cost of servicing and repairing some high-tech engines coming onto the market but the Holden V-6 has the rugged reliability and ease of maintenance they were looking for. In addition, it has 10 per cent more power and 20 per cent more torque than the VL Commodore engine, producing a 10 per cent improvement in 0-100 km/h acceleration time. Although the engine capacity has been increased from 3 litres to 3.8 litres, there is no increase in fuel consumption under normal operating conditions.

The V-6 is extremely smooth running. Its crankshaft is supported by four main bearings and counterbalanced by the flywheel (or torque converter), crankshaft balancer and by weights cast into the crankshaft. Additional counterbalancing is provided by the balance shaft which rides in the block and is located above and parallel to the camshaft (and driven via the camshaft gearing) and is designed as an integral part of the unit.

96

The cylinder block is made from cast iron. The tin-plated aluminium alloy pistons have full skirts and are cam-ground to present a perfectly round shape at normal operating temperatures. The bore is 96.5 mm, stroke 86.3 mm and displacement 3.791 litres.

The camshaft is supported in the crankcase by four bearings and driven from the crankshaft by sprockets and chain. The cast-iron, cross-flow cylinder heads have integral valve stem guides. They also incorporate combustion chambers with 'fast burn' characteristics achieved through the special shape and by locating the spark plug as close to the centre of the chamber as possible. This ensures more even propagation of the flame front. Large inlet and exhaust ports improve the volumetric efficiency by allowing a greater concentration of air into the combustion chambers and a faster, more complete exit of exhaust gases.

The one-piece aluminium intake manifold is bolted to the inner faces of both cylinder heads so as to connect with all inlet ports. Each exhaust and inlet valve has a dual valve spring to ensure positive valve seating throughout the rpm range. The valve rocker arms for each bank of cylinders pivot on pedestals which bolt to the cylinder head. The latest technology hydraulic roller valve lifters differ from conventional spherical foot lifters by having a roller bearing assembly in place of the spherical foot. This assembly rolls over the cam lobe and turns on low-friction needle bearings as it follows the rotating camshaft contour. In this way, the sliding friction contact of the conventional spherical foot lifter is eliminated. Tubular push rods operate overhead rocker arms. In addition to the normal function as a cam-follower, each hydraulic valve lifter serves as an automatic adjuster. It maintains zero lash in the valve train under all operating conditions, promoting very quiet valve operation. The design also eliminates the need for periodic valve adjustment.

Holden's V-6 runs on 91 octane unleaded fuel with an 8.5 to 1 compression ratio and uses an Australian-manufactured catalytic converter to control exhaust emissions. Located in the exhaust pipe, the catalytic converter has much less precious metal than the VL design, resulting in a substantial saving both for the original equipment and future replacement units.

The engine features port fuel-injection which uses a Bosch fuel rail and Bosch electronically controlled latest-technology Director plate-style injectors developed to be immune from clogging and provide a precise fuel spray pattern. The fuel system is controlled by a locally developed Delco electronic speed-density engine management system with a comprehensive diagnostic capability.

'We regard the Delco GMP4 management system as the most advanced, compact and cost-efficient in the world', says Errol Croll.

The high-tech ignition system has a computer-controlled coil ignition system with three ignition coils and an electronics module. The three discrete coils are packaged in one unit and only one is fired at any one time, depending on which cylinder is to be fired. Each coil fires two spark plugs simultaneously but the plugs allocated to each coil are grouped so that when one plug is fired on the compression stroke, the other plug will fire on an exhaust stroke. Dual electro-magnetic Hall-effect sensors are mounted at the front of the engine behind the harmonic balancer. These sensors measure the crankshaft rotation by virtue of two slotted rings mounted behind the harmonic balancer. The inner ring has three slots cut into it and the outer ring has 18 slots. Thus, for each crankshaft revolution, two signals of three pulses and 18 pulses respectively are generated and delivered to the ignition control module.

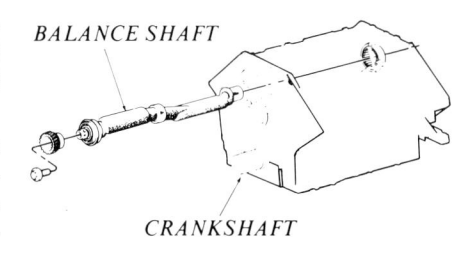

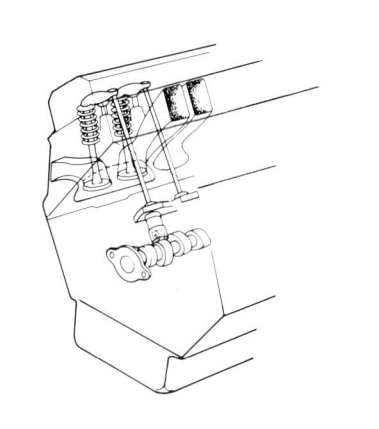

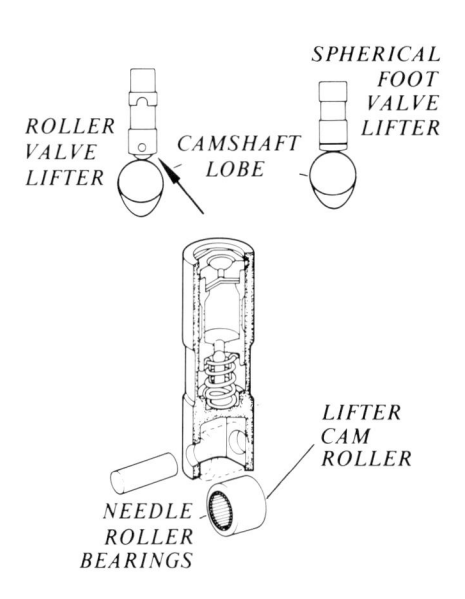

The module determines the proper firing sequence and, using spark control timing information provided by the onboard computer, selects and sequentially triggers each of the three interconnected coils to fire at precisely the correct time. Also included in the system is a closed loop electronic spark control in which a piezoelectric (ceramic-based) sensor transforms engine detonation vibrations into electric signals. These are fed to the control module which adjusts the spark timing accordingly. An electronic filter with integrated circuitry blocks out any vibrations not related to detonation. The coils fire the spark plugs through special wires designed to withstand thermal cycling. The ignition and engine management systems are virtually maintenance-free.

Full-pressure lubrication supplies oil to the crankshaft, connecting rods, camshaft bearings and valve lifters and a controlled volume of oil is routed to the rocker arms and push rods. All other moving parts are lubricated by gravity flow or splash. The 'gerotor-design' oil pump (i.e. a gear within a gear) is located in the engine front cover and driven by the crankshaft. The full-flow oil filter is mounted externally on the engine's lower right front. Oil is pumped at the rate of 49 litres per minute at 4000 rpm, against 24.5 for a conventional spur gear oil pump. At idle speeds, the gerotor pump delivers 5.6 litres per minute, compared with the more usual 2.8 litres. The greatly improved oil delivery reduces engine wear through more effective lubrication and cooling of the critical components.

A special feature is the single 'serpentine' belt drive (with automatic tensioner) which drives the water pump, generator, power steering pump and air-conditioning compressor. The system was adopted to avoid the need for periodic checks and tensioning.

A major design achievement is that complete oil and water sealing has been effected through extensive use of moulded silicone seals and O-rings. Holden's V-6 is the first engine in the Australian industry to use sophisticated new sealing methods employing rubber seal bonded silicone gaskets.

Although based on the US design, the local V-6 has important differences. BOC's unit is designed for east-west installation in a front-wheel drive car and is sold in the USA with automatic transmission and power steering as mandatory equipment. Holden's VN version is the world's only rear-wheel drive application of the latest BOC 3.8 V-6 and is mounted longitudinally.

Over 25 000 hours of design and development time were spent modifying and localising the V-6 for Australia. To have it ready for the car's launch date, Senior Design Engineer Peter Shepherd-Smith successfully overcame a number of problems which others had thought were 'insurmountable' in the available time.

Minor changes were needed because VN customers have a choice between manual and automatic transmissions, with power-assisted steering fitted to most cars but with manual steering offered as a delete option.

A modified crankshaft and a new flywheel were required to accept the five-speed manual transmission. Holden's also decided to use a different engine management system, the Delco Speed Density unit, with which they have had considerable experience with Family II engines. The Aussie-developed system replaces a Delco sequential injection system fitted to the BOC unit which has to meet more stringent US exhaust emission standards.

'One of the reasons for using the Delco system is that we have had so much success with it', says Peter Vawdrey.

'We have developed a very effective software package for it here and a similar management system will be used in the V-8. We can simplify service support by using the software in several applications.'

Changing to the longitudinal configuration and adopting a different engine management system kept HEC engineers busy for several months. The intake manifold had to be locally designed to make provision for the manifold air temperature sensor required by the Delco engine management unit. The manifold also needed changing to suit the different engine location. Not only is it placed north-south in the VN but the engine is inclined at a 3 degree angle. Early on, the development engineers found the angle created some water circulation problems in the manifold and cylinder heads and considerable work was required to find and test the eventual solution.

Holden's installation ran into difficulties with the exhaust system because routing the exhaust pipes to clear the rack-and-pinion steering and transmission created an interesting engineering challenge. At one time, the exhaust piping was so complex that the right-hand bank went over the top of the transmission to join the left bank in front of the firewall, close to the cockpit module. This created heat and noise problems which would have made a special adhesive necessary to secure the cockpit module in place. After several alternatives had been tried without success, engineers called in the pipe-bending supplier to find out how far they could go with intricate bending. Over a period of three months, at least six separate systems were built and installed before, finally, they produced one which followed a route similar to that used on a V-8. Finding the answer was far more difficult than it sounds and was only achieved when new techniques were found to volume-produce some very complex bends.

The engine mounts also created an unexpected share of problems because Holden's was determined to exploit the inherent smoothness of the counterbalanced V-6.

'The job of taking an engine and putting it in an entirely different structure almost guarantees you will have work on the noise and vibration aspect', says Peter Vawdrey. 'The VL was an exceptionally hard act to follow, but we set ourselves the task of matching it at the very least.'

The early prototypes required further refinement and colleagues in the NVH department determined that the ideal mounting system involved using two hydraulic mounts at the front of the engine and a traditional rubber isolation mount at the rear. Though this solution involved redesigning the front cross-member and increased the production cost, the results justified it.

Other changes to suit the VN configuration included a new oil pan and pick-up pipe to clear the front cross-member. It was also necessary to revise the accessory drive to lower the power steering pump and to avoid engine hood interference. A new drive plate was needed to match the THM 700 automatic transmission and new exhaust manifolds and throttle controls to suit the new packaging.

According to Peter Vawdrey, the in-house objectives for fuel economy were to match the VL Commodore in both the city and highway operating cycles.

'Even during the early days of calibrating and testing the engine', he said, 'I was surprised how good it was on highway trips. But we had to do a lot of work to meet our city cycle objectives'.

The V-6 was judged to have such potential for performance, reliability and ease of maintenance that the Confederation of Australian Motor Sport (CAMS) announced in mid-1987 that it would be used in a new Formula Australia for open-wheeler racing. With permissible modifications under the formula, the V-6 is expected to develop over 225 kW.

At the time of VN's launch, the program called for over 100 different components to be manufactured locally, including intake manifold, throttle body, sump pick-up pipe, flywheel, flex plate, fuel rail, throttle body adaptor and oil filter adaptor. The local content is expected to increase rapidly.

V-8 POWER

The V-8 is of major importance to the VN program, not only because of the proven demand and high local content but because it gives Holden's a major advantage over all competitors. The V-8 also has considerable export potential, with inquiries received from around the world, including Germany and Japan.

Holden's experience in designing, developing and manufacturing V-8 engines dates from 1965 when work started on 4.2-litre and 5-litre units which went into production four years later. By 1988, no less than 12 V-8 outright victories in the gruelling Hardie-Ferodo and James Hardie races at Bathurst, New South Wales, give testimony to the company's ability to combine power with reliability.

For standard application on the SS 5000 (and optional across the VN range from late 1988), HEC has developed a greatly upgraded version of the 5-litre, 90 degree, OHV V-8 design, featuring port fuel-injection. The

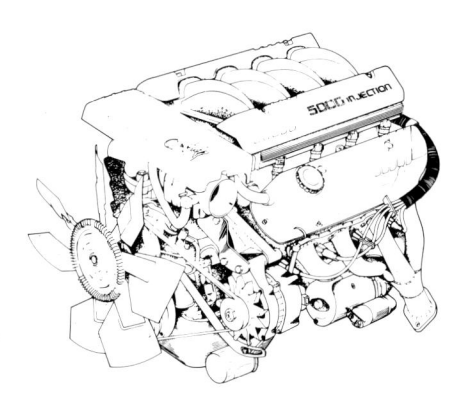

This huge transfer machine can deliver 30 fully machined V-8 cylinder blocks per hour.

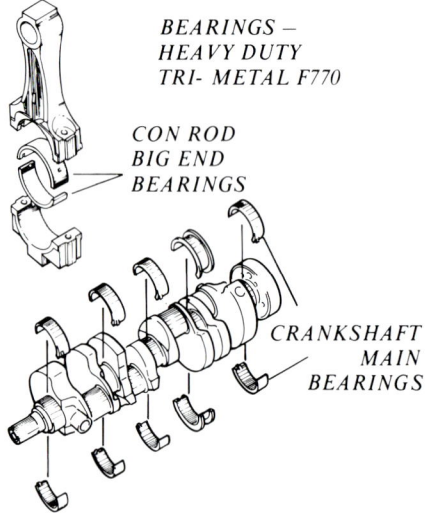

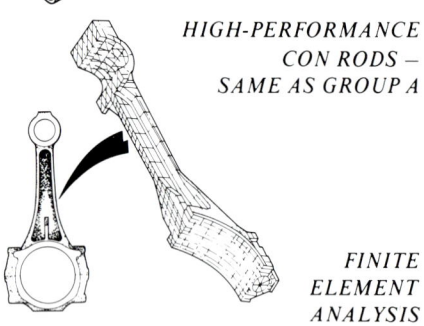

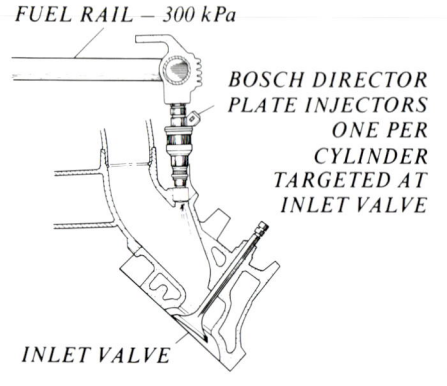

BEARINGS –
HEAVY DUTY
TRI- METAL F770

CON ROD
BIG END
BEARINGS

CRANKSHAFT
MAIN
BEARINGS

HIGH-PERFORMANCE
CON RODS –
SAME AS GROUP A

FINITE
ELEMENT
ANALYSIS

FUEL RAIL – 300 kPa

BOSCH DIRECTOR
PLATE INJECTORS
ONE PER
CYLINDER
TARGETED AT
INLET VALVE

INLET VALVE

company first investigated the use of port fuel-injection (PFI) for the V-8 in 1972 and subsequently reviewed the position at regular intervals. It was not until May 1985, however, that a full study was made on a PFI V-8 for use with VN.

Although the decision was made to proceed in July 1986, it was recognised from the start that the PFI V-8 could not be made ready in time for the start of VN because priority had to be given to the V-6. Naturally, the marketing people were greatly disappointed. Early tests had shown the VN V-8 is much faster off the line than the turbocharged version of VL, and this means it will be Australia's liveliest production car.

HEC engineers have also calculated that the V-8 would use less fuel than the turbo, especially at high road speeds.

Although based on the VL carburettor V-8 (with the same capacity, bore, stroke and compression ratio), the VN PFI V-8 has electronic spark timing, the Delco engine management module and port fuel-injection. It also has new cylinder heads, inlet manifolds, exhaust manifolds, camshaft, rocker covers and camshaft followers. It has revised crankshaft, crankshaft bearings, connecting rods (and bearings) while minor changes were made to stiffen the cylinder block to handle the extra power.

The new cylinder head design has higher flow inlet ports and permits better breathing thanks to a large single-throttle body, larger diameter ports, larger manifold runners and tuned inlet manifold ram tubes. A feature of the design is the unidirectional porting in which all inlet and exhaust ports come out of the cylinder head in the same direction. On the previous V-8 they were located in mirror image fashion but the new arrangement allows the fuel injectors to target their sprays directly at the intake valve.

An important part of the VN V-8 story is the VL Group A engine developed to allow the production early in 1988 of the minimum 500 units required to achieve homologation of the fuel-injected unit for Group A touring car racing. It has a unique inlet system and special features such as dual throttle bodies, four-bolt main bearings and roller rockers. Developing this engine provided valuable experience which was applied to the mainstream PFI V-8 program.

The V-8 has a spectacular appearance and looks unlike any previous Holden engine, thanks to cast aluminium rocker covers and tuned aluminium inlet manifold. The technology has been proved both in the conventional arena and on the racetrack with the very potent Group A PFI V-8 competition cars.

The Holden V-8 PFI employs the same electronic fuel-injection design used with the Holden V-6, which is one of the most modern available. It uses eight injectors and a combination of Bosch and Delco parts. It provides fuel in proportion to the engine speed, load, temperature and throttle position and has a fuel cut-off on deceleration. The computer-controlled ignition system advances the spark based on engine temperature, rpm and load. A detonation sensor automatically retards the spark if detonation should occur.

As a result of the changes, the Holden PFI V-8 has numerous advantages over the highly regarded carburettor V-8 it replaces. Power has risen from 122 kW to 168 kW net and torque from 323 to 400 Nm net. Engineering tests show the VN can accelerate from rest to 100 km/h in just over six seconds.

The V-8 is highly refined by any standards and gives virtually instantaneous starting, outstanding drivability and full power immediately after a cold start. The idle is smoother and the fuel consumption reduced compared with the carburettor version of the same engine.

'The Holden PFI V-8 complements the V-6 engine and both will provide outstanding service in the hands of our customers', said Alistair McKinnon.

'The choice is simple. Customers can have outstanding economy with excellent performance with the V-6 or outstanding performance and adequate economy with the V-8.'

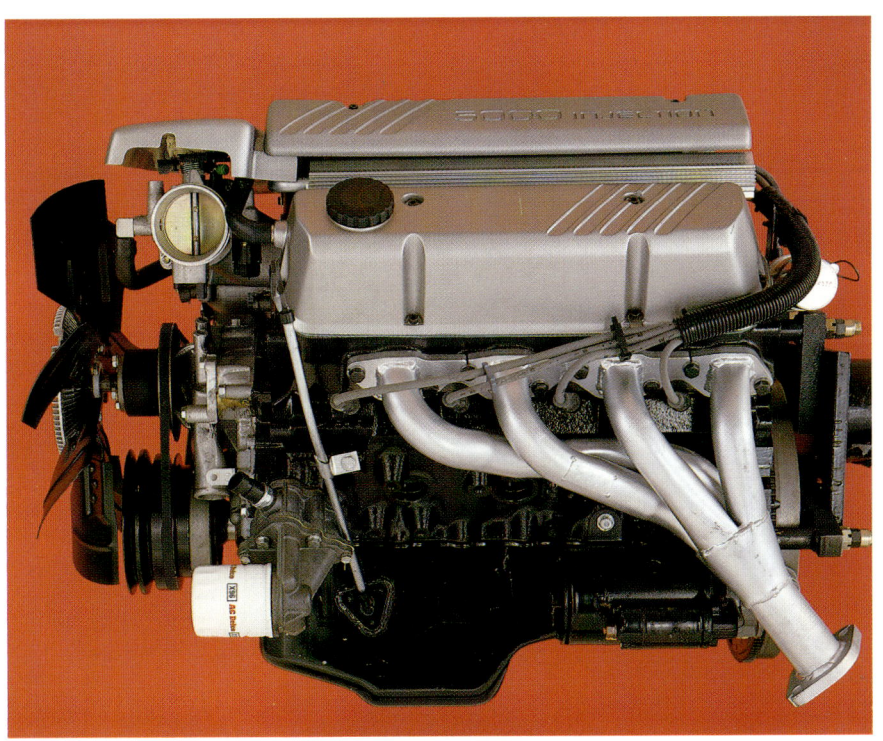

Holden's handsome and potent V-8.

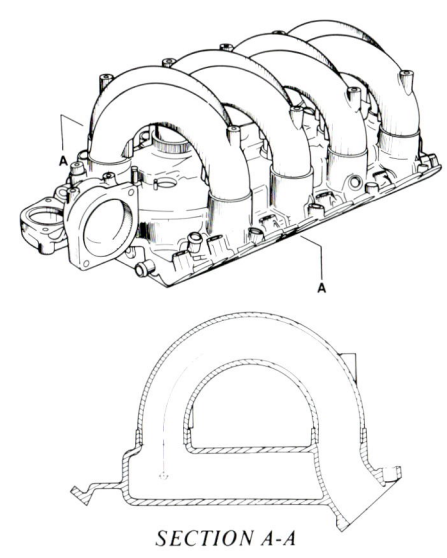

OPTIMISED RUNNER LENGTH AND DIAMETER

SINGLE THROTTLE BODY

RAM-TUNED INLET MANIFOLD

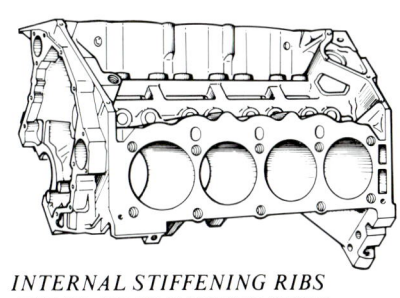

SECTION A-A

INTERNAL STIFFENING RIBS ADDED TO ELIMINATE BORE DISTORTION

An experimental Group A V-8 is ready for its first on-road test run.

Australia's first mass-produced V-6.

Peter Thomas and Errol Croll

Peter Thomas has a long commercial background, starting in GM-H's purchasing department and later serving as supply manager from 1978 to 1981 with GM, New Zealand. He became purchasing manager at Holden's in 1983, then moved to manufacturing where his considerable administrative skill led to his appointment as head of the manufacturing complex at Fishermans Bend. In late 1986, he became Managing Director of the newly formed Holden's Engine Company (HEC). At the same time, Errol Croll was appointed Manager, Engine Development and Sales.

Errol Croll, who has served Holden's in a number of capacities over 25 years, has both technical and commercial responsibilities with HEC. He is in charge of design, development and testing engines, and is also involved in developing new markets, a recognition of the fact that the company sells technical products to technical people. The four-cylinder Family II engine is already a major success in Europe where it is fitted to Opel Omegas and Vauxhall Cavaliers and the company is working hard to secure contracts in developing industries closer to home: Taiwan, Thailand, Malaysia, Indonesia and China. HEC is also looking to develop markets for the V-6 and PFI V-8.

Errol believes that motor sport is one key to success.

'Australia is not the place where people expect to buy serious things like engines', he says. 'We have an image problem to overcome. There are several answers and we need to explore them all. We are already involved with Group A cars in motor sport overseas to give our products credibility. At trade fairs we display race cars and use them to promote our capability in engine technology.'

'At the 1987 Australian Grand Prix we spent some time talking to Formula One racing teams. Although we have no immediate plans in this direction, producing a F1 engine is very interesting to think about.'

Putting it together
... building cars in the new age

'ONCE WE CHASED NUMBERS, NOW WE CHASE QUALITY'

'Until the time we were building the last of the VKs, the most important job was to keep up the production schedule', says Vic Beesley.

'Production numbers took priority and some cars went off the line with water leaks, poorly balanced wheels, paint blemishes and incorrectly adjusted headlamps.

'The poor quality caused a number of complaints and they began to affect sales.

'Even so, when they told us late in 1985 that quality was to come first, many people were skeptical. They had heard it all before and thought nothing would really change. However, the assembly line stopped one day and the operators were told that the quality was not up to scratch and the line would continue to stop every time a quality problem arose.

General Supervisor of Assembly Technical Services Graham Mesecke inspects the massive multi-spot welder installed as part of the main VN body line at the Elizabeth plant, South Australia, during the try-out stage.

New technology is indispensable for production efficiency but human resources are even more important. Fiona Kerr leads one of many discussions on human resources management held by senior management at the Elizabeth plant when the manufacture of the all-new VN was being planned.

'The assembly line is king in a plant like this and stopping it for any reason practically needs a letter from the board of directors. So when the line stopped, and the reason was given as poor quality, everyone here realised that Holden's was fair dinkum.

'At just about the same time, another major change took place. The factory superintendents were made responsible for the quality of the work done in their shops; they could no longer hide behind the excuse "Ah, but the quality control inspector passed it".

'Then we got a resident engineer who could make decisions without reference to head office and the quality control picture was transformed. The changes affected everyone. They dramatically improved the manner in which the VL was built and set the stage for the VN, which I think is the best car we have ever made.'

Vic Beesley is Technical Manager of Assembly Operations at Holden's plant at Elizabeth, South Australia. He is a leading executive at the 123 hectare complex located 25 km north of Adelaide. The plant was born during the late 1950s when Holden sales forecasts indicated that additional production facilities would soon be needed. About the same time, the South Australian Housing Trust was looking for industrial organisations to take up land near the growing township of Elizabeth. GM-H purchased 95 hectares in 1956 and the new hardware plant opened in 1959, the bodyshop in 1962, the trim and paint areas in 1963 and the stamping plant in 1965. Additional land was acquired during the 1960s, giving a total of around 123 hectares. Of this, almost 21 hectares are under roof.

The Elizabeth site has developed into one of Australia's most advanced sheet metal plants and motor vehicle assembly facilities. The operation, which employs 5000 people, presses sheet metal panels for Holden, Nissan and Toyota and manufactures plastic components for Holden. Elizabeth is the birthplace of VN cars. Here the sheet metal panels are stamped, the bodies fabricated and the vehicles assembled and trimmed. The mechanical components are supplied by Holden's Victorian operations and by outside suppliers.

THE ROBOTS ARE MARCHING

Recognising that improved productivity alone is not the key to the 1990s, Holden's spent about $200 million on new facilities at Elizabeth to substantially raise the quality of the finished product. Two fully automatic transfer presses cost $30 million, the tooling for the body assembly ran to $42 million and sophisticated measuring machines added a further $8 million to the bill. Countless other expensive items were bought. The alternative to this expenditure was to build the VN in two plants, but this would have increased the unit cost of each vehicle by about $200 at retail level. It would also have been necessary to forgo many of the quality control improvements which come with the latest technology.

The equipment is formidable indeed. In August 1987, Holden's commissioned the two largest and most advanced transfer presses yet seen in the southern hemisphere. Built by Hitachi Zosen of Japan, the giant 2700 tonne machines stamp out about 2.5 million VN body panels per year. Each press has six work-stations and a tri-axis feed mechanism which automatically advances the sheet metal from one work-station to the next. The continuous striking rate can be varied from eight to 16 per minute, giving a production rate up to $2\frac{1}{2}$ times faster than a conventional large press line.

In addition to the substantially better efficiency, the transfer presses provide increased flexibility and quality of finish. Advanced computer technology allows them to switch from one job to another at the push of a button and for dies to be changed in ten minutes instead of the usual two hours. The transfer machines join over 90 large presses in the Elizabeth stamping plant.

Other equipment installed specially for VN includes a massive multispot-welder for the main body line. Completely automatic and remarkably precise in action, this unit is so large it weighs 23 tonnes. It cost almost half-a-million dollars in freight alone to ship the body assembly lines from Japan!

Less spectacular to watch, but equally vital to quality control, is the new LK 3-Dimensional Coordinate Measuring Machine used to accurately measure structures such as the body shell. This remarkable piece of technology can scan components and measure up to 120 points in one minute. It is also capable of measuring up to 140 critical points around the body shell, comparing them with the design specifications and reporting the results in less than an hour. To ensure the big machine remains accurate under all conditions, the X-axis is made from a 26 tonne piece of granite, the most dimensionally stable material known. The Y-axis is fashioned from rigid carbon fibre and was made in the same factory as many Formula One racing car chassis.

Because flush glass poses new problems relating to door fit, Holden's spent $5 million on equipment to manufacture door frames in a completely new way. John Oldenhove, the Senior Process Planner, says the system is a combination of computerised rolling and bending machines operating in conjunction with robotics and single-point tooling fixtures. Working with Okaya, Miic and Mori in Japan, Elizabeth engineers have pioneered a system which very accurately produces the complex shapes needed for door frames. The 40 metre long system manufactures frames for 360 vehicles per day.

The concept, which was conceived at Elizabeth, took 18 months to develop and is a world first. Where previously 35 people and 35 items of equipment were needed to fabricate the door frames, the new system allows the work to be done by ten people using one fully integrated line. A far higher degree of accuracy is achieved and the equipment automatically measures each frame as it is built. If any measurement is wrong, the line stops until the fault is fixed. John Oldenhove says the concept is so advanced that engineers from Opel, Fisher Body and GM have studied it with a view to adopting some of the technical concepts themselves.

Holden's plastics plant, located within the Elizabeth complex, was commissioned in 1982, and is regarded as one of the best of its type anywhere. By utilising the appropriate plastic materials, greater flexibility is available to design bumper facias which meet the company's impact criteria. The facias also incorporate the lower valance panel and other features not possible with the steel bumper bars previously used. Automotive plastics have the added advantage of being lighter than steel and resistant to corrosion.

Sophisticated robotic-oriented assembly fixtures have been developed to meet the exacting quality standards required on the sedan tail-lamp assemblies and the larger instrument panel.

New state-of-the-art injection moulding machines allow large components to be made in one piece, thus eliminating joint lines and parts proliferation. One machine can make 24 VN front bumpers per hour using an 18 000 kilonewton clamp-pressure press and a single die. In contrast, producing the steel bumpers and separate valance panels used for the early Commodores required a rolling machine, stretch bender and press tools to trim and pierce. Another advantage is that the plastic VN bumper is 4.5 kg lighter than the earlier chromed steel unit.

Top:
Pattern-makers in the toolroom at Woodville, South Australia, inspect these polystyrene patterns which are about to go the foundry for casting as press dies to stamp out sheet metal panels. The polystyrene melts as the molten metal is poured.
Above:
One of the largest transfer presses in the southern hemisphere, this Hitachi Zosen unit at the Elizabeth plant dwarfs the gantry crane operator who is repositioning a press die.

Janet Dissinger is one of several operators from the Elizabeth plant who went to Japan to study the die-setting and press operation techniques needed for the highly computerised Hitachi Zosen transfer press.

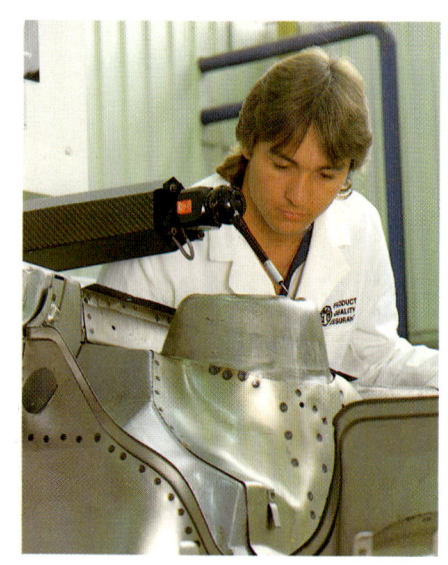

Michael Lloyd uses the incredibly accurate LK 3-Dimensional Coordinate Measuring machine to check a VN front suspension strut tower.

Right:
Craig Palmer (foreground) and Ralph Boyce check the conformity of a VN decklid panel on a master check fixture.

WHO OWNS THE PROBLEM?

Some of the biggest problems associated with car-making never reach the ears of the public. These are the endless headaches which occur when the manufacturing engineers start to design the equipment needed to manufacture a completely new car.

Their very difficult job — one which receives little recognition — is to work out the best way to produce each of the thousands of parts which make up a single car.

'The previous practice', says Rod Filmer, 'was for our colleagues to design a car in mid-air at Fishermans Bend, then hand us the job of producing it'.

'We would run into all sorts of difficulties trying to turn the designers' dream into a production reality. We'd have a dozen teams working on the various aspects of production but, when something went wrong, no one wanted to know. The problem always belonged to someone else. The production guy blamed the designer and vice versa.

'Two new concepts were introduced for VN, and they made an enormous difference. One was Simultaneous Engineering in which the manufacturing process engineers had a say in the car's design; the other was the NDCT (New Design Control Team) process in which groups of technicians and suppliers, offering a variety of skills, helped pilot the VN from concept to completion.'

As Manager of Manufacturing Engineering Services at Elizabeth, Rod Filmer heads a 90-strong group of engineers and technicians who provide the indirect manufacturing engineering support required by the fabrication side of the business. His group handles industrial engineering, plant and equipment engineering and the provision of all equipment and tooling needed for fabrication operations.

'Getting the VN ready for production put a tremendous strain on our people', says Rod. 'We spent over a million dollars sending key players to Japan. Some were away from home for months on end and they worked in a strange environment harder than they had ever worked before'.

'Single-point tooling, which has some major advantages in terms of quality control, caused our biggest headaches. To make the concept work, we must start with perfect dimensional accuracy. That's our job.

Top:
These GM-Fanuc robots are being prepared for installation on the underbody line in the body plant.

Above:
Senior Production Engineer Phillip Smith tests the robot welding sequence for part of the cockpit module.

Left:
A Cincinnati Milacron robot gun-welds several components as part of the three-stage robotic line where the complex dash panel is built.

Top Left:
First Class Machinist Stefano Desciscio observes the robot action from a finishing fixture control panel. This robot places in position and removes the formed door frames from the finishing fixtures which reset, pierce, joggle and trim them.

Top Right:
Maintenance Electrician Robin Rayment at the robot control console on the underbody line at the Elizabeth plant during the tryout stage.

Bottom Left:
Production operator George Delorenzo completes the shuttle transfer of station wagon underbodies on the main body line.

Bottom Right:
John Quinn, Klaas Neef and Paul Robinson spot-weld body-side assemblies on the shuttle system adjacent to the main body line.

'We've also seen a higher degree of training during the past three years than I've seen in the previous 30 years in the company. For example, it cost $50 000 to train the operators involved on the door frame line alone. This covered not just the routine operation but fault-finding, diagnostics and maintenance. My colleagues, who look after engineering support for the assembly side, are doing a similar job for the body shuttle assembly operation.'

The Production Engineering Manager, Bob Miller, reports to Rod Filmer and manages 55 technical people involved in process planning, tooling, materials handling and other industrial engineering support functions. He identified another major change of emphasis developed for VN production.

'My people are originating planners', he says. 'They take a part designed by engineers in Fishermans Bend or Opel and conceptualise the tooling and process requirement by which it will be produced'.

'For VN, we were responsible for finding the best and most economical way to fabricate 800 separate sheet metal parts. We look after each from

108

the raw material to the point where it is ready for shipment to the body shop. One of our main objectives is to achieve a process capability ratio of less than 75 per cent in Total Quality Control terms. This ensures that fabrication consistently produces only high-quality parts.

'The original way of doing things was to have a number of planners handle several aspects of producing a number of parts. Invariably, if something went wrong, there was a temptation to pass it off as someone else's problem. With the new approach, we have deliberately developed a sense of "ownership". Each process planner is assigned the job of completely planning the production of each part. He takes responsibility for all aspects of that job. In our language, he "owns" the part and he "owns" the problems. But he can also take the credit when the tooling concept works and produces good parts.'

To help their task, Bob Miller's people use a new device they call a UCF/PCF, or Unit Checking Fixture/Parts Checking Fixture. Essentially, it is a type of clothes horse on which they can try out a skin surface metal panel or a complete subassembly — such as an engine hood, door, decklid, roof or fender — and make sure it fits perfectly. The UCF/PCF is invaluable for checking tooling and fixtures during the pre-production stage as well as routinely checking production parts.

George Delorenzo (right) instructs Michael Johnson on the new roof bow fitment technique developed for the VN body line.

A fully automatic weld station on the main body line where the body sides are assembled to the underbody.

109

Below left:
GM-Fanuc robots spot-weld the roof panel to the VN wagon body sides in the Elizabeth plant body shop.

Below right:
Starting with a straight frame section, a computer-controlled bending machine starts to form a door frame (centre of picture).

Bottom left:
Electrical Engineer Noel Wyett at the control console of the rear door final assembly line. The robot in the foreground is about to apply hem adhesive and anti-flutter compound to the panel.

Bottom right:
Production Leading Hand Albino Pancione unloads and inspects finished door frames received from the unique rolling and bending machine developed at the Elizabeth plant.

When Bob Miller's department has decided how each sheet metal part will be made, and what equipment will be needed, it hands the information to another section headed by Ron Stevens, Plant and Equipment Engineer. This section analyses the equipment requirements and comes up with the appropriate specifications. It also procures the equipment if not already available within the plant. In many cases, this means going through the very difficult process of working closely with a machinery vendor and having the item purpose-built to exacting requirements. Even with so-called turnkey contracts, Ron's engineers are deeply involved in solving the initial technical problems.

The section is also responsible for making sure that the rules and regulations of government and society — safety, environmental and other issues — are in place. The job has been made more difficult than usual because robots, which Ron calls 'a mixture of brutal force and electronic genius', are potentially dangerous, unless programmed very carefully and fitted with fail-safe circuitry, and appropriate allowances are made for operator interface.

'We've had to take on some young people who are comfortable working with equipment incorporating a high level of technology', Ron Stevens says.

'It's paid off because we now use effectively some of the most sophisticated robots available anywhere in the world. They are mainly GMF Robotic Inc. designs, developed by General Motors in conjunction with Fanuc of Japan.'

Newly pressed VN front fender 'skins' await transport to the paint area for corrosion protection before being fitted to the body.

Bottom left:
A VN pilot body is immersion primed as an anticorrosion measure.

Below:
Production Leading Hand Barry Satterley hoists a cockpit module assembly from the subassembly floor conveyor for delivery to the body station.

111

Senior Production Planner Stewart Underwood readies the module for fitment to a VN body.

HOW NOT TO ASSEMBLE BODIES

VN's contoured body shell consists of several hundred steel stampings joined by 4532 spot-welds. The accuracy with which the shell is built affects the way in which the doors close, the windows wind, the various panels fit and whether the bonnet and boot lid sit squarely in their allocated spaces. It also affects wind noises and other characteristics. To make sure the new car lives up to its 'world class' target, Holden's decided to depart from the previous way of building the body.

The original Elizabeth body assembly shop was laid out in 1964 to build bodies for forthcoming Holden models and was designed to allow a number of different bodies to be built on the same track. At the time, the state-of-the-art technique was to build various subassembly structures, such as the side panels and underbody, on a number of similar jigs which moved around a closed loop. The subassembly started with one panel and, as each jig reached a work-station, a new panel was welded in place. At the end of the loop, the subassembly was complete.

The body sides were built on detachable frames (known as side gates) to which the metal panels were clamped by hand before being spot-welded into place. The side gate, complete with the body side, was then moved to the main body line and welded to the rest of the shell.

The main body line was virtually an enlarged version of the system used for the subassemblies and consisted of a circular loop with 30 or more work-stations. Travelling around the loop was a series of 'trucks'. A complete body was progressively built on each truck as it moved from one work-station to the next.

The operation started when the underbody was clamped to the truck, followed by the body sides, roof, windscreen surround and other parts added in turn. Most subassemblies arrived suspended from an overhead conveyor and were lowered at the appropriate work-station. The side gates (still carrying the body sides) were temporarily attached to the truck while the sides were spot-welded to the shell using a hand-held gun. In effect, these gates controlled the body's dimensional accuracy.

Although all side gates were identical in theory, some variations occurred, especially after the gate had been in use for some time. These led to small differences in critical body dimensions and customers saw these differences as ill-fitting panels or hard-to-close doors. Although they do not affect the body's strength or durability, the gaps between the panels and the poor door fits were noticeable and undesirable.

SINGLE-POINT TOOLING

To eliminate the problems associated with the traditional way of building bodies, Holden's switched to a new system called Single-point Tooling for VN. Instead of employing a number of similar assembly fixtures, all producing near-identical products, a series of fixtures is used, with each one doing a different part of the overall job.

Graham Mesecke, General Supervisor of Assembly Planning, explained that each body-framing operation is completed on the same piece of tooling so the bodies are as close to identical as technology can make them. This in turn provides a near-perfect match for the panels. The single-point tooling approach also lends itself to the use of several modern production techniques. For example, as it is being built, the body is transported from one operation to the next on a shuttle conveyor; hence the operation is also known as 'shuttle assembly'. Holden's adopted this system when building the last of the Gemini range in order to gain the experience needed for the much higher volume VN.

The 'lift-and-carry' shuttle itself plays no part in jigging the body, as in the conventional method of body building, but it eliminates the need for a number of similar fixtures to carry out the same basic operation. The shuttle lifts the incomplete body out of one work-station, transports it above the line and lowers it at the next station. The system provides much greater control over dimensional accuracy and, using the 3-Dimensional Coordinate Measuring Machine, it is possible to quickly and accurately measure the finished result. If any discrepancies show up, there is only one work-station where the fault could have occurred; previously, it could have been caused by problems in any of 30 trucks or 18 pairs of side gates.

In the old system, the major panels were manually clamped in place prior to spot-welding, a time-consuming job which caused problems if not correctly done (or even omitted!) due to human error. The shuttle system allows the use of automatic pneumatic clamps which are quick and consistent. Pneumatic clamps are used for 30 subassembly fixtures as well as the main body assembly, thus speeding the entire operation. A programmed logic device automatically operates the clamps in the correct sequence. All spot-welds are done while the body is stationary and none has to be hurried to keep pace with a moving line.

Because each body is built through the same set of fixtures, it is identical to all other bodies. In the event of a collision, a replacement door and body panel would fit correctly. Vic Beesley says that the switch from the traditional way of building bodies has resulted in a number of major customer benefits as well as improved productivity. From a quality point of view, he says, shuttle assembly is a significant leap forward, giving accurate door fits, flush body panels and uniform gaps between the boot lid and bonnet surround. The system also reduces the time required to build a body by about 2.2 hours, thus helping to contain costs. With VL it took 212 people to make 200 bodies a day but 174 can build 240 VN bodies with a higher degree of precision.

The improved productivity is partly because the complete body-building operation employs sophisticated robotics, sensing and monitoring devices.

About 40 per cent of the spot-welds are done automatically. Automatic checking devices are also used and, in some cases, the spot-welding machine stops immediately a weld current monitoring check shows that the weld is not up to specification.

There is less need for spot-welding than there used to be, because new metal-to-metal adhesives, which are induction-cured by low-frequency heating, have been introduced to secure the engine hood assembly, decklid and other components.

An interesting detail is the method used to attach the doors to the body. The previous practice was to weld half of the hinge to the door and the other half to the door frame. The two parts were then expected to mate correctly to accept the hinge pin after the body had been assembled.

Because the theory did not always work in practice, two 'fine-tuners' were employed to encourage the doors to fit, using whatever tools were necessary. With VN, half of the hinge is welded to the door during fabrication and the other half is welded to the body only after the door has been jigged into its final location. The fit is then very close to perfect and no dedicated fine-tuners are required.

'The culture and attitude of people is changing', says Ray Grigg. 'Out of every 100 people employed in the old way of doing things, you had maybe 94 operators and six technicians. The way we are heading, we will soon need 94 technicians and six operators.'

'So we are giving our people, particularly the older tradesmen, the opportunity to upgrade their skills to be ready for the time when further change is needed. It is done on a voluntary basis but already we have more volunteers than classroom space.'

PRACTICE BEFORE PRODUCTION

Long before production of VN bodies started at Elizabeth, 58 Holden production engineers and technicians went to Japan, staying for periods between ten days and two years. Working with Nissan people and other equipment vendors, they confirmed specifications, designs, and tested the equipment. Considerable coordination was necessary because they had to bring together parts manufactured in Australia and Japan, conduct the test program and build 41 bodies for shipment to Australia.

These off-tool bodies were then used by the Engineering Department for prototype testing, by the Materials Management group for development and fitment checks and by Manufacturing for development and proving purposes.

Following Japanese tradition, a buffet dinner was held in May 1987 to celebrate the completion of the last of these bodies. It was exactly 28 months since Holden's had first decided who would manufacture the tooling and it was two years since a full-time representation had been established in Tokyo to manage the large VN tooling and equipment project.

The celebration dinner was attended by Nissan people from the variety of departments involved in the project during its lifetime, together with the Holden personnel in Japan at the time.

Satisfied that the tools produced bodies to the correct specifications, Holden's transferred the tools and components to Elizabeth in mid-1987 and the first Australian tryout bodies were built in November to prove the shuttle system which had just been installed. Trim and mechanical components were added in January 1988 with the commencement of the Phase One pilot vehicle program.

The first vehicles built to saleable specifications were completed in mid-May 1988 (they were used as test cars). Three months later, the assembly line was fired up on a continuing day-to-day basis. At that time, the production schedule called for 220 vehicles per day (on a two-shift basis) with the output rising to 432 units per day as experience was gained. The current plant capacity of 100 000 units annually is designed to meet the anticipated local and export demand.

EVEN ROBOTS GO TO SCHOOL

Robots are of course mechanical devices which can be programmed to automatically do almost any kind of manual job. They are invaluable in unpleasant work situations (e.g. where fumes are present), for monotonous routine jobs and for tasks where extreme accuracy and automatic checking of each operation is required. Some robots are built to do a single task; others can be taught a variety of skills which are captured electronically so the robot can change from one job to another at the touch of a button.

For example, a skilled spray paint operator can teach a robot how to spray a sedan body of a given shape by guiding its arm through the exact movements it is required to make. The operator then shows the robot how to spray bodies of a different shape using other movements. The robot can even be taught to recognise the shape and automatically select the correct spray action to handle the next job, be it a sedan or wagon.

Holden's Elizabeth plant has 58 robots engaged in a variety of tasks. Many are fascinating to watch. Some spot-welding equipment, for example, goes into a rest mode and cleans its own fingertips, or rather weldtips, automatically after a predetermined number of welds. Six very intelligent robots handle work on the shuttle body main line; another tirelessly assembles an endless stream of brake pedal stands. A mini-army of 18 robots handles door assembly and a further 18 look after the underbody and body shell fabrication areas. One particularly useful robot draws the bumper facia from the dies, a job which is difficult to do manually without damage.

BLACK GUNK COMES BEFORE THE GLOSS

When a complete body shell has passed inspection, it goes through a seven-stage spray process during which it is thoroughly cleaned and coated with zinc phosphate. According to Geoff Bayly, the Central Laboratory's Chief Materials Engineer (Body), the phosphate serves both as an anti-corrosion measure and to help the primer bond correctly to the surface. It also inhibits rust from creeping under the paint if a stone should chip the paint.

After this initial treatment, the body is immersed to the waistline in a 16 000 litre tank of black primer so that paint runs into every crevice of the metal structure including the interior of the box sections. The gunk is there to protect inaccessible areas of metal from corrosion. Drain holes are necessary in some areas of the body to allow it to enter and to stop the body from floating in the tank. Next comes a coat of thicker primer-surfacer paint which is sprayed using an electrostatic process in which the negatively charged paint is attracted to the grounded body shell. The primer-surfacer is lightly baked for 22 minutes at 150 degrees Celsius.

All joints are filled with PVC sealant, a toothpaste-like material which goes hard after baking in the paint ovens. The sealant is brushed down to penetrate the joints and wiped to a smooth surface. The areas under the bonnet and boot, which cannot be reached in the first spray booth, are painted with primer-surfacer in a second booth. The body is baked again, this time for 40 minutes at 150 degrees Celsius. The process leaves a very hard primer-surfacer undercoat, 30 to 40 microns thick, which provides additional corrosion protection and an even base for the final colour coats. It also fills minor imperfections in the metal surface.

The primer-surfacer is wet-sanded to a smooth finish by hand and the body is cleaned, dried and moved to a computerised spray booth. Here it is sprayed with an acrylic sealant which provides good adhesion and chip resistance for the top coat. Three coats of acrylic lacquer are applied, the first two coming from electrostatic spray guns. A normal compressed-air gun is used to apply the final coat to prevent disorientation of the metallic flakes should a metallic finish be specified. The body is baked for 14 minutes at 77 degrees Celsius and thoroughly inspected. After any minor touch-up work which may be necessary, it receives a final reflow bake with sufficient heat (135 degrees Celsius) to make the paint surface flow and fill any light scratches which may be present. The reflow bake also brings out the full gloss potential of the acrylic lacquer colour.

Although the VN is finished in an acrylic lacquer similar to that used with VL Commodores, automatic spray equipment has improved both the way in which it is applied and the quality of the finish. The $4 million modernisation program includes a completely new 42.6 metre long spray booth with three programmable paint machines. Program logic controls ensure an even colour and a uniform paint thickness. About $1 million has been spent upgrading the current facilities to paint the polypropylene bumper facias using a clear-over-base urethane finish.

GOODBYE DASH PANEL WELCOME COCKPIT MODULE

Few things in the VN illustrate the new design approach more than the way in which the conventional instrument panel has been replaced by a cockpit module.

In almost all other cars, the bare dash panel is welded in place while the body is being fabricated. When the operators come to fit the instruments and wiring harness, they are forced to work in the very cramped space behind the dash. This leads to mistakes, poor workmanship and other problems. It is also extremely difficult for the quality assurance inspectors to check behind the instrument panel and make sure everything has been correctly assembled.

Steve Scaife and Bert Paul carefully place the cockpit module in position.

The new way is to assemble the entire instrument panel outside the car, have it checked for quality and then fitted to the body as a complete unit. Known as the cockpit module, the unit comprises the dash panel, instrument panel, sound deadeners, heater/ventilation/air-conditioning unit, ducts and the appropriate controls for the heating and air-conditioning systems. The sheet metal section of the module is fabricated by 12 operators at Elizabeth using a multispot-welder for some subassemblies and robots for the full assembly task. Elsewhere, other operators fit all parts to the module using a small production line with 26 rotating fixtures set at normal height. They install the complex wiring loom, instruments, sound system and air-conditioning (if specified). The steering column, brake pedal assembly, wiring, plumbing, foot pedals and other components are attached and an electrical check made.

After assembly, the module is picked up by a transporting fixture and delivered to the body assembly point on the trim line. The adhesive is applied, then the fixture aligns with the body and the module is lowered into position and bolted to the front body pillars and floor.

A two-part silicone adhesive bonds it to the body structure and provides a seal which prevents noise, fumes or moisture travelling from the engine compartment into the passenger area. Once in place, the module is permanently fixed but the instruments and wiring can be serviced in the normal way. The main reason for the off-line assembly operation is to make it easier to both install and inspect the mechanical and electrical parts which make up the panel. Much better quality is achieved because the operators and inspectors do not work in a cramped area, as is necessary with the conventional arrangement. Another advantage is that it is easier to trim parts of the body, prior to the cockpit module being installed, because the operators have easier acccess.

JUST-IN-TIME

Also known as Kan Ban, the just-in-time (JIT) parts system was developed in Japan to reduce the large inventory investment and space normally needed to store components prior to assembling cars in volume.

The conventional system was to fill a warehouse with sufficient parts to keep the production line moving for days or even weeks on end. Thanks to computerised ordering systems and controls, it is now possible to substantially reduce the size of the storage area without loss of production. In its most refined form, the components arrive from the supplier a matter of minutes before they are needed on the assembly line, hence the name. Things are not cut so fine at Elizabeth, however.

According to Don Nicholson, Materials Manager, the company has introduced the program cautiously. Initially, the JIT system was installed progressively for some Gemini components with a view to gaining experience for VN. It took two years to build a system in which 20 suppliers delivered 152 different parts, effectively reducing the supply of some components from an average of six to 1½ days. Nearly 30 vendors now deliver over 200 separate components with JIT scheduling.

The concept also extends to fabrication plants where it is used to control the flow of materials. Naturally, JIT is designed to minimise possible shortages but it is only one of 35 possible causes of component delays, ranging from vendor quality rejection to incorrect identification.

The advantages of JIT range from better quality control to less congested work areas, better utilisation of space and reduced parts inventories.

THE FINAL FITTING

The assembly operation follows conventional lines. Building a VN starts with a painted body which proceeds down an assembly line where the mechanical components, accessories and trim are added progressively

Top to bottom

Senior Production Planner Brenton Maidment lowers a VN pilot body onto its 'mechanicals' in the Elizabeth plant pilot room. At this point in its life, the unit becomes a car.

A VN pilot body receives the second of three colour coats in the automatic stage of the spray booth.

Sewing Machinist Daphne Ward works on VN Calais seating in the Elizabeth Trim Fabrication plant.

Mark McRitchie (left) and Gary Howarth, production operators in the trim assembly area, fit the one-piece headlining to a VN pilot body.

The first VN pilot car built in the Elizabeth plant is flanked by a group of production operators and management people.

until the complete car rolls out of the factory. As each order is received from a dealer, the customer's requirements — such as colour choice, trim level and options — are keyed into a computer. Electronic signals are used to ensure that each vehicle is assembled in a way which complies exactly with the customer's order.

The most important part of the assembly operation is the final checking and testing which is done before the car moves out of the door. The car is run on a roller test for six minutes giving ample time to reveal any of a number of possible faults. A diagnostic test is made of the engine management system; a highly advanced automatic pressure test, done at 1200 kilopascals, can disclose even the smallest leak in the braking system. A 'sniffer' probe checks for gas leaks from the air-conditioning unit and the wiring harness is functionally checked out. The doors are opened and slammed closed, the wheels and headlights aligned and all aspects of the interior and exterior appearances scrutinised.

A TOUCH OF CLASS

Graham Douglass, General Supervisor of Final Assembly Planning, is very impressed by the trim used in VN, regarding it as a big advance in appearance and ease of assembly. This, he says, is particularly true of the moulded headlining which is initially attached using Velcro tape. The grab handles, sun visors and decorative rear strip are then fixed and serve as the primary method of securing the headlining. An added virtue is that the headlining can be easily removed in the event of roof repairs, such as hail damage, being needed. The main trim material is cut in multiple layers to the required pattern and hand-sewn using a variety of specialist sewing machines.

The moulded door trim is attached in one piece by fir-tree studs and by the door handles and window winders. The new moulded trim is less of a problem than conventional trim and brings several customer benefits.

The job is done.

TOTAL QUALITY CONTROL

Good workmanship is related to good morale and, recognising this, Holden's operates a Quality of Work Life (QWL) program designed to emphasise democracy in the workplace and respect for everyone in the work force. Although voluntary, a large number of employees at the Elizabeth plant have attended QWL workshops and the program is judged to be extremely successful in raising morale and improving workmanship.

As part of a major campaign to improve customer satisfaction, Holden's launched the Total Quality Control program (TQC) in May 1984 and immediately began training the work force and management in its principles. A key factor in the program is to make people responsible for the standard of work they do, rather than have separate departments monitoring all quality.

Over 2000 employees in the Elizabeth complex have undergone training in TQC. At least half the work force has also been trained in the use of various problem-solving techniques, in group skills and in group leadership. After training, these people are formed into 'family groups' — that is, operators working together on similar jobs — and the groups jointly help solve difficulties arising in their daily work. Such problems vary from complex technical snags to environmental concerns. The groups meet formally for an hour or so each month, more often if necessary.

A fascinating group technology program was developed jointly by Holden's and the Adelaide division of the CSIRO. The basis is that the production process for a given product is controlled by a cell of personnel representing a variety of skills. The cell is responsible for such activities as product quality, material handling, die sets, scheduling and productivity. Attached to a group of three or four cells is a core of tradesmen handling the maintenance of tools and equipment. Working with the cell, the trades group also helps solve problems of a technical nature.

Another innovation involves the commissioning of new equipment. The past practice with complex machinery was to have the supplier make the installation and cure any teething troubles which might arise. These days, the company has its own team which works with the supplier during the commissioning period and helps integrate the new equipment into the overall operation. This approach has proved particularly valuable in systems which involve data transfer, another area where HMC engineers have established a reputation as being second to none.

During the initial stages of VN production, every vehicle coming off the assembly line is test-driven over a six kilometre test course. The reports are studied to provide a database which shows if a recurring problem area can be identified. The routine testing of all production vehicles will continue for at least six months after the start of production and for as long as necessary to ensure that the TQC objectives are met. Even then, all Calais models will continue to be tested as well as a high proportion of other models.

'Quality is our number one objective', says Ray Grigg. 'It's a continuing battle which can never be completely won. But, since the introduction of TQC, the number of customers who have found problems with their Holdens has already dropped by 50 per cent. I aim to make the VN the most trouble-free Holden yet.'

Ray Grigg

Raymond G. Grigg was handed the brief of planning the VN project back in 1980 and now has the job of manufacturing the car. As General Manager — Operations, he runs Holden's South Australian and Dandenong plants with the mixture of skill, dedication and determination he showed when playing VFA football for his home town of Box Hill, Victoria.

Much of Ray's early life revolved around Box Hill where he was born and educated. He received his first engineering training there and joined GM-H in January 1957. Ray continued playing professional football and chalked up about 75 games before hanging up his boots when his career began making too many demands on his leisure time.

Ray studied part-time for many years at the Swinbourne Technical College (Victoria) and took courses at the University of New South Wales, Northwestern University, Chicago, and Vevey in Switzerland. He is a Fellow of the Society of Automotive Engineers (A/sia) and a Fellow of the Australian Institute of Management.

Since 1975, when he went to Opel as a Project Engineer, Ray has been deeply involved in new designs. After working on VBs in Germany, he was appointed Program Manager at Fishermans Bend, and was responsible for coordinating all aspects of the Commodore program. After the VB was launched, Ray became Manager of Product Planning and, in October 1982, Director of Planning. This put him in charge of strategic business direction, new products, marketing planning and the conceptual development of business opportunities.

In August 1985, Ray Grigg was appointed Director of Product Quality Assurance, heading the drive towards better-made cars. Within three months of this appointment, he was elected a Board Member of GM-H.

He currently controls all activities associated with the company's vehicle purchasing and assembly operations at Elizabeth, South Australia. He directs the facilities at Dandenong, Victoria, and the stamping, fabrication and plastics operations in South Australia. He is also a Director and Board Member of Holden's Motor Overseas Corporation, a subsidiary of General Motors Overseas Corporation.

'The technology used to build VNs is a huge leap forward', Ray Grigg says.

'But the theme I'm trying to get across is this: Technology is an indispensable tool to beat the competition but, no matter how good the equipment, it takes people to operate, maintain and service it. The most important part of new technology is to make sure it produces a better product.'

Powerful friends
... worldwide support

There's a saying in the automobile business that 'numbers are the name of the game'.

In short, the argument is that a company producing two million vehicles per year can afford to invest considerably more in the design, development and testing of a new car than a firm selling half a million.

With the motor industry immersed in a technological explosion, the cost of keeping pace with the competition has become a problem of nightmare proportions for all but the largest companies.

How then, can Holden's remain 'world class' in its design and manufacturing processes with an output of approximately 100 000 new cars per year?

The answer is to receive a little help from powerful friends.

No one in the automobile business is more powerful than General Motors. With an annual output running at around six million cars and nearly two millions trucks and buses, it produces almost twice as many motor vehicles as its nearest rival.

It's hardly surprising therefore that General Motors has the world's most extensive research laboratories and that Holden's, a subsidiary of the giant corporation, has unlimited access to the design, manufacturing and other technology developed by the parent company.

General Motors first ventured into international markets in 1911, only three years after its inception. General Motors Australia was formed in 1926 when plants were established in Brisbane, Sydney and Melbourne. By 1928, Chevrolet tourers were being produced with 65 per cent local content. Three years later (1931) GMA merged with Holden's Motor Body Builders and this combination set the scene for the first successful all-Australian car. It went on sale in late 1948.

Today, General Motors Corporation regards General Motors-Holden's Automotive Ltd as an essential part of its global strategy. This position is acknowledged by the fact that Holden's exports complete vehicles and specialised components and that Holden's Engine Company ships over 200 000 complete engines a year to other GM divisions.

To meet the challenge of the rapidly changing times, GM has become a veritable powerhouse of new technology. Its many recent acquisitions include two major high-tech companies: Electronic Data Systems (EDS) and Hughes Aircraft Company. Hughes is the firm which built the AUSSAT satellite and, like EDS, has extensive expertise in advanced electronic systems and high-speed computer software. It is also a world leader in laser applications, artificial intelligence and other forms of new technology. GM has also acquired Group Lotus, the consulting and performance car manufacturer world-renowned for its work in engine applications, vehicle dynamics, composites and aerodynamics. Lotus has also demonstrated the virtues of active suspension to countless millions of television viewers via the International Formula One Grand Prix series.

GM owns numerous component specialist companies and has assembly, manufacturing or distribution organisations in 35 countries, including the the USA and Canada. It is involved in over 30 joint ventures with major partners around the world (including the Holden's-Toyota joint venture announced in Australia in late 1987). In addition to its Cadillac, Chevrolet,

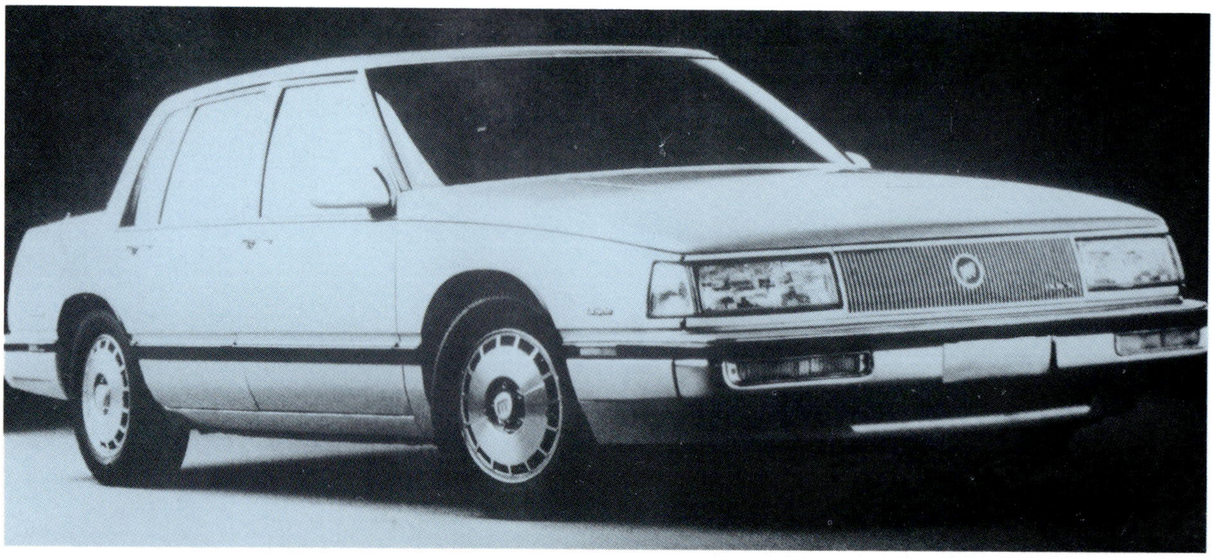

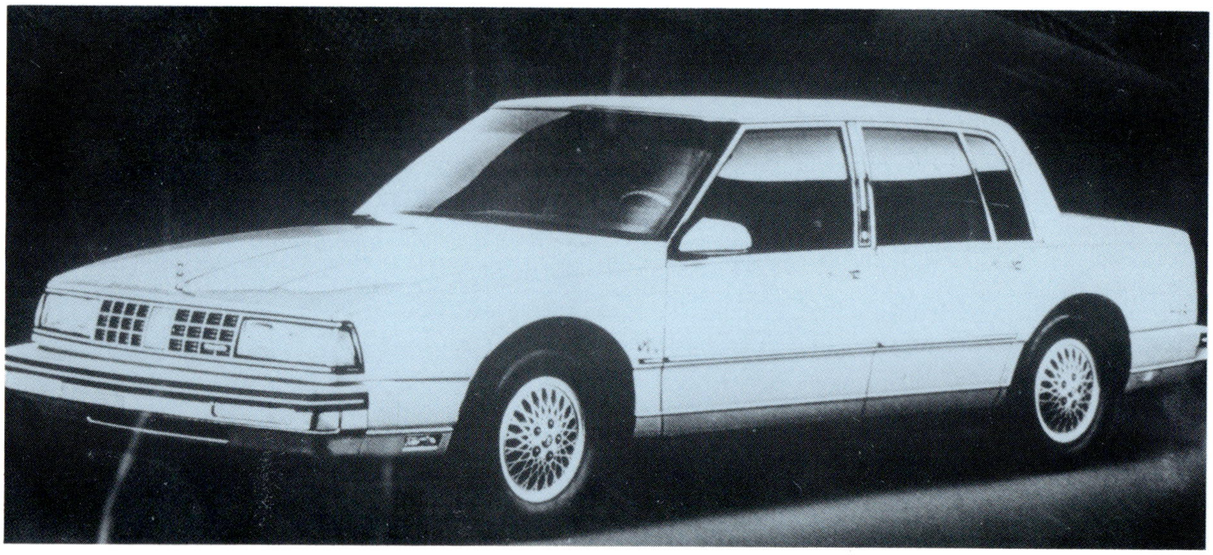

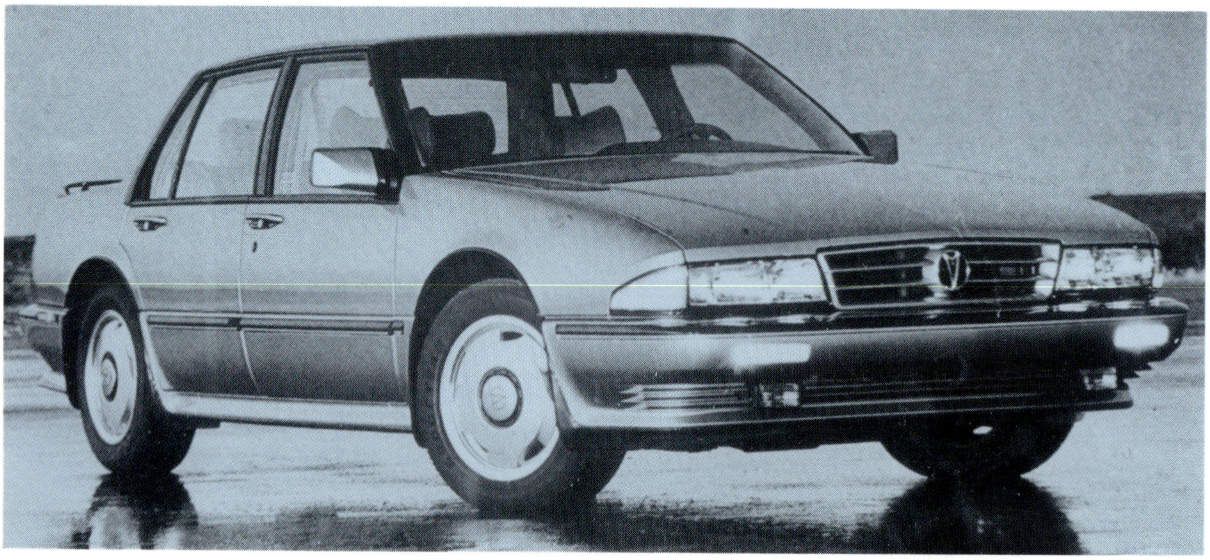

Pontiac, Buick and Oldsmobile nameplates, GM marques include Holden in Australia, Opel in Germany and Vauxhall and Lotus in Britain. The company also has a financial interest in Isuzu and Suzuki in Japan and Daewoo Motor Company in South Korea.

The heart of all General Motors' technology lies in the GM Technical Centre, located in Warren, Michigan, USA. It acts as the principal research arm and the coordinating force behind GM product engineering centres worldwide. The Vice-President in charge of the Technical Centre's research operation, General Motors Research Laboratories (GMR), is Dr Robert A. Frosch, a former head of the National Aeronautics and Space Administration (NASA).

'Scientists and engineers work with lasers, electron microscopes and other scientific instruments to unravel nature's secrets and lay the groundwork for tomorrow's technology', Dr Frosch says.

'It is the task of the Labs to help ensure that General Motors is not taken by technological surprise. Our scientists and engineers strive to anticipate technologies of the future, and to develop expertise in those areas.

'And GM divisions can call on GMR expertise in many different disciplines to help unravel knotty technical problems relating to GM products and manufacturing processes.'

Holden's is, of course, a prime recipient of such information. Its engineers make frequent visits to Detroit and have the opportunity to obtain up-to-date briefings on GMR activities. To help all technical staff keep abreast of new developments, Holden's also receives a wide range of GMR publications designed to keep GM's associate companies fully informed on matters as diverse as the chemistry of acid rain and the latest developments in the fluid dynamics of fuel-injection. Other types of published information are received from the company's Advanced Engineering Staff (AES) which is one of five divisions of the GM Technical Centre serving GM operations worldwide.

'One very useful document is the Quarterly Review produced by the Advanced Engineering Staff, which cannot be disclosed outside the corporation', says Geoff Chamberlain, Holden's Advanced Product Studies Engineer.

'The second major source of technical information comes from papers given at the annual Product Engineering Technology Conference. We are always represented at these conferences and the papers are detailed and strictly in-house. They make some forthright comparisons between corporation technology and competitive technology.

'The engineering staff who run this conference have what they call a "Mona Lisa process" which establishes what is the best in the world in each product feature and analyses what makes it the best. The product is then

Opposite page and above: American cousins Pontiac, Oldsmobile and Buick front-wheel drive GM70 models share the same basic V-6 engine as the rear-drive Commodore.

compared with the current corporation equivalent. If you are going to talk world class, you have to compare yourself with the best, and this makes fascinating reading.

'We also have a constant stream of GMR reports which are not on specific product features. They can be on subjects as diverse as software for designing space frames to the nature of smog formation. If we want to buy a software package, we contribute toward the cost but there could be ten corporate customers, so the charge to us would be relatively small. Many of the reports are in condensed form, but they act as contact information and we can have the full report on any subject which interests us.'

GMR employs about 1600 men and women in 19 separate technical departments, all involved in fundamental research. Its library houses 90 000 technical books and is supplemented by access to a further 200 computer databases located in leading university and public libraries.

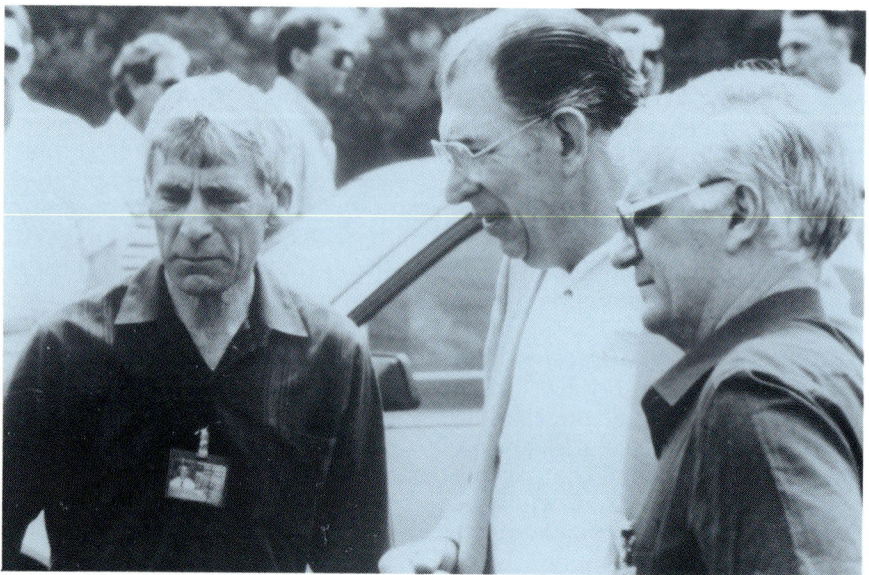

GM has devised a special technique to foster technological transfer. When a study is being undertaken by Advanced Engineering Staff, an individual from a sponsoring division is assigned to the study team when the project is near to the point where it could be implemented. The selected person works on the project for one or two years as part of the team and then takes the newly acquired knowledge and skill back to the sponsoring division, in time for the new product to go into production.

Operating separately, but in close cooperation, are several vehicle proving grounds located in North America and around the world. The largest is the GM Engineering Staff proving ground at Milford, Michigan. It was here that the corporation established the world's first purpose-built automotive proving ground in 1924. The facility now covers 1600 hectares and is designed specifically for the 'real world' testing of cars, trucks and other vehicles.

Its work is supplemented by the Desert Proving Ground in Mesa, Arizona, the GM Mountain Test Facility at Pikes Peak, Colorado, the Emission Test Facility at Van Nuys, California, the High Altitude Test Facility at Denver, Colorado, and the Cold Weather Test Facility at Kapuskasing, Canada. Most overseas divisions also have their own proving grounds, Holden's facilities being at Lang Lang, Victoria. Holden's also has access to other proving grounds where more specialist work can be undertaken. For this reason, VN was extensively tested at Lang Lang and at several other GM facilities.

The way in which Holden's and GM work closely was demonstrated in November 1987 when a combined GM-Holden's team entered and convincingly won the first-ever transcontinental solar car race. The 3200 km

Opposite page and Below:
In late 1987 General Motors' President Robert Stempel made a special trip to Holden's Lang Lang proving ground to inspect a VN prototype and compare it with competition models. He was greeted by Tony Brougham and Don Wylie.

Pentax World Solar Challenge started in Darwin where 23 vehicles from six different countries raced to Adelaide. Only six vehicles were deemed to be official finishers, although some other competitors struggled to the end and reached Adelaide outside the allotted time.

The GM entry, appropriately named SunRaycer, was a fascinating team effort which embraced expertise contributed by Hughes Aircraft, GM Research Laboratories, GM's Advanced Engineering Staff, GM's Advanced Concepts Centre, Lotus and AeroVironment Inc. These specialists provided the technology support required to design, test and race the unusually shaped car. Holden's weighed in with race strategy, reliability development and testing, logistics support and the lead driver, racing champion John Harvey. Ray Borrett, an engineer who is also Holden's Reliability Manager, was race manager for the SunRaycer team. He was associated with the Holden Dealer Team for many years and is now a consultant to Holden Motor Sport.

The SunRaycer is the most advanced solar car ever built and completed the 3200 km journey in less than 45 hours — almost 24 hours ahead of its nearest rival — with an average speed of 66.92 km/h.

High-technology was the secret of its success. The aerodynamic shape was refined by the use of an advanced computer program developed by the National Aeronautics and Space Administration. This work resulted in the lowest coefficient of drag for a road vehicle ever measured at the Californian Institute of Technology. Because temperatures up to 50 degrees Celsius were expected, the SunRaycer's canopy was gold plated to protect the driver. Gold reflects 90 per cent of visible light and 98 per cent of infra-red radiation.

The car's drive power is generated by 7200 tiny solar cells of the same type used by the Hughes-built communication satellites. These cells have a nominal efficiency of 16.5 per cent which means they convert into electrical energy about one sixth of the solar energy received. The complete solar panel typically operates at 150 volts, providing 1000 watts of electrical power. This energy flows to a special high-efficiency Magnequench electric motor jointly developed by GMR and the Delco Remy division. The motor drives one of the rear wheels.

Special silver zinc rechargeable batteries accept any electrical energy not immediately required by the motor and store it for use as indirect power when needed. This power was used early and late in the day to supplement the reduced solar energy. It was also invaluable for accelerating and hillclimbing.

The SunRaycer has a space frame chassis weighing only 15 kg which supports a vehicle with a total weight of 248 kg (including the driver and the ballast required under the competition rules). It has four-wheel independent suspension (designed by a member of GM's Advanced Engineering Staff) and custom-built wheels with small disc brakes. The body is made from a sandwich comprising layers of Kevlar and Nomex, and has great strength and low weight.

On a broader level, Holden's has become increasingly involved with other GM divisions in the electronic transfer of digital data over standard telephone lines through an international data transmission network called 'GM Net'. The drawings and parts list for the V-6 engine, for example, were received electronically from Buick. Holden and Delco regularly exchange software files for electronic engine control modules, Opel sent drawings for car body components while GMR transferred a variety of engineering and computer software data. Because of time constraints, some drafting work for the station wagon was done in England and the drawings transferred via satellite to Holden's drafting office.

According to Tony Roessen, a leading draftsman in the chassis and drive-train office, it would have taken months to tranfer the engine data alone using traditional means such as microfilm. But all the working drawings initially needed, involving about 150 components and 200 drawings — many of them major layouts — were transferred by telephone within two weeks.

Geoff Chamberlain's current responsibilities include looking at developments which could have potential for Holden's future programs. These include GMR's highly sophisticated software packages which enable components to be designed and tested on a video screen, the output of an engine to be assessed before a prototype has been built or a space frame to be designed with minimum weight and optimum strength.

It is through GMR and AES that Holden's keeps track of the latest developments in alternative engines, such as turbines and two-stroke units with direct fuel-injection, which are amongst numerous concepts being developed or tested by GM. The corporation did serious work on four-wheel steering during the 1960s and is currently working on continuously variable transmission, viscous drive and active suspension systems. Geoff Chamberlain says the latter is a system in which there is no compliance between the wheel and the vehicle frame, except a computer-controlled hydraulic cylinder. Both power input and power absorption are present in a true active system.

He says active suspension systems offer very real benefits. There is no need to compromise between the car's ride and handling characteristics, for example. It is possible, he says, to design the exact riding and handling characteristics required without having to worry about the car rolling on corners, dipping the nose under braking or squatting during acceleration. Such a vehicle can have different damping characteristics on smooth roads than on rough roads. He says the suspension's entire nature can be varied by changing an integrated chip. This means, for example, that the characteristics of the car could be instantly changed if a caravan is to be towed or the driver decides to enter a weekend motor sport event.

GM's Advanced Engineering Staff also keeps Holden's up-to-date in developments concerning electronic anti-lock braking. The accent here is on designing less expensive systems which could be fitted as standard equipment in some models. Similarly, AES is working extensively on more effective anti-thief systems, superior engine management modules and electronic traction control devices. The latter prevent wheelspin on slippery surfaces and could be used with two-wheel or four-wheel drive cars. Full-time four-wheel drive is another development being thoroughly researched by General Motors, along with a wide variety of new forms of technology.

In the past, Australia has given the world such automotive inventions as the first four-wheel drive cross-country car, the downdraft carburetter, coupe-utility, self-parking windscreen wipers, the tipper truck, the Repco-Brabham World Champion winning V-8 engine (based on a GM cylinder block) and numerous other inventions. No doubt, Australian innovations will continue to spread around the world but the cost of originating many aspects of technology is now so high that very few companies can afford to undertake the basic research.

But having powerful friends in America and around the world has enabled Holden's to keep pace with the latest and best in automotive design and production technology. This is a sure pointer to the company's future success.

The GM SunRaycer streaks across the plain on its way to Adelaide. It averaged 66.9 km/h.

To market, to market
... selling the product

During the heady days of the late 1950s and early 1960s, Australians queued for blocks to see a new Holden and salespeople got writer's cramp taking orders. Holden's was single-handedly producing more cars than the entire Japanese industry, yet it found that its biggest problem was keeping up with demand.

Needless to say, those days have gone. By 1987, Australia had developed into one of the world's most competitive markets, with five local manufacturers vying for a share of a pie which amounted to about 375 000 new sedans and station wagons. About 300 000 of them were made locally which sounds a lot, until you consider that the Japanese industry now builds that number in nine working days.

At the time of VN's launch, the major players on the Australian scene offered a dozen basically different locally made models and 14 fully imported cars. In addition, no less than 27 other firms imported and sold nearly 70 basically different cars, plus an even larger number of four-wheel drives, minibuses, light commercials and other vehicles which, to some degree, compete against the local car-making industry. Obviously, such a fiercely competitive selling environment means that nothing can be left to chance.

The automotive business is one in which a number of factors play a crucial role in determining how each competitor will fare. They include styling, performance, value-for-money, brand loyalty, word-of-mouth reputation and package size. The competition to retain existing customers and capture some opposition business is so great that sophisticated and subtle sales techniques have been developed. However, car companies are only too aware that the marketplace is the ultimate judge. No amount of hype or hard-sell will save the day if they have a product which the customers do not like or think is too dear.

The customer is the only arbiter when it comes to deciding what is the right car and what is the right price. There are no courts of appeal and no higher authorities to complain to. Not surprisingly, car companies go to enormous trouble to research customer expectations long before a new vehicle goes into production. The first thing the average customer notices, irrespective of the car's merits, is the appearance. If it doesn't look to be the right shape and size, its sales appeal plummets. This is why styling 'clinics' are widely used throughout the motor industry.

WHY CARS GO TO CLINICS

A clinic is a session where potential customers have the opportunity to see an anonymous prototype alongside several competitive vehicles and make a judgment on its styling and apparent roominess. It is usually held in a neutral venue and the participants are not told which company is seeking their opinions in case brand loyalty influences their answers.

Clinics provide a worthwhile measure of what the general public likes and dislikes and are therefore taken very seriously by car-makers. In 1974,

GM's winning entry in the world's first cross-continental solar race was a triumph in both marketing and technological terms. Holden's made a significant contribution to the SunRaycer's success and the lead driver was racing champion John Harvey. (Photos: Ray Berghouse).

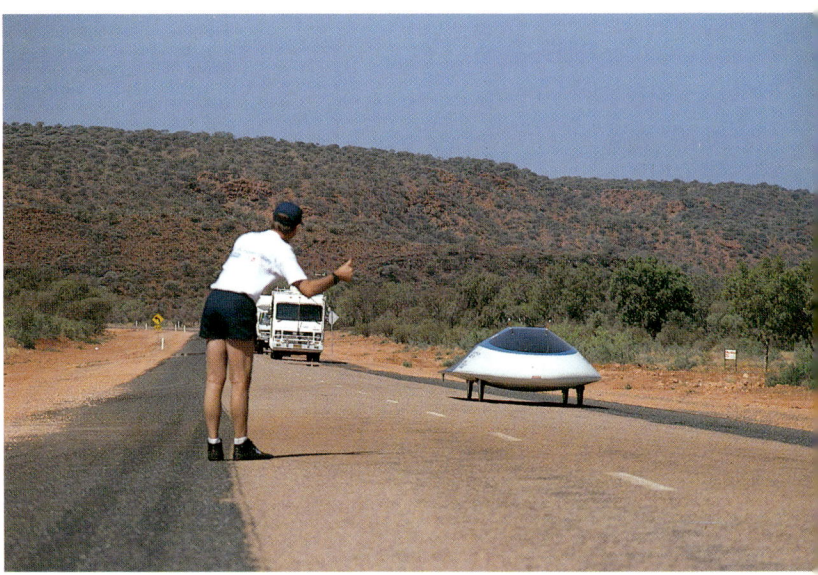

for example, Holden's conducted a 'clinic' on the proposed WA model scheduled for release as a successor to the HZ. The car was poorly received at the clinic and the design was scrapped.

Holden's first became involved with clinics in 1965 after running into an adverse reaction to the sharp-edged front guards featured on the HD. It learned a valuable lesson. Although it costs about $100 000 to conduct a styling clinic, Tony Winkleman, who has looked after Holden's market research for 20 years, says the money is well spent. A clinic to help guide the VN during its formative days was considered essential.

During eight days in October 1984, a VN clay mockup was displayed alongside seven other sedans in the Wool Board building at the Melbourne Showground. Alongside were a yet-to-be-released VL Commodore, a Cadillac de Ville, a JD Camira, a 1985 Japanese Sigma (the basis of the still-secret Magna) and current Falcon, Commodore and Cressida models. The other cars had been borrowed or hired for the purpose and each had its badges removed and was identified by a code number.

A representative group of 800 potential car buyers was invited to view the display. The participants were paid a small fee (around $25) and given suitable refreshments. Each was asked to give his or her opinion on a number of factors relating to the vehicles on display. The questions ranged from the appearance of the tail-lights to the perceived value of one car against another. Although it usually takes about 1½ hours to fill the 30 or so pages of questions, some people became so involved they spent up to three hours studying the various models.

After the participants had recorded their preferences and ratings, or otherwise expressed a reaction to each car, it was found that the clay model had scored well in some ways but not in others. Some respondents considered it to be modern looking, even sporty, but others considered it too avant-garde.

This polarised reaction was possibly because the VN's appearance was radical for 1984, a time before the so-called aero cars had come from Europe. As a group, the younger married buyers without children favoured the VN's appearance but the problem was that the bulk of the market lay with different groups: families with children and business fleet operators. Even so, of the Australian cars on display, 26.5 per cent of respondents gave their first preference to the VN's appearance, compared with 22.6 per cent for Ford's Falcon, 17 per cent for Holden's Camira and 14.9 per cent for the Sigma. Most popular of all was the forthcoming VL Commodore, which in appearance was something of a stepping stone between the squarer Holdens of the early 1980s and the full aero design.

In an unusual question, the respondents were asked who they thought should manufacture the mystery clay mock-up if it were to go into production. Almost half named Holden, 14 per cent mentioned Ford and, surprisingly, Mazda came next with 9 per cent. Toyota scored 8 per cent and Mitsubishi 4 per cent.

Despite an overall favourable reaction, there was some criticism of the VN's front and rear styling. Holden's Design department made various changes and a second clinic was held in October 1986. This time different

From the time the first VNs became available, seasoned marketing and merchandising people have been hard at work filming and photographing.

132

vehicles were chosen as the basis of comparison because the public was becoming aware of the aerodynamic flush glass look. The VN was pitted against an Audi 100 and Honda Legend and there was some jubilation when its front and rear appearances came ahead of the others. The VN and Legend collected the bulk of the first preferences, with the VN being rated as the most spacious.

The results delighted Dutch-born Tony Winkleman whose previous research had indicated that the lack of rear seat room for three adults had damaged sales of previous Commodores. Tony, who holds a degree in Law and Economics and is a Bachelor of Arts, is regarded as one of the industry's top research analysts.

His department looks at new car buyers as a group, studying age, sex and occupation. One favoured method is to contact people who have just bought any brand of new car and ask the reasons for their choice. Mail is used to make contact because this is the least intrusive approach. Such surveys involve 40 to 50 questions and are so expensive that several carmakers sometimes join forces in a single study, each drawing from the survey the results they require. In addition to participating in such surveys, Holden's conducts independent studies.

THE PHILLIP ISLAND THINK TANK

To examine the marketing issues objectively and without interruption, Holden's held a couple of 'think tank days' on Phillip Island, Victoria.

For special glamour shots, cars photographed in the studio with special lighting can be 'stripped in' to any environment the photographer desires.

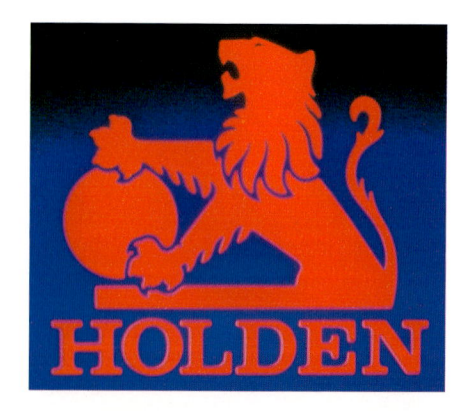

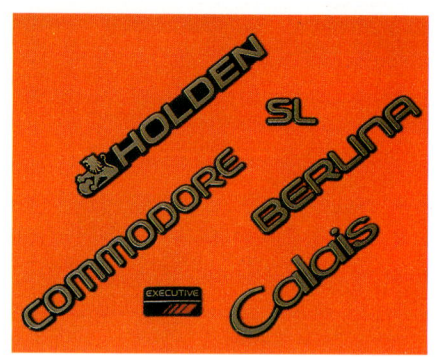

Present were the Director of Marketing, Marketing Manager, Merchandising Manager, key marketing personnel, Product Planning Manager, Advertising Manager, Sales Promotion Manager, Fleet Manager and Distribution Manager and representatives from Public Relations. The advertising agency was also there. The group met to develop a total strategy which would become the bible for the months ahead. Everyone was given a chance to make an input into the program and throw in ideas — no matter how bizarre — which might prove helpful.

Contrary to popular opinion, merchandising and marketing people don't do the same job. Like many companies, Holden's divides its sales activities into distinct groups. Marketing is basically looking at the product, determining who will buy it, at what price and with what level of equipment. To do this, it is necessary to carefully analyse competitive products. Merchandising, on the other hand, covers those activities directly relating to selling, including dealer operations. For Holden's at least, merchandising means national advertising, sales promotion and dealer marketing activities. In short, the marketing people decide what to sell, the merchandisers go out and sell it. There's another factor in the sales equation — Public Relations — which is concerned with the broad image of the company as well as the promotion of individual products.

According to Director of Marketing Rob McEniry, planning the VN sales campaign began in mid-1985 when Holden's started to consider how best to communicate the major changes and what marketing strategies to use. This work was completed in late 1986.

Holden's has a committee which examines the expectations of potential buyers and recommends the target customers, the required levels of standard equipment and the price positioning relative to the competition. This group did most of the lead-up work.

The Phillip Island think tank first considered the possibility of changing the name of the new car and/or the designations applied to the various models. Tony Winkleman had ready a kaleidoscope of alternatives to the Commodore name and had narrowed them to a manageable few. However, the group agreed that the Commodore name is so widely respected that a change would be a negative rather than a positive factor. They felt the same about a possible name change for Calais or Berlina, and plenty of research was presented to support the view. The first major decision was therefore that the existing names would continue with the VN.

Research had revealed that most customers expect more comfort and a higher level of standard equipment in a family car than in previous years, so it was decided to make the Commodore Executive the standard model. Animated discussion centred around the name Executive and whether it would be perceived purely as a business model or would be acceptable to the retail public as well. The feeling was positive, so the Executive became the base car in place of the SL. The latter became a 'delete option', that is, a de-specified model aimed at government purchasers rather than retail customers. The Executive thus became the main model for fleets as well as private buyers.

This was an important decision, because the group felt that the VN would be far more competitive than its predecessor for the fleet market and that a dedicated merchandising campaign should be directed toward fleet sales.

Another important decision was that, in the months leading up to the launch, the Commodore name should receive as high a profile as possible. This was partly because of the hype which would follow the release of the rival Falcon in early 1988. The refining of the VN advertising program would, to a large degree, be left until they could see what Ford did during the Falcon launch.

The run-out campaign, to clear stocks of VL Commodores, was considered next. No major hurdles were foreseen in this department and it was decided to follow a standard run-out program including special advertising and factory incentives if required. Someone suggested that existing Commodore owners should receive a letter during the three months April-to-June 1987 saying in effect: 'There are some pretty good Commodore deals available now but, if you are not sold on these, don't forget that the all-new car is just around the corner. Please wait a bit longer'.

The group discussed market opportunities, anticipated sales volume and the various ways of explaining the car's virtues to the buying public. Because of the flush glass appearance, a different communication strategy than had previously been used was recommended. It was felt that some lead-in strategies were desirable, prior to launch, to educate the public on the worldwide trend to more 'slippery' shapes.

The think tank agreed that the VN's modern appearance is its most exciting marketing advantage and that this will enable the company to go well into the 1990s without being embarrassed when newer competitive models arrive.

Another important plus mentioned was that VN could match its major competitor in package size internally whilst retaining a sleek, compact looking external appearance. The new engine and drive train were considered big competitive virtues, as were the more opulent trim levels.

Although the new manufacturing techniques promised to make the VN extremely price-competitive, the group agreed that it would be a premium product and should not be underpriced to gain additional sales.

After the Phillip Island session concluded, a marketing strategy document was prepared to serve as the handbook for everything relating to VN marketing and merchandising. Subsequent meetings were held to refine some concepts and take in new factors but, basically, the original strategies remained unchanged.

As expressed by Rob McEniry, the most challenging aspect of the job would be to convince the public that the new car is fully competitive in package size. VL had been able to consistently outsell the Falcon to private buyers but not to fleet operators. It would be necessary, he said, to convince business and government buyers that the VN is a genuine five-seater and a better buy than the alternatives.

The VN is unveiled to the motoring press. This is the 'long lead' release for magazine journalists at the Lang Lang proving ground.

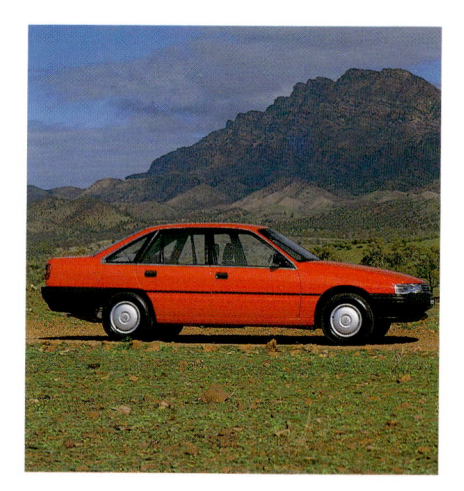

Above:
The Executive caught in the Flinders Ranges.

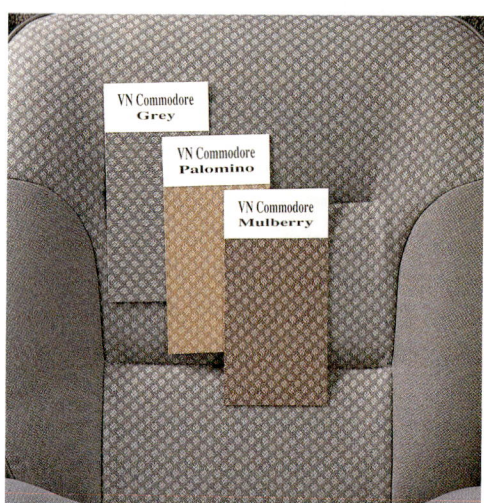

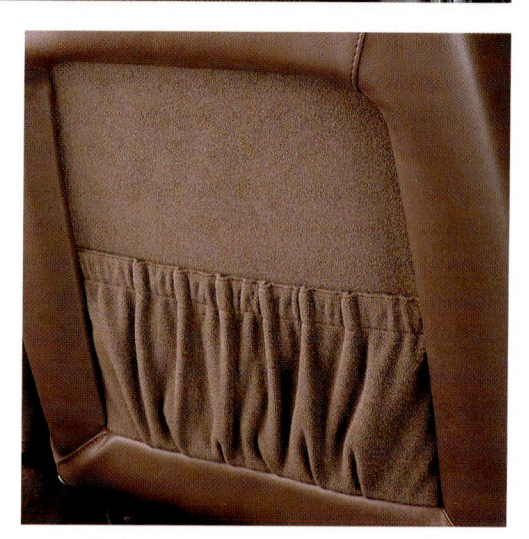

The Commodore Executive.

The Commodore Berlina.

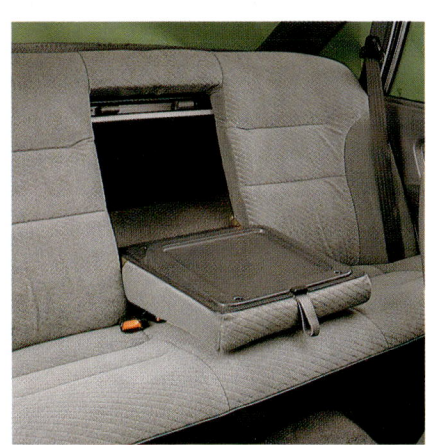

The Commodore Berlina

The Calais

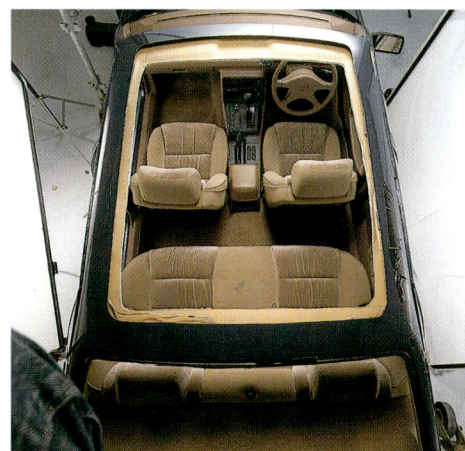

Brochure shots are the result of meticulous work which involves more than skilled photography. Cars are sometimes dismantled and even 'chopped up' to allow difficult angles to be captured on film.

The Calais.

Above: The VN and its predecessor, the VL (Photo: Kent Mears).

(Kent Mears)

Above: The Commodore sedan and wagon.

Above: The Calais and Commodore 'S' sports version.

(Kent Mears)

(Photos: Kent Mears)

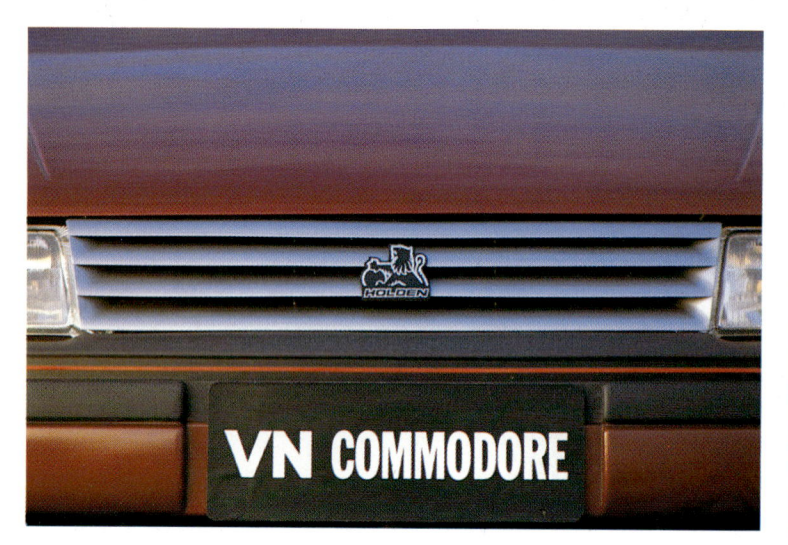

NO SUCH THING AS A FREE LAUNCH

A 'good launch' is the elusive target that all car companies strive for when releasing a new model. In search of this, they have been known to illuminate entire islands, helicopter cars into the least likely place and produce firework displays to rival the Bicentenary celebrations.

By such standards, Holden's approach was subdued. The company was looking for effectiveness rather than spectacle. Nevertheless, something close to $8 million was budgeted to cover dealer conventions supported by six months of merchandising and advertising. An additional $5 million per year is likely to be spent to maintain the impetus.

Such figures are not drawn out of a hat. They are necessary to be competitive, to match the money spent and the coverage gained by opposition companies. Although the expenditures by rival companies are never revealed, they can be calculated by determining each 'share of voice'.

This industry expression refers to the percentage of the total car advertising that the major players obtain. It is calculated by monitoring all car advertising on television and radio and in the print media. Using the standard rates, analysts work out the total amount of advertising done and the comparative share bought by each firm. Because Holden's knows exactly how much it has spent to achieve its own share of voice, it can estimate the total amount spent by other companies.

DEALING WITH 371 DEALERS

Car companies do not sell directly to the public but through a network of authorised dealers.

Designer Phil Zmood says the flush glass 'allowed us to achieve the total shape we have been striving for'.

Holden's V-6.

These dealers each have a 'sphere of responsibility'. This is an exclusive area in which they are responsible for sales and service, advertising and promotion, customer satisfaction and ensuring that Holden's has a respectable market share. Holden's has 371 dealers nationwide. In each case there is a Dealer Sales & Service Agreement binding both parties to certain conditions.

Rob McEniry defines a good dealer as 'one who concentrates on all aspects of his business, particularly customer satisfaction'.

This area of dealer/customer relations plays an increasingly important role in Holden's marketing philosophy. In the past, Rob says, there was a tendency to concentrate on sales but it is now Holden's policy for dealers to put maximum emphasis on pleasing existing customers so that they will be retained and also spread the good word for future business.

'We are working closely with our dealers to ensure they have an environment which welcomes each customer', he says.

'The dealers are concentrating on improving customer satisfaction and we have introduced some interesting training programs to improve the professionalism of the entire sales force.'

THE HARD SELL

Don Bowden, the Merchandising Manager, draws a clear line between marketing and merchandising activities. Merchandising is the sharp end of the business, where they strive to cut out a bigger share of the available market. He loves the job and regards every day as a new opportunity to get the message across.

Don oversees all national advertising, dealer marketing activities, dealer merchandising, motor show development, dealer manpower training and the various sales promotion and dealer ideas which range from a give-away book of matches to a full-scale dealer convention.

FOLLOW ME OVER THE MOUNTAIN

The most important day in the life of any new car is the occasion when the company presents it to the dealer network. If the dealers are enthusiastic, the sales campaign takes on a vigorous life of its own. If they are not, there's a long, hard slog ahead.

'The biggest thing in this business is to maintain and improve the morale of the retail sales force', said Don Bowden as he fine-tuned the details of the VN dealer launch.

'In this industry, a large share of any company's advertising is done to motivate its own people. If their morale is not right, the retail sales force can kill a car as easily as it can make it a spectacular success. With something as major as VN, there is no way we would take risks.

'We made a point of consulting our key dealers while the VN was being planned, so we knew we were on the right track. Even so, when we formally present it to the dealer network, we will generate as much enthusiasm as possible. I want them to leave the convention convinced they have a real winner on their hands.

'If we put on a good launch, the odds are that the dealers will go back and put on a really good retail sales campaign. Had we just fed the car onto the market, without hype or excitement, and without the dealers squarely behind it, we could not possibly meet our sales targets. It is essential that the dealers enter the sales arena fully charged with the smell of success.'

At that point, Don was deciding whether to release the VN to the dealers at conventions around the country, or at one central location. Either way, the bill will be at least $1.5 million, money the company regards as well spent.

'I expect an outstanding dealer reaction', said Don. 'We organised a VN preview for the dealers six months before its official release. This was partly to keep them informed but also to stiffen morale during Ford's promotion for the new Falcon. The first dealer meeting was not the full bells-and-whistles convention we will have for the official launch, but it showed them what the new car looks like, how it is engineered and specified. It also gave them a close look at the competitive advantages, and the dealers were suitably impressed.'

'A full-scale launch is a much more elaborate affair. We normally hold the convention in an attractive setting to give the dealers a brief respite from normal business. Sometimes we also invite the dealers' wives. Sometimes, as with the VL model, it's a two-day affair with a very comprehensive program which starts with a dealer business meeting during which we talk about the economic outlook, how the car market is going, sales opportunities and other pertinent matters. We also talk about company progress, service and parts, the importance of improving customer satisfaction and what we are doing to further improve our quality standards.

'This meeting involves a series of talks from key executives, with the Managing Director leading the way.

'In VN's case, the task falls upon John Bagshaw. He is a merchandising manager's dream. He'll ask the dealers to follow him over the mountain and get the job done — and they will.

'After the business meeting, we break before going into a full-scale theatrical release of the car. For this we have all the retail sales force present including dealers, sales managers, service and parts managers and sales people. The presentation includes a full documentary of how the car was conceived, planned and manufactured. This is followed by the "product reveal" often with dancing girls, music, smoke, lights, movement, turntables, cars coming out of the sky — you name it. If it is exciting and can be done, we do it. It's this reveal that gets the adrenalin stirring — and that's my job.

'We go into all the detail on the product, its features and benefits compared to the competition. We show the advertising program and point-of-sale material. I guess we go for overkill because we want everyone to leave the show thinking "Wow, what a car!" '

Like many aspects of the dealer launch, the advertising campaign is handled by an outside agency. The agency's assignment is based on the marketing strategy document, the key points of which are used to create an advertising strategy document. This goes to the advertising agency which generates the creative approach. Well before this point, however, the agency had been fully briefed on the new car. Along with the audiovisual group, convention company and a firm which makes promotional items, key agency members attended a three-hour presentation in November 1987. Almost every facet of the car was described in detail by Engineering and Design executives.

After a further briefing from Holden's advertising manager, the agency came back with a suggested advertising theme and several concept campaigns. These were extensively studied and discussed by Holden's merchandising and advertising people who, after research and some revisions, approved one for further development.

Holden allocates about 65 per cent of its advertising budget to television but makes extensive use of newspapers and specialist magazines. The VN campaign started with a series of television 'teasers' prior to the official unveiling, with glimpses of flush glass and other unusual features to build excitement and expectation.

Because the wagon with its increased size is seen as a major new business opportunity, the possibility of launching it as a separate model several weeks after the Executive and Berlina sedans was considered. The plan called for the VN Calais to make its debut after the sedan but before the wagon. Later still, V-8 variants of both the sedan and wagon were to be announced.

The advertising material was designed to stress the VN's enhanced roominess. This concept is easy enough to communicate, but explaining why the car has flush glass is trickier.

'We have to be careful how we advertise the aerodynamic factor because many people don't understand the implications', says Don Bowden.

'If we take an aggressive stand, we might turn people off. This is one advantage we have to explain with a lot of caution.

'We are also keen to emphasise the improved performance, because the 3.8 V-6 has gained over the previous 3-litre engine, good though it was. Style and performance have always sold motor cars — usually in that order — and must be the basic ingredients of our advertising campaign.

'Fuel economy, which is comparable to VL despite the extra power, is not a strong merchandising point in a television sense because we have to be single-minded about what we communicate. A TV commercial can handle only one or two major points, but a press advertisement allows us to discuss in detail many more subjects including fuel economy.'

Don believes the car's performance should be a key feature in motor magazine advertisements and he would like print advertisements to also stress handling and other performance-related characteristics.

'We will of course be using other forms of promotion', he says. 'For one thing, we need to emphasise the car's ride and drive characteristics and the best way to do so is by an actual demonstration. We are considering approaching existing Commodore owners via direct mail and offering to let them drive the new car.'

'Finally, we must get across our total commitment to improved quality.'

Prior to the VN going on sale, the marketing department had the job of overseeing the run-out of existing stocks of VL Commodores. This perennial industry headache creates a dilemma for all companies. There's a need to clear stocks at a time when word has leaked out about the new models and many buyers prefer to wait, unless there's a big financial incentive. Companies, however, are keen not to make it look like a fire sale. Advertising big discounts or factory bonuses makes the public wary and cheapens the company's image.

To limit the run-out problem, Holden's locked itself into producing a definite number of VLs as early as November 1987. Don therefore knew exactly how many cars had to be sold before the VN launch. One reason for the approach is that Holden's would be selling VLs throughout Ford's Falcon campaign and the accompanying hype. Fortunately, the VL had been Australia's top-selling car to private buyers during 1987, so Don was convinced the momentum would keep rolling throughout the traditionally difficult run-out period.

Don Bowden is one of Holden's most experienced merchandisers. He started with the company in 1951 working in Adelaide as a junior sales clerk. By 1960, he was Acting Zone Manager for South Australia but his hopes of being confirmed in the job were dashed when it went to a colleague with more service. He was John G. Bagshaw, the current Chairman and Managing Director. Instead, Don was transferred to head office in Melbourne as Assistant Advertising and Sales Promotion Manager and, for six years, worked in advertising and promotional activities.

He then returned to Adelaide to join the retail side of the motor business, becoming General Manager of United Motors, South Australia's largest Holden dealer. After 18 months there, he started his own new car dealership which he ran successfully, employing nearly 300 people at its peak. Twelve years down the track, and after some bad eyesight problems, he left the day-to-day grind of retail selling to become a consultant. After a while, Holden's then Sales Director, John Loveridge, heard that Don was available and invited him back to head office. With his health no longer a problem, Don was delighted to combine his retail and wholesale experience and rejoined Holden's in 1983 as Sales Promotion Manager. He assumed his present job in 1985.

FLEETING OPPORTUNITIES

The fleet market, which comprises business vehicles owned by government agencies and private companies, is far larger than many private motorists realise. Approximately 180 000 cars and station wagons were sold to the fleet market in 1987. Of these 40 per cent were six-cylinder models.

This means that almost one out of every two new passenger vehicles goes into a government or company fleet. The market is so large that it influences the design and type of vehicle some manufacturers produce.

According to Rob McEniry, the switch to a local engine and the use of very modern manufacturing processes means the VN's cost structure has been exceptionally well controlled. This in turn places the company in a better position to bid for fleet and government sales than had been the case with the VL Commodore. He expects Holden's share of the fleet business to increase considerably.

The job of masterminding the campaign on a national level falls to Tyler Halsted, who came to Holden's from General Motors Overseas Corporation ten years ago. He says the period following VN's launch will be the most exciting and challenging he has faced since joining the company.

A 'fleet' is considered to be anything from ten units upward registered in one name. It can range from the vehicles on a large farm to a major mining and steel-making company with over 5000 vehicles on strength.

The competition is so fierce that, in 1984, Holden's set up Holden National Leasing (HNL) to sell vehicles directly to those fleets running 100 or more vehicles. HNL, a limited liability company jointly owned by Holden's and 200 major dealers, has been very successful.

Ford, Holden and Mitsubishi are the big players in the passenger fleet market and Toyota is the strongest in commercial vehicles. Of the overall fleet business, 20 per cent goes to government and its affiliates, 7 per cent to rental car firms and the rest to private companies. Large fleets with 100 vehicles or more account for 25 per cent of passenger fleet sales, the smaller fleets (20 to 100 vehicles) take about the same percentage. The remainder is bought by operators with less than 20 vehicles.

Tyler Halsted says his immediate objective with fleet sales is to catch and overtake Ford, the 1987 market leader. He believes this objective will be quickly realised.

'At last we have the right product at the right price', he says. 'And we no longer have to apologise to customers for the size of the car.'

Holden has fleet executives in all States, with head-office specialists who handle large business fleets, rental cars and government areas. Each zone fleet manager is supported by a fleet service group dedicated to helping customers who run into problems which their dealer cannot quickly fix.

'We tend to bend over backwards to make sure fleet customers are happy with our service', Tyler says.

Like the general fleet market, the rental business is surprisingly large. It has been a growth area for several years and rental companies see the tourist boom as nothing but a plus to them. They say the growth will continue for as long as the country can attract overseas visitors.

WHAT PRICE A VN?

Glenice Simmons, Manager of Pricing until late 1987, played a significant role in the development of the VN, partly because of her size.

'I was the resident guinea pig during the two years they were designing it', she says.

'As the smallest person with a suitable security clearance, I was repeatedly called out of my office because someone wanted to know if I could reach a bonnet catch or the heater controls, or whatever they were working on at the time.

'Because cars are often frustrating for people like me, I took great delight in not being able to reach things, so they had to change them!'

Glenice also contributed to the VN in a more formal role, first as Operations Planning·Manager and later as Manager of Strategic Planning, which gave her a coordinating role in a variety of objectives and plans.

From here she took charge of the department concerned with pricing new vehicles, ex-company cars and those components which Holden's sells to other companies. Though new car prices are generally arrived at by market forces, a delicate juggling act is done to reach a figure which is fair to the company and also achieves the desired sales volume.

'We have to determine which features of the car the customer will be prepared to pay extra for', says Glenice.

'For example, if it's a new design like the VN, customers expect it to look different, so they won't pay extra for more modern styling. The previous Commodore had a four-speed automatic transmission, so has the VN. Again we can't expect the customers to pay extra. However, we have a more powerful V-6 engine and that has a market price. My job is to determine how much this extra feature is worth to a retail customer. The VN is also larger than the car it replaces. This is a bonus feature with a market value.

'We have to make a judgment on the value of each such feature as far as the customer is concerned. Occasionally, we are guided by what the competition charge, for example, for an optional extra such as a bigger engine. But the end result must be to produce a retail price which is acceptable to the customer and which provides the company with a reasonable return on its investment.

'When this office arrives at a final figure, we meet with the marketing people and try to come up with a joint recommendation. We take that recommendation to the Price Review Committee which comprises the Managing Director, Marketing Director, Finance Director (or Comptroller) and the Executive in Charge of Planning. That's where the final decision is made.'

LET THE CAR SPEAK FOR ITSELF
– THE ART OF PUBLIC RELATIONS

Holden's Public Relations Manager, John Morrison, says his department has a fairly broad role, acting as a go-between for the company and the public. In the context of a new car, he says, the job is to relate the facts as best he can to a well-informed and experienced press.

Australia's motoring journalists are exposed to product launches on a frequent basis and John says that Holden's policy is not to outdo other companies but to launch a new car as professionally as possible.

A typical guest list covers between 35 and 42 full-time motoring journalists, many of whom have worked together for a long time.

'I've been in the business for more than two decades', John says. 'And I've found that the motoring press takes a very professional approach to a new product and its likely impact on the market. We respect that knowledge and present the car to them in a way which acknowledges their background and technical understanding.'

'We try to make a press launch essentially a non-commercial affair without any hard-sell. Unlike a dealer convention, it is a straightforward, information-sharing process.

'This is not because we don't like the hard-sell but because it would be counterproductive. It is important that we get what is sometimes called a "good press" because that gets us off to a good start in public esteem. In my experience, if a new car is not up to the expectation of the motoring press, they will say so, regardless of how we package the information.'

Marc McInnes, Public Relations Manager for NSW and Queensland (whose responsibilities include organising national new model release programs), adds that it is important to communicate effectively with the motoring press because they are the first source of information on the new car for potential owners.

'Essentially the members of the press enable us to get the message out more quickly', he says. 'This is not only because many potential buyers read their material but because the opinion formers, the enthusiasts and others who devour the motoring columns, spread the word. It is common for widespread opinions about a certain model to develop at a time when relatively few people have driven it or even seen the car in question.'

After a few months, the opinions of journalists has less impact than the opinions of owners, but if the message that first comes out is complimentary, a car is almost guaranteed a good start.

John Morrison says he has found that writers never go out of their way to deliberately criticise a car. They invariably give it a fair go but, on past performance, he knows they will not hold back and refrain from criticism if they think it is justified.

'We are very sensitive to the close examination the group gives to the car and we try to keep the launch as efficient and effective as we can', he says.

'There's a number of key elements in the process which bring a degree of difficulty. For any successful car launch, you need a large fleet to allow every guest to drive a car and, indeed, an appropriate mix of models. You need to give each writer a good cross-section of body styles and transmissions, along with plenty of time to explore the car and not feel restricted by lack of access to it.'

John says that his department tries to set up a press launch in an environment of some visual interest which the motoring group may have not previously experienced. An area with a good mixture of road surfaces is selected so that each writer can drive the cars over a wide variety of roads and conditions.

The full-scale press launch always comes after the dealer convention and, in comparison, is a fairly low-key event without the same razzamatazz. Even so, an enormous amount of detail and coordination is required. The typical press launch starts with a meeting during which key executives present various features of the engineering, design, specifications and merchandising plans, supported by visual aids if necessary. At most Holden launches, the Managing Director talks about the car's broad philosophy and objectives. Other executives describe the car itself, with special emphasis on engineering or design features which are different from the previous model.

'We go through all the technical details associated with the product', says John. 'Of course this information is available in printed form, but the press likes to hear it from the people involved. They also have the opportunity to ask questions on any points which are not clear.'

'Next comes a manufacturing guy to talk about the new production technology and the quality standards. Marketing people reveal how they will introduce the car to the public, our anticipated sales volume, market share, marketing theme and why we think the public will relate to it. We probably also show examples of our television and press advertising campaigns.

'Next on the agenda comes a drive program during which the guests change cars several times and travel with Holden people as passengers so they can ask questions as they go along. After the drive program, there's usually a group question-and-answer session during which curly questions may be thrown at the people best able to deal with them.

'The final part of the press launch is a wrap-up social gathering, usually a dinner, which gives us all a chance to reflect and talk about the product and exchange views.'

English-born John Morrison has been with Holden's public relations office for over 20 years, serving initially as a speech-writer and later as the company spokesman. He says the job has many facets, such as being the front man for the organisation in good times and bad and, where necessary, talking on television or radio on a variety of issue-related subjects. Some can be very difficult to grapple with and explain briefly, he says, mentioning as examples the implications of the Button Plan (to restructure the motor industry) and the social problems associated with car theft.

He adds that no matter how much thought and time goes into a press launch, it is the car which speaks for itself. The design has to be exceptional to command respect from the press and ultimately from the buying public.

'The press launch can only be as good as the product', he says.

Rob McEniry

Robert James McEniry, Director of Marketing, has been with VN from Day One and is the resident guru on its commercial potential. Prior to his present assignment, he was the VN Program Manager and, having a marketing background, ensured that the marketing department made a major contribution to the design concept.

Now married with a young family, Rob was born in Bendigo, Victoria. By the age of 12, he was buying as many motoring magazines as he could afford. In later years he also found time for scuba diving, snow skiing, tennis, photography and art. Rob did his tertiary studies at the Bendigo Institute of Technology and at the Royal Melbourne Institute of Technology. He received a Master of Business Administration from the University of Melbourne and undertook further studies in the USA and Switzerland.

During his student days, Rob worked part-time as a systems analyst and programmer, then joined the Myers retail group to help implement a computerised credit system. His interest in motoring continued and, in 1976, he joined GM-H as a zone manager for dealer business management. Rob progressed rapidly through the organisation and, by 1982, was National Merchandising Manager. This put him in charge of all GM-H merchandising programs, including advertising, sales promotion, manpower development and program planning, with an annual budget in excess of $40 million.

After a stint as Sales Staff Manager, Rob became the divisional manager in charge of reorganising GM-H's Parts and Accessories division. This accomplished, he was appointed Project Manager for the VN program. Concurrent with that assignment, he was a member of the strategic analysis and planning team which recommended the overall direction the company should take.

In 1987, Rob McEniry became Director of Marketing, responsible for selling passenger, light commercial and heavy commercial vehicles as well as the export, service, replacement parts and accessories divisions.

Getting on track
... motor sport and special vehicles

In 1986 an official from a large Australian car company frankly admitted he would swap all of his company's motor sport successes for just one victory at Bathurst.

But fate did not allow such a bargain. The 1986 James Hardie 1000 brought the familiar sight of Holden cars taking the first two places. For the 12th time in 19 years, 'The General' had won the race which, to many Australians, is the only one that matters.

While eyes were fixed on Allan Grice's all-conquering Commodore VK on that sunny October Sunday, work on Holden's 1988 race car was already underway.

For more than six months, engineers had been engaged in developing a high-performance, fuel-injected version of the race-winning Holden V-8. They were also making plans for the ultimate sporting evolution of the VB-VL Commodore package.

Although unknown to anyone at the time, this '1988 Group A' would signal a new age for Holden's racetrack and high-performance road car activities. It would not be produced by Peter Brock's Holden Dealer Team (HDT) organisation, as in the past, but through the offices of two new groups: Holden Motor Sport and Holden Special Vehicles. And the 1988 Group A super-car, based on the VL Commodore, was designed to pave the way for a string of spectacular VN specials planned for the years ahead.

HOLDEN MOTOR SPORT

Many of Australia's most acclaimed motor racing drivers — Peter Brock, Larry Perkins, John Harvey, Allan Grice, and others — have spent the major part of their driving careers behind the steering wheels of Holden cars.

The Commodore V-8 has brought these men enormous success. Its performance and reliability, their talent plus their teams' skill and dedication resulted in an extraordinary number of motor sport victories between 1980 and 1986.

It is no secret, however, that during 1987 the once-dominant Holden V-8 fell behind. The 'big boys' had arrived from overseas with new-generation, purpose-built, small capacity power plants and the 1987 Touring Car Championship ended without a single Holden victory.

The 1987 Bathurst race was a messy affair, preceded by bickering over the rules and the eligibility of certain cars. It was conducted in confusion and ended with protests and counterprotests. When the considerable dust had cleared, Peter Brock's Holden Commodore was awarded first place. This took his personal tally of Bathurst victories to nine and Holden's to 13, but it was not the sort of win that Holden's or Peter Brock would have preferred. The victory effectively closed a year of racing that both parties would otherwise like to forget.

A fightback was clearly needed.

The 1988 Group A, with its sensational 180 kW fuel-injected V-8 and radical wind-tunnel-developed fibreglass body-kit, was unveiled at the Sydney Motor Show in late 1987.

Since 48-215 and FJ models first took to the circuits in the 1950s, race fans have seen Holdens at the fore in production car racing. Here a young Dick Johnson pushes his EH to the limit (1968) and Peter Brock and Colin Bond leave all behind them in their XU1 Toranas (1973).

Perhaps the most versatile production car ever on the local scene, the fast and nimble Torana took scores of chequered flags in races, rallies, rallycross and other forms of motor sport. Its racing successor, the Commodore, has had a big act to follow.

The building of a limited run of 750 1988 Group A road cars was not done with profit in mind. It was undertaken to make the fuel-injected engine eligible for use in Group A Touring Car racing, as Holden's considered it sound marketing sense to keep the Commodore competitive until the VN, for which the fuel-injected engine had primarily been developed, was ready for the track.

The company's determination to uphold the winning tradition was underscored by the setting up, in late 1986, of Holden Motor Sport (HMS). Designed originally to work with HDT to provide support to all teams racing Holden products, the new group found itself something of an orphan by the time it was officially launched in early 1987. Holden's and HDT had, by then, gone their separate ways in one of the most publicised and debated incidents in local motoring history. The two companies had run into irreconcilable differences over a Brock-designed Commodore variant called 'Director' and Holden's had ended the partnership. Until then, HDT (in collaboration with Holden's) was responsible for the development and production of special vehicles. HDT also took care of the racing end of the business, running a semi 'works' race team with Brock, John Harvey and Allan Moffat as the leading drivers.

The top men at Holden's insist to this day they did absolutely everything possible to keep the HDT partnership intact and they admit that the split with the idolised Brock was a public relations nightmare. The other problem resulting from the break-up was considerable disruption in the development of the 1988 race car. At least 500 examples of the 1988 Group A had to be completed for homologation and, although HEC was well on track with the fuel-injected engine when the split occurred, the wind-tunnel development of the much-needed new body-kit had not begun.

Holden versus Ford battles have been a highlight of local motor sport for much of the 1960s, 1970s and 1980s, with the 'Great Race' at Bathurst the major highlight. By 1987 the Bathurst score was Holden 13 and Ford 10. Six of the Holden victories were achieved by Commodores.

152

The role of HMS was quickly reshaped, with homologation road-car development (and other duties previously taken care of by HDT) falling into its lap. According to the Manager of Holden Motor Sport, John Lindell, HMS started life as a proposal endorsed by Peter Brock.

'The 1988 Group A would certainly have been a joint HDT/HMS project, all other things being equal', he said.

'Following the demise of the Holden/Brock relationship, a partnership with Tom Walkinshaw Racing was struck and wind-tunnel work commenced in England. In late 1987, Holden Special Vehicles, an organisation to develop and produce high-performance Holden cars, was formed under an agreement between Holden's and Tom Walkinshaw Racing. By that time, Holden's had made a comprehensive review of nine formal tenders.'

John says Holden's has no intention of becoming directly involved in motor sport. HMS has three areas of responsibility.

'The first is to support those people engaged in motor sport with our product. The second, which is directly linked to it, is the conception, design, development and manufacture of the Group A road car, which is the base for the race car. The third part of the exercise is to work with the Holden Special Vehicles organisation. Although Special Vehicles is owned largely by Tom Walkinshaw Racing, HMS is the Holden arm of the equation and liaises with Special Vehicles on day-to-day operating.

'In terms of motor sport support, we will continue to provide assistance to drivers in the form of parts and technology. For example, we recently

The Commodore of Allan Grice pressures race-leader Peter Brock in the 1982 Castrol 400 at Sandown circuit (Victoria). Under the prevailing Group C rules, touring cars sprouted enormous flared guards to house the widest possible tyres.

With the international Group A touring car rules now in force, the Commodore is restricted to its road-going body shell. This situation has led to a succession of Group A road cars. Larry Perkins — seen here at full-tilt in a VL — was the leading Holden driver in 1988.

had a car here for a week doing numerous elaborate measurements that the team couldn't do itself. That sort of back-up is available. We also assist with transport, publicity, trackside facilities and allied matters.'

John says that, with the lead times involved, it is necessary to start planning a new race car at least 18 to 20 months in advance of its debut. The feedback from drivers and knowledge gleaned in the VL program provided the basis for the VN race car, which was conceptualised in early 1987.

Asked about the racetrack advantages of the VN, Lindell points out that 'all Holden's cars are designed firstly as passenger cars and are only raced because of man's competitive nature'.

'There is always a great deal of development to be done but naturally some vehicles lend themselves more to racing than others', he says.

'Purely from a motor sport point of view, the VN's major advantage is its aerodynamics. It will give us a starting point pretty close to that of the final development of the VL. We have spent a massive amount of time in the wind-tunnel in England getting the VL's Cd figure down by 25 per cent [the 'Cd' is the coefficient of drag].

'With the VN, even in race configuration, with wide tyres and other paraphernalia including aids to increase downforce, I believe that we will be able to sustain a Cd of about 0.3 and maybe a bit better.'

The fact that VN is a bigger, longer, wider car is also an advantage says Lindell, who adds that the VL was a little narrow for competition.

'The wider VN track will allow further suspension development and we will also get a slightly lower roll centre with VN. But I still see the major advantage in that it will be much more aerodynamic without having to carry extra weight.

'By lowering the Cd as we have, we now require 56 kW less to push the car through the air at 240 km/h. This gives other advantages, such as fuel economy. It is difficult to quantify this in a race environment, but it could make the car up to 15 per cent more economical. You can go further without having to pit for fuel.'

A fuel-injected V-8 with around 375 kW on tap is another advantage. Under Group A regulations, Commodores have been restricted to the same fuel distribution system as on the road car.

'Until 1988', says John, 'we were struggling with a carburettor which, although excellent and very reliable on the road, was far from ideal for the track.

'Moving to a fuel-injected engine gives very much better distribution of fuel. It enables us to do a better job on the manifold and provides the ability to electronically tune the engine for a greater range of conditions. Where we couldn't alter the conventional carburettor for racing, fuel-injection enables us to have specific electronic modules for Bathurst, for Calder, for wet weather, dry weather and so on.'

Touring Car racing is designed for vehicles based on high-volume production cars and, for many years, it has been the biggest crowd puller in Australian motor sport. The international Group A rules, adopted here in 1985, are designed to allow as many different cars as possible to compete on relatively even terms. The rules allow a race car to be developed from a 'sporting evolution' of a base production model, providing that a minimum number of each have been built. For Australian manufacturers, the required number of production cars is 5000, followed by 500 sporting evolutions.

The aim of successful homologation is to determine the weaknesses of a car under race conditions, examine which parts the rules allow you to evolve and, using this information, produce a batch of 500 road cars which make the best base for a race car.

'We will carry on the tradition with the VN and its successors', says John Lindell.

Before the sporting evolution VN can be built, race rules require Holden's to build 5000 standard VN road cars fitted with the V-8 engine. This will take Holden's about 12 months (as V-8 models will make a relatively small proportion of total VN production) so the VN V-8 won't be homologated until the 1990 race season.

John and his team — consisting of himself, engineer John Hocking and parts procurement man Tony Porrit — drove the early VN prototypes at the proving ground and were immediately impressed by the handling qualities.

'We were given the opportunity to input what we, in the motor sport group, would like to see in the production car', he says.

'Not only has the new vehicle the potential to deliver better handling than the VL in a motor sport application, it will gain from lessons learned with the VL.'

The three-man Holden Motor Sport group, set up within Holden's Marketing department, has a budget and an objective, but it is entirely up to them how to go about things.

'We have used the good offices of Holden's Engine Company and the Engineering Group in Holden's Motor Company [now GMHA Ltd] wherever possible', says John.

'But most departments here have been so heavily committed to working on VN that, to some extent, we have had to take our work outside. For the race engines of the 1988 VL Group A and the VN Group A, we used the facilities of racing driver/engineer Larry Perkins. The wind-tunnel work, of course, was done in the UK by Tom Walkinshaw Racing.'

A handbuilt VN prototype was shipped to England late in October 1987 for wind-tunnel work. Afterwards, it was used by Tom Walkinshaw Racing (TWR) and Holden Special Vehicles to develop an upgraded VN for road use.

Two complications with the VN Group A exercise were the demise of the Group A World Touring Car Championship after the 1987 season and the looming shadow of the Silhouette category. As the name suggests, this new category has a formula based purely on the silhouette shape of a car and there is no need to base the mechanical parts around a production vehicle. The rules require a 25 000 production run of the body shape but the race car itself is allowed to be powered by a mid-engined turbocharged engine, and the body may be steel-framed with reinforced carbon fibre panels. Understandably, it is an exceedingly expensive form of motor racing.

'There is no doubt that Silhouette racing will appeal to a lot of manufacturers who don't have a production car suitable to be competitive in Group A', says John. 'Nevertheless, we decided to press on with a VN for Group A racing, which we are sure will continue to be the most popular category

Group A Commodore number 500 comes off the line at Holden's Dandenong Plant in March 1988. Greeting it were (left to right): Plant Manager John Fenner, Larry Perkins, John Harvey, John Crennan, Andy Morrison and the manager of Holden Motor Sport, John Lindell.

in this country. Sadly, the ending of the WTCC robs us of the chance to compete in, and possibly win, a world championship.'

Motor sport is expensive and getting more so with each year. According to John, it would cost roughly $2 million to set up a two-car team good enough to secure victory in the Australian Touring Car Championship.

'When you start to add up your transport costs, fuel, accommodation, entry fees, tyres and engines ... I mean the race engines alone are well in excess of $20 000 apiece and the top Commodore teams change them after every race. Every component is "lifed" so, if a conrod has done so many hours, out it goes. It is the same with a transmission, and they cost well over $10 000 apiece. The costs can build up alarmingly!'

Although we are unlikely to see a Holden V-6 used in Australian Group A racing, the 'six' will be heard on local racetracks. It has been chosen by the Confederation of Australian Motor Sport as the standard engine for the Formula Australia competition, designed for open-wheeler cars. In race trim, the V-6 is good for well over 200 kW.

John Lindell has had a lifelong love of motor sport. He was involved briefly as a driver and, to use his phrase, discovered that his talents lay elsewhere. Instead he became a preparer of motor cars.

'Subsequent to that I had 20 years at Holden's, mainly on the manufacturing side', he says. 'I was involved in industrial engineering, which is a generic term for all the things that cannot be accurately described by any other form of engineering, and later I became Program Manager. That's the guy who takes an approved program and ensures that it all comes together at the required time. When I took on that job, I had the JE Camira, the VL Turbo, VL V-8 and the 1986 Group A car to look after.'

The men responsible for the setting up of HMS are Reliability Manager Ray Borrett, who proposed the concept and wrote the operating guidelines, and John Crennan who, as the (then) Marketing Manager of Holden's, 'sold' the Board of Directors on the benefits of having a dedicated group within the department.

Ray Borrett has been involved in the development of racing Holdens since the 1960s. Of the Commodore he says:

'The good old Holden V-8 provides the basis for a very highly tuned engine and the Commodore, in VL form, has reliable components, exceptionally good torque "for climbing mountains" and a good pool of drivers who are experienced with the car. They are supported by experienced teams plus, of course, factory technical support.

'The VN will be even better with sophisticated aerodynamics, well-developed brakes and a new racing transmission. Changes to its suspension, plus the wider track and longer wheelbase, will ensure better handling.

'The Group A body-kit', he adds, 'will be designed to allow us to exploit rules to the maximum in terms of tyre widths and other specifications.'

HMS finds plenty of opportunities to tap Ray's experience and enthusiasm. John Crennan also plays a major role. He is now Managing Director of the other arm in Holden's race and performance network — Holden Special Vehicles.

SPECIAL VEHICLES

The entire staff of Holden Special Vehicles was gathered at the company's Notting Hill (Melbourne) headquarters at 11.00 pm, Sunday, 3 January 1988. It was then that the final touches were put on the first 'pilot' of the 1988 Group A road car. It had been such a struggle to get the car finished that Christmas and New Year's Day had passed almost unnoticed by most of the team.

When the last panel was attached and the staff stood back to take a look, there was a shock in store. The appearance was even more extrovert than the models and drawings had suggested.

Managing Director John Crennan looked at the completed car and drew a long breath. He knew it wasn't going to be everybody's cup of tea but it was obvious that the wildly styled silver VL, with its 65 kg of fibreglass aerodynamic aids and radical lines, would not fail to turn heads. And performance car enthusiasts would be over the moon.

'As the first car for Special Vehicles', he said, 'this is a good strong statement from us. To some people it may be over the top but everything on the vehicle is there for a good reason. In many ways this is the most advanced car ever produced in Australia and we have to get that message across'.

No matter which way you look at it, the connection between Holden Special Vehicles (HSV), GMHA (nee HMC), HEC, HMS and TWR is complicated. The relationship changes from one project to the next but every group has its input and each party knows the job it has to do.

With the 'homologation specials', the captain's hat is on the head of John Lindell at Holden Motor Sport. For the 1988 Group A, the sequence was something like this. Lindell liaised with Holden's Motor Company and

John Crennan, John Harvey, Ian Dorward and Rex Nesbit raise the Special Vehicles standard.

157

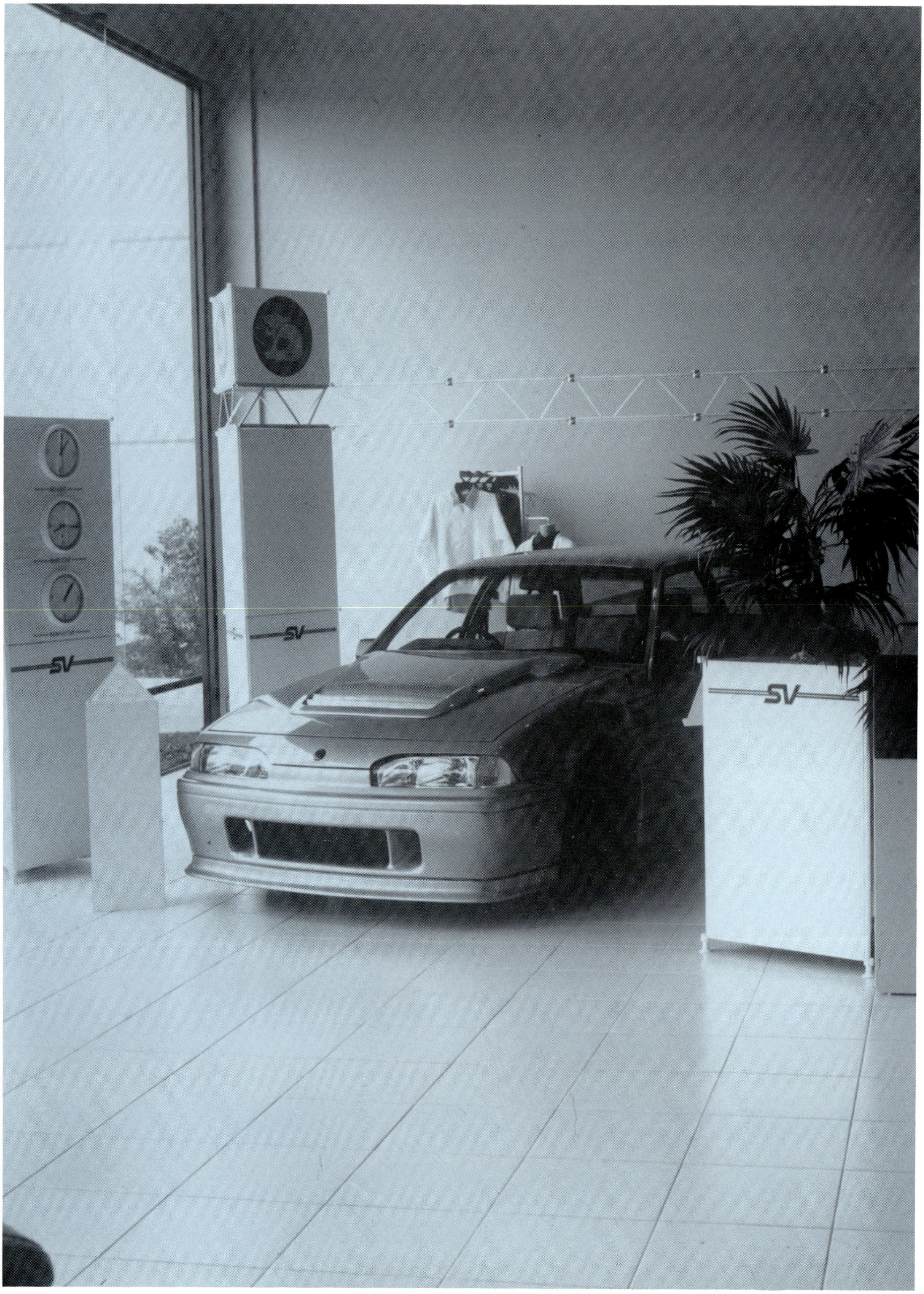
SV
SV
SV

Holden's Engine Company to get the mechanical specifications he needed for the base car. Larry Perkins was brought in to assist with engine development, as were other groups including Tom Walkinshaw's international operation, which later signed a ten-year agreement with Holden's to set up and run the Australian-based Special Vehicles Group. During the development of the body-kit, HMC's Design department was given the job of striking a balance between the ideal aerodynamic shape and an attractive, workable package.

Holden Special Vehicles came into the picture at the manufacturing stage, being contracted as overall project managers. This job included the production and fitting of the new body-kit and other equipment. Holden's Motor Company/GMHA then came back into the act to collect the final product and sell it through the dealer network while Holden Motor Sport began homologation proceedings and started liaising with drivers and teams.

Although Holden Special Vehicles input in the 1988 Group A was almost nil, it is now playing a significant role in the VN Group A development.

For projects other than the homologation cars, HSV has a free run to dream up requirements although Holden's, which warrantees the final product, retains the right of veto.

Holden Special Vehicles started with a work force of 30 in November 1987. John Crennan was under no illusions about the work needed to fill the big shoes of his predecessor. Unlike Brock's HDT organisation, however, which produced hot Commodores and Statesmans, HSV was set up to produce performance versions of large and small Holden models.

HSV has exciting plans for upgraded and upsized engines to be fitted to the smaller models and also some spectacular VN variants. The group is working two years ahead with engine plans, basically by supplying the required specifications to Holden's Engine Company which then investigates whether the objective is possible and how much it will cost.

Crennan is very mindful of export possibilities, something that could be facilitated greatly by international motor sport success. New Zealand and Great Britain are the major targets initially. It is unlikely that left-hand drive cars will come out of HSV in the foreseeable future though to the enormously enthusiastic and energetic John Crennan, this and virtually anything else, is possible in the long term.

'We want to be the Porsche of Australia', he says, 'with superbly presented cars that are advanced, functional, classy and exciting'.

To this end, HSV has gone to great lengths to maintain a decidedly upmarket identity in its corporate signs, symbols and advertisements and has set up, within existing Holden dealerships, some of the most stylish showrooms in the business.

As well as producing better and more exciting cars as time goes by, there is a determined effort to increase the company's flexibility.

'We would like to make very personalised cars, almost with a menu approach', says Crennan. 'We probably couldn't promise someone a complete one-off, but we would like to be able to have our dealers offer such a wide choice of colours, equipment and mechancial specifications from our brochure of goodies that people can have exactly the car they want.'

As well as building its own production models, HSV will produce showcars and conduct contract work for Holden's.

The Japanese car company Honda, whose ambitious Formula One project has taken it to the top-of-the-tree in that category, claims it has one major reason for racing. The excitement associated with this branch of its operations attracts the brightest young talent to the Honda ranks and brings out the best in the people already there.

Crennan has a similar philosophy with HSV.

'HSV offers a big chance for the people here and at Holden's. Everyone at Holden's is very keen and many have spent a lot of their own time helping us get the best into our products.

'When we advertised for apprentices at the start of the year, we were literally swamped with applicants.'

Opposite:
A Holden Special Vehicles showroom.

Few sedans will turn as many heads or move as quickly as the first product of HSV — the fuel-injected V-8-powered Commodore SS Group A.

John Crennan's right-hand man is John Harvey, the Bathurst winner, Monza winner and former manager of Peter Brock's HDT organisation. He was also present when HSV's first car was finished just before midnight on 3 January.

'It's outrageous', he said with an emerging smile. 'No one's going to fail to notice this one.'

Harvey had already driven the car without the body-kit and was enormously confident of its capabilities.

'The performance is spectacular', he said. 'If you're going to race a Commodore this year and you don't have one of these, you might as well stay at home.'

Harvey has raced each successive Commodore model and has been closely involved in the development side.

'The first requirement of a good Touring Car', he says, 'is a basically sound design. The Commodore is excellent in terms of weight distribution and so on, but I think its biggest asset is its reliability. In all the years I've been campaigning Commodores, I can't recall a single structural problem. This is particularly remarkable because until the advent of Group A in 1985, we were required to use virtually standard suspension, axles, steering and other components'.

'I think the VN will be excellent, particularly in aerodynamics', he adds. 'Until the 1988 Group A, the Commodore has always been a little nervous over humps at race speeds, due to a lack of downforce. That has now been largely corrected but the VN should be better again.'

Harvey has been very enthusiastic about HSV from the start.

'We have set up an impressive new building, a very enthusiastic staff and all our equipment is brand-new so there are no compromises. Most importantly, we have 100 per cent Australian employees working on Australian cars for Australians.'

When Holden's severed its ties with Peter Brock's HDT organisation, it needed a new special vehicles group. There was an enormous response to the call for tenders, so why did Holden's go with Tom Walkinshaw?

'TWR is a British-based company', says John Harvey, 'and I suppose this made some people wonder why it was chosen. But TWR is so vastly experienced and professionally run, it is the ideal choice. Everything is well planned and executed and the company achieves its objectives'.

(Interestingly, the paths of Holden's and TWR had crossed earlier when TWR was making plans to participate in the 1987 World Touring Car Championship with a team of Commodores. TWR later withdrew from the WTCC following restructuring of the Championship sponsorship but, nevertheless, gained a lot of experience with, and confidence in, the Commodore V-8.)

Tom Walkinshaw has made a great success of motor racing, John Harvey points out, both in terms of chequered flags and the business side. He actually makes a profit out of racing, which is quite a feat.

'Equally importantly, he is a new car dealer. The bottom line is that we have to sell our cars through dealers and Tom has special knowledge in that area.

'In respect of the Brock situation', adds Harvey, 'I think people recognise that Holden's had no alternative but to do what it did. As a result, they should greet the new set-up enthusiastically'.

The link with TWR gives Holden Special Vehicles and Holden Motor Sport access to state-of-the-art performance technology.

To emphasis the identity of Holden Special Vehicles, all models (except the Group A) will be simply identified by the prefix of 'SV' followed by the engine capacity and/or other information relating to specifications or year

The SV 88, a luxurious version of the V-8 Calais, was the second model from HSV. Options included a phone and fax machine, making it a very rapid office indeed.

161

Larry Perkins (left) is not only an excellent driver. As an engineer, he has played a significant role in the development of the fuel-injected V-8 race engine. On the right is engine-builder Neill Burns.

of production. John Harvey believes that, in time, the cars will be generally known as 'SV Holdens' in the same way that all HDT products have collected the tag 'Brock' cars.

The building of the SV 5000 (based on the VN Commodore 5-litre V-8) in late 1988 caps an extremely busy first year for HSV. During this time it has produced the VL Group A, the SV 88 (a luxury high-performance VL Commodore), SV 1800s (based on the Astra) and SV 2000s (based on Camira).

The VN Group A is expected to be built in late 1989 and will be seen on the racetrack during the 1990 season.

As well as building cars for race homologation, the major benefit of Holden Special Vehicles is to allow Holden dealers to cater for a larger cross-section of buyers without General Motors-Holden's Automotive becoming further involved in model proliferation or capital outlay.

SV cars, like their HDT predecessors, already look like becoming appreciating assets. At this stage, at least, the new set-up appears to have created an 'everybody wins' situation.

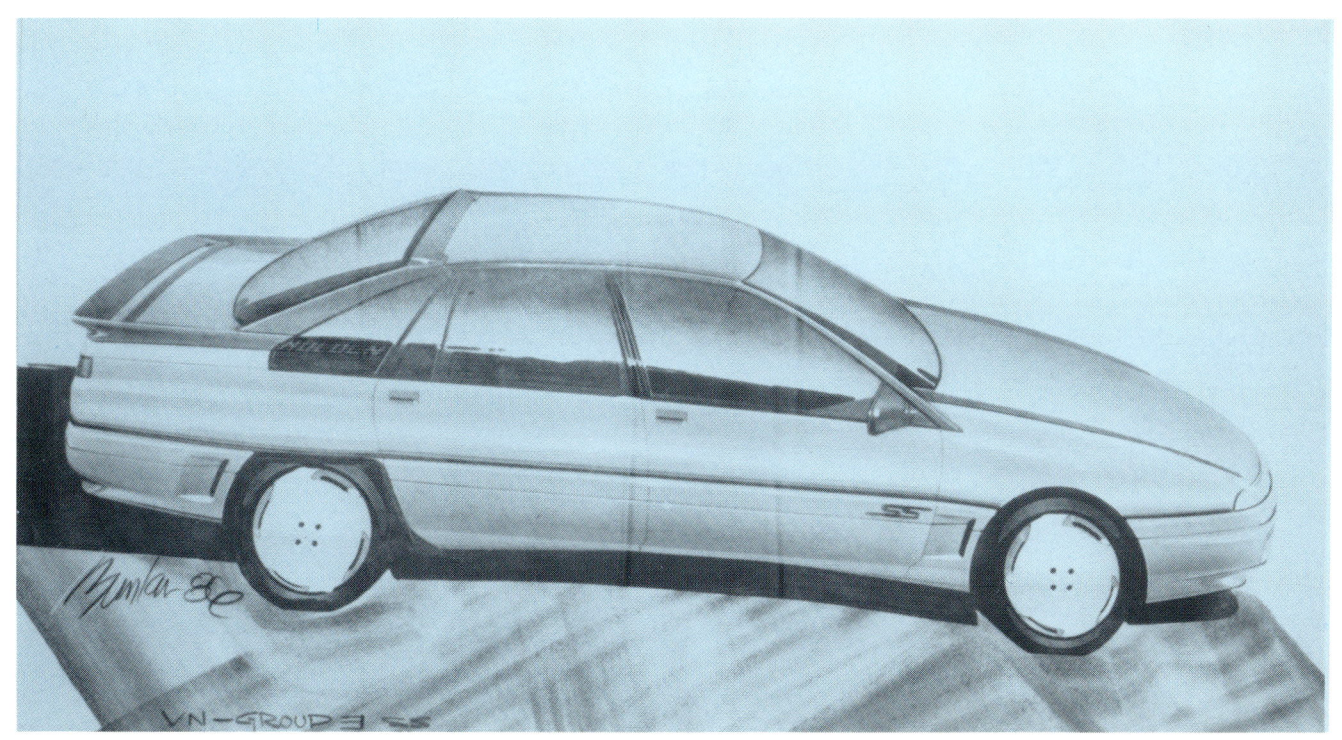

And the VN Group A? Work is already well underway. This is an early sketch from Holden Design.

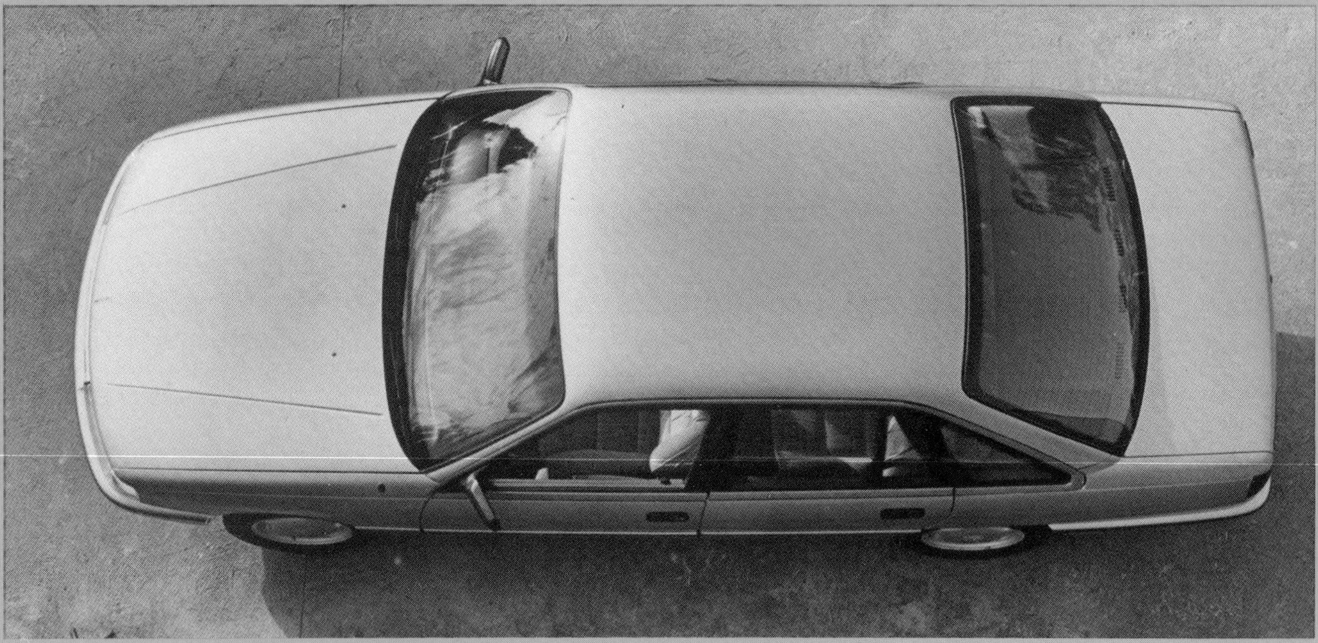

The end result
... specification details

VEHICLE TYPE	All new four-door, five-seater sedan and five-door, five-seater wagon with choice of V-6 and V-8 engines and three distinct levels of equipment.
MODELS	Holden Commodore Executive Holden Commodore Berlina Holden Calais
CHASSIS/CONSTRUCTION	All steel unitary body construction.
ENGINES	• V-6: 3.8-litre overhead valve 90 degree vee, even firing configuration. Four-main-bearing crankshaft. Port fuel-injection. Balance shaft. Hydraulic valve actuation with roller valve lifters. Single-belt accessory drive. • V-8: 5-litre overhead valve 90 degree vee configuration. Five-main-bearing crankshaft, hydraulic valve actuation. Port fuel-injection with RAM-tuned single-throttle body inlet manifold.
TRANSMISSIONS	• Manual: M78 Five-speed, all synchromesh with floorshift lever in console. • Automatic: MD8 Turbohydramatic 700 four-speed torque converter with planetary gears. Solenoid-operated downshift switch, part throttle kickdown. T-Bar floor shift in console.
PROPELLER SHAFT	Two-piece straight tube shaft with rubber insulated centre bearing and constant velocity centre joint.
CLUTCH	Single dry plate. Beville diaphram spring. Mechanical cable operation, connected directly to pull fork throw-out lever.
RADIAL TUNED SUSPENSION (RTS)	• Front: Independent MacPherson wet-strut design. Front cross-member assembly bolted to the engine body side rails at four points carrying all the suspension, steering and front engine mountings in one assembly. Struts are attached at their upper ends to the body through rubber insulated self-aligning bearings. Tranverse location of the lower end of the strut is controlled by a U-section pressed steel lower arm with a tuned rubber inner bush and an outer nylon seated ball stud pivot. Fore/aft location is by a forged tension rod with rubber bushings at either end. Linear rate springs offset in relation to the strut centre line are mounted on seats welded to the strut tubes. Polyurethane concentric bump stops are used. A 26 mm stabiliser bar is linked directly to MacPherson strut and mounted in rubber pivots on the sub frame. • Rear: Rigid axle. Five-link type with parallel short upper and long lower trailing arms and a Panhard rod between axle and underbody. Tuned rubber bushes are used throughout. Progressive rate rear coil springs are mounted on the lower control arms forward of axle housing. 16 mm decoupled stabiliser bar is mounted on the axle and connected to the underbody through pivoted links. 30.2 mm diameter shock absorbers.

REAR AXLE — Salisbury type with tubular steel axle tubes which are pressed into the cast-iron centre differential section.
Axle shafts have rolled splines and are fitted with taper roller bearings. A 191 mm ring gear is standard.

STEERING
- Hydraulically assisted rack and pinion. Variable ratio (17.2:1 on centre to 11.8:1 on lock). Direct linkage (rear of front wheels) from rack to steering arms. Turns lock-to-lock — 2.7.
Soft padded 408 mm diameter circular steering wheel.
- Manual rack and pinion (optional). Variable ratio (19.7:1 on centre to 23.3:1 on lock). Turns lock to lock — 4.5.

BRAKES — Four-wheel power-assisted disc brakes working on split circuit hydraulic system with proportioning valve. Power assistance — integral vacuum, mechanically operated 230 mm booster.
- Front: Ventilated disc, 271 by 22 mm single piston sliding head caliper. Heavy-duty system for V-8 has disc diameter of 289 mm.
Front swept area: Standard disc: 109 562 mm sq. Heavy-duty disc: 118 044 mm sq.
- Rear: Solid disc. Rear swept area: 98 922 mm sq.
- Total swept area: Standard disc: 208 484 mm sq. Heavy-duty disc (with V-8 engine): 216 966 mm sq.
- Brake lines: Double wall 360 degree wrapped steel Bundy tube lines.
- Parking brake: Centre console-mounted pull-up type with push-button release. Operates mechanically on separate drum in centre of rear disc hub.

FUEL SYSTEM — Electronic control port fuel-injection on V-6 and V-8. V-6 and V-8 incorporate speed density fuel control, Bosch director plate style fuel injectors (to provide a precise fuel spray pattern) and Delco electronic control module.
Electric fuel pump in fuel tank.
Fluid treated paper element in air cleaner.
V-8 has aluminium RAM-tuned inlet manifold. V-6 has aluminium inlet manifold designed and tuned for maximum efficiency.
Underslung fuel tank with fuel filler on right-hand rear quarter-panel behind flap.

ELECTRICAL — 12 volt negative ground.
Batteries: V-6 — 75 min/350 amp nine plate. V-8 — 80 min/400 amp 11 plate.

IGNITION SYSTEM — Electronic ignition system with copper core tapered seat spark plugs and television and radio suppression carbon core cable.
V-6 has computer-controlled three-coil ignition (distributor deleted). V-8 has breakerless electronic ignition.

COOLING SYSTEM — Fully sealed liquid 103 kPa pressurised cooling system.
Front-mounted cross-flow radiator and radiator coolant recovery bottle.
Centrifugal water pump driven by belt from crankshaft with choke-type thermostat.
Full-length cylinder water jackets.
Four-blade 375 mm cooling fan on V-6.
Air-conditioned V-8 models also have thermostatically controlled seven-blade 457 mm diameter electric auxilliary fan.

EXHAUST SYSTEM — V-6: Fabricated dual exhaust manifolds.
V-8: Cast-iron dual exhaust manifolds with single crossover pipe. Single seam welded steel exhaust and tailpipe with two reverse-flow mufflers.

WHEELS — Executive and Berlina: Ventilated pressed steel 6.00 JJ by 14 with plastic wheel trims.
Calais: Styled cast light alloy 6.00 JJ by 15.

TYRES — Steel-belted radial tyres, all models.
Executive and Berlina: P185/75 HR 14.
Calais: P205/65 HR 15.

EXTERIOR LIGHTING	• Front: Single quartz halogen rectangular semisealed headlamps in glass housing. 55 watt low beam, 55 and 60 watt high beam. Front park lamp and indicators incorporated in headlamp assembly. • Rear: Square rear lamp cluster in rear panel for indicator, park light, stop light, reflector, white reversing light.
INTERIOR LIGHTING	Illuminated glovebox, rear compartment, instrument panel, heater/ventilation controls, ashtray and cigar lighter, all models. Central lamp with spot lamps (Berlina and Calais), rear quarter lamps on Calais. Executive has a central dome lamp.
INSTRUMENTS/CONTROLS	Centrally located around steering column in four groups: 1. Instrument panel. 2. Central switch bank. 3. Control panel. 4. Steering column control stalk. • Commodore Executive/Berlina: 1. Semicircular speedo. 0-220 km/h with odometer and tripmeter. Quadrant temperature gauge and fuel gauge. Central warning system in horizontal cluster (high beam, oil pressure, battery, brake, park brake, optional trailer light). 2. Illuminated heated rear window switch. 3. Illuminated ashtray. Illuminated cigar lighter. Windscreen wiper dwell control. 4. Steering column control stalk: indicators, flasher, headlamp dip. Other controls on binnacles: light switch, instrument lamp rheostat, hazard warning switch, interior light switch, windscreen wiper/washer switch. Digital clock in radio. • Calais: additional instruments/controls: 1. Tachometer. 2. Illuminated power antenna switch. 3. Electronic AM/FM radio stereo cassette player with PIN security feature. Plus: Cruise control and trip computer switches on instrument binnacles. Power window controls on centre console. Power exterior mirror switch on driver's armrest.
VENTILATION	• Flowthrough air blending system incorporating: Two centrally located adjustable face-level fresh air vents. Four adjustable heating and fresh air vents on each end of instrument panel including side window demisters. Foot-level heating and fresh air outlets. Two rotary controls above central console for adjusting temperature and mode, four-speed electric blower fan switch. • Air-conditioning: Fully integrated system (original equipment on Calais, optional on other models). All vents release air-conditioning, including additional vents at rear of centre console.
SEATING	'Z' spring-supported, contoured full-foam front and rear seats. Reclining front buckets with non-removable head restraints, rear bench on all models, central folding armrest on Berlina, Calais. Mechanical ratchet vertical height adjustment on driver's seat. Also lumbar support adjustment on Berlina and Calais. Boot access flap in centre of rear seat. • Seat covering: Executive – knitted material. Berlina – woven fabric. Calais – velour, with leather also available.
SOUND INSULATION	• All models: Upper instrument/dash panel – Triflex. Lower intrument/dash panel (including pedal stand isolation) – moulded triflex, rubber-backed. Floor pan – Heat fusible sound deadener; flat triplex bonded to carpet in floor area; moulded triflex bonded to carpet with rubber backing in specific locations. Pillars – polyurethane foam. Roof insulation – Moulded headlining (all models); moulded headlining plus flat triflex (Calais). Inner bonnet – Fibreglass insulation (Berlina and Calais).

CORROSION PROTECTION	• Zinc precoated: floorpan. • Zinc precoated steel (single-side): inner engine hood decklid, front fenders, outer door panels, rocker panel inner, wheelhouse brace, door belt outer reinforcement. • Zinc precoated steel (double-side): fender connecting panel. Selected body structural members, air outlets, fender facing, frame upper brace. • Rust preventative wax: rocker inner box section, lower doors, engine hood forward nose, decklid inside rear edge. • Acid resistant enamel: panels adjacent to battery and washer bottle locations. • Protective clear lacquer: engine and engine compartment. • Epoxy black dip: body to top of wheel arches, engine hood and decklid.
INTERIOR DIMENSIONS	Front leg room (mm) — 1042 (sedan and wagon). Rear leg room (mm) — 930 (sedan and wagon). Front headroom (mm) — 977 (sedan and wagon). Rear headroom (mm) — 968 (sedan), 1004 (wagon). Front shoulder room (mm) — 1518 (sedan and wagon). Rear shoulder room (mm) — 1518 (sedan and wagon). Front hip room (mm) — 1528 (sedan and wagon). Rear hip room (mm) — 1520 (sedan and wagon). Glass area (sq mm) — 27 698 (sedan), 29 865 (wagon).
EXTERIOR DIMENSIONS	Total length (mm): 4850 (sedan), 4896 (wagon). Total width (mm): 1794 (sedan and wagon). Total height (mm): at kerb weight: 1403 (sedan), 1422 (wagon). Wheelbase (mm): 2731 (sedan), 2822 (wagon). Front track (mm): 1451 (Executive and Berlina), 1453 (Calais). Rear track (mm): 1478 (Executive and Berlina), 1480 (Calais). Kerb weight (kg): 1290 (Executive), 1329 (Berlina), 1482 (Calais) (estimates). Turning circle kerb to kerb (mm) 10 380. Fuel tank capacity: 63 litres with optional tanks of 85 litres (sedan) and 68 litres (wagon). Cargo capacity (litres) SAE: 566 (sedan) 2475 (wagon).
ENGINE SPECIFICATIONS	• V-6: Bore and stroke: 96.5 by 86.3 mm. Displacement: 3791 cc. Power output (DIN): 125 kW at 4800 rpm. Torque (DIN): 292 Nm at 3600. Compression ratio: 8.5:1. RAC rating: 34.6 HP. • V-8: Bore and stroke: 101.6 by 76.8 mm. Displacement: 4987 cc. Power output (DIN): 168 kW at 4800 rpm. Torque (DIN): 400 Nm at 3600 rpm. Compression ratio: 8.5:1. RAC rating: 51.2 HP.
ENGINE/TRANSMISSION COMBINATIONS	• Commodore Executive: Engine: 3.8-litre V-6. The 5-litre V-8 is optional. Transmission: M78 five-speed, all syncromesh gearbox (manual floorshift). The MD8 Turbohydramatic four-speed automatic transmission with torque converter clutch is optional. • Commodore Berlina and Calais: Engine: 3.8-litre V-6. The 5-litre V-8 is optional. Transmission: MD8 Turbohydramatic four-speed automatic transmission with torque converter clutch. The M78 five-speed, all syncromesh gearbox (manual floorshift) is optional.

TRANSMISSION RATIOS	● M78 (V-6) five-speed manual: 1st: 3.25 2nd: 1.99 3rd: 1.29 4th: 1.00 5th: 0.72 Reverse: 3.15 ● MD8 Turbohydramatic four-speed automatic: 1st: 3.06 2nd: 1.62 3rd: 1.00 4th: 0.70 Reverse: 2.30 ● M78 (V-8) five-speed manual: 1st: 2.95 2nd: 1.94 3rd: 1.34 4th: 1.00 5th: 0.73 Reverse: 2.76
REAR AXLE RATIOS	V-6: 3.08 V-8: 3.08
SAFETY FEATURES	Automatically retracting seat belts for driver and three passengers. Lap/sash belt for fourth passenger. Energy-absorbing steering column and steering wheel. Anti-theft combined steering/ignition lock. Tandem brake cylinder — split hydraulic circuits. Spring-loaded knockout-type internal rear-vision mirror mounting with shatter-resistant mirror. Remote control external rear-vision mirrors — glare reduced. Shaded upper laminated windscreen. Tinted safety glass windows. Glare-reduced safety-padded instrument panel. Recessed instruments. Glare-reduced intruments and controls. Low-profile window regulator handles. Sun visors — energy absorbing. Flush-fitting lift-up exterior door handles. Safety door locks — handles freewheel. Two-jet electric windscreen washer. Two-speed windscreen wipers with glare-reduced arms and blades (matt black). With intermittent wiper facility. Cigar lighter operates on ignition or accessory positions only. Reversing lights. Flowthrough ventilation. Fusible link in wiring harness. Fan-assisted heater demister. Brake failure lamp. Safety flanges on both rims of road wheels. Front seat head restraints. Underslung fuel tank and external fuel lines. Skid header panel. Centre floor-mounted parking brake. Parking brake warning lamp. Lane-changer facility on traffic indicator control. Hazard warning flasher. Child restraint anchorages for rear seats. Side-mounted intrusion bars.

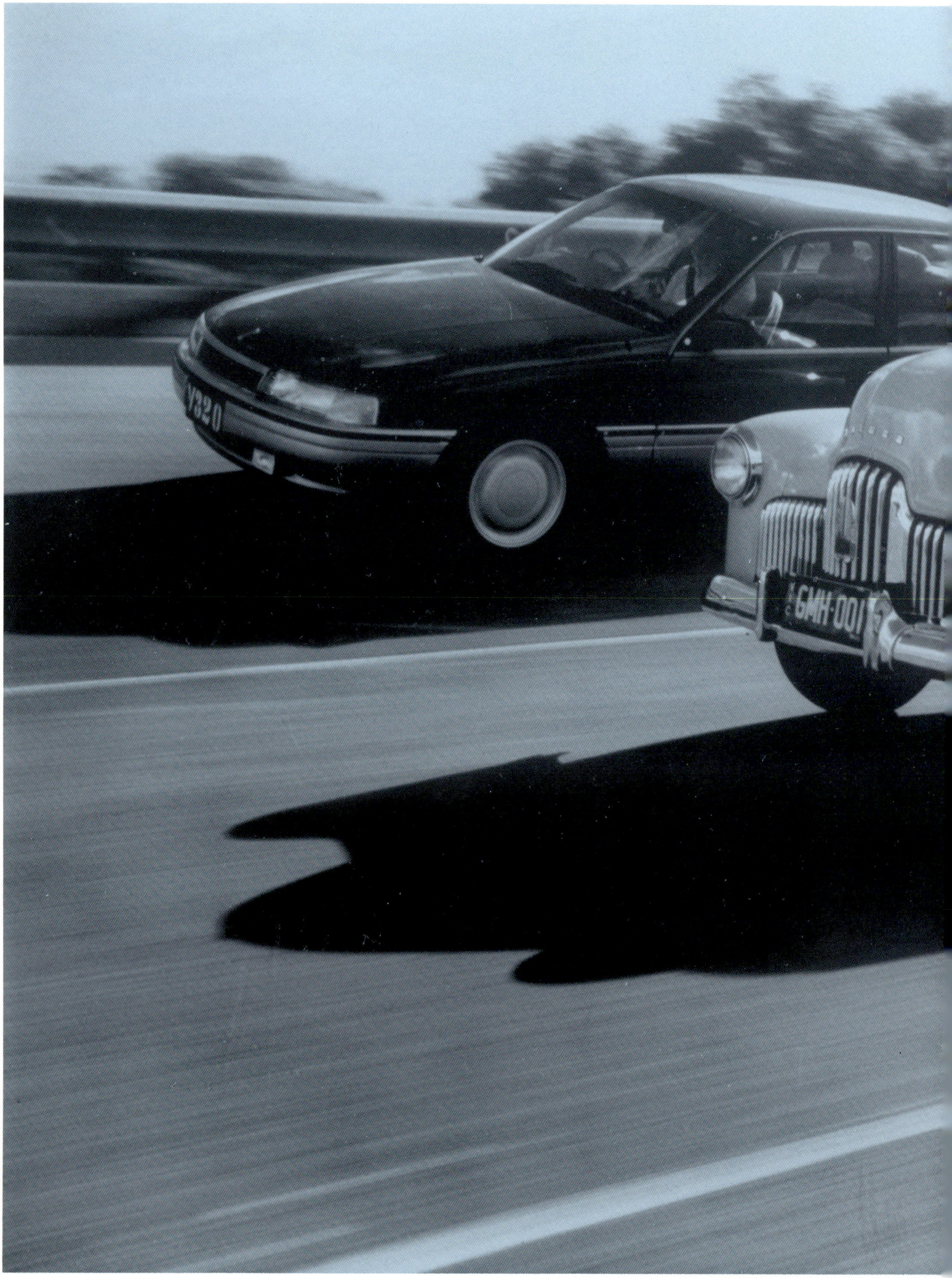
V320
GMH-001

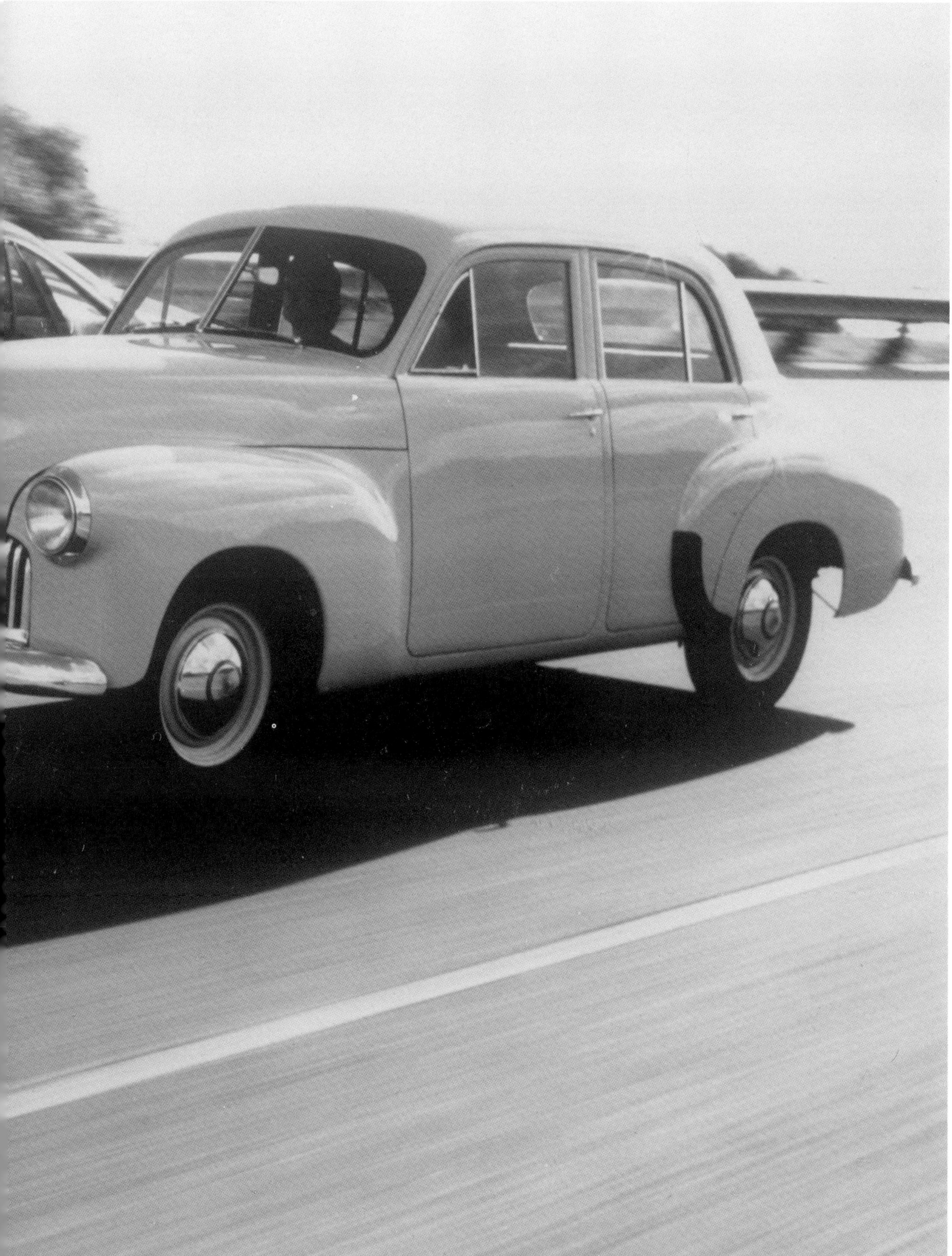

*The man who started it all
James Alexander Holden.*

Appendixes

The Holden heritage ... a chronology

1852: • Seventeen-year-old James Alexander Holden arrives in South Australia from Staffordshire, England.

1856: • James Alexander Holden sets up shop in King William St, Adelaide, as a leather-worker and saddle-maker.

1865: • Business booms for J.A. Holden and Company and the firm moves to bigger premises.

1872: • A new partnership is formed: Holden and Birks.

1875: • Holden and Birks is dissolved and J.A. Holden and Co. reestablished.

1879: • Holden takes his 20-year-old son Henry James into the business and the name is changed again, this time to J.A. Holden and Son.

1885: • German-born Henry Frederick Adolf Frost becomes a junior partner and the company name becomes Holden & Frost. It continues in leather-work and small-scale ironmongery, then graduates to repairing (and eventually building) horse-drawn carriages and coaches.

1887: • James Alexander Holden dies, aged fifty-two. Henry Holden becomes the senior partner.

1905: • A third-generation Holden — Henry's son Edward Wheewall Holden — joins Holden & Frost.

1908: • Holden & Frost engages in minor repairs to car upholstery and is soon manufacturing hoods and side-curtains.
• In the USA, General Motors Corporation (GMC) is founded by William Crapo Durant. GMC expands at a great rate; during the first year, 14 000 employees build 25 000 cars and trucks.

1909: • Henry Frost dies.

1911: • The GM Export Company is formed.

1913: • Holden & Frost begins production of complete motorcycle sidecar bodies.

1914: • Holden & Frost produce their first complete custom-made car body, using laborious carriage-building techniques.
• The GM Export Company appoints a field representative to Australia, based in Sydney. The first GM cars arrive just before WW1.

1917: • The Australian federal government's wartime trade restrictions (which decree that only one complete car could be imported for every three chassis) leads to the decision by Holden & Frost to commence large-scale production of car bodies.
• Holden & Frost buy up another Adelaide motor body builder, F.T. Hack Ltd, to increase the production facilities. They produce a total of 99 car bodies during 1917, mainly for Dodge and Buick chassis.

1918: • Holden's Motor Body Builders is set up as a division of Holden & Frost. It produces 587 bodies in its first full year.

1919: • Holden's Motor Body Builders becomes a registered company.
• Business takes off rapidly and HMBB starts to revolutionise the industry with state-of-the-art production machinery and designs which take a minimum of hand-finishing. Innovative shipping techniques mean Holden's bodies are price-competitive across the country.
• Holden's produces nearly 1600 bodies for the year, fitted to a wide variety of marques.

1920: • A boom decade starts for Holden's which, by the early 1920s, has a timber mill and production line in operation. Production time is cut to just five man-hours per body (from 160-plus man-hours per body in 1917). As the USA produces a constant string of new car designs and marques, HMBB responds with a vast array of suitable body styles.

1923: • Holden's builds 12 771 car bodies.
• A site at Woodville, South Australia, is purchased for the construction of a massive new plant.

1924: • Holden's new Woodville plant is opened, featuring the country's most modern production line. The new set-up is so impressive that GM Export Company (Aust.) shelves plans to open its own body-building factory; instead GM strikes a contract with Holden's ensuring that Woodville will manufacture bodies only for GM vehicles. The deal allows HMBB to import blueprints of forthcoming GM models. By designing a structure around these blueprints, HMBB is able to have the bodies ready by the time the new chassis hit Australian shores.
• Now sole local body supplier for GM vehicles, Holden's continues production for other car-makers at the original King William St plant, which is further extended.
• In 1924 Holden's produces no less than 65 body styles and a total output of 22 150 units (including 11 060 for GM). Holden's output represents about half of local production – a feat General Motors-Holden's will repeat with complete cars in the late 1950s and early 1960s.

1925: • Holden's produces 34 309 car bodies, including the first closed body types. The company's body-building operation is now the biggest outside North America and Continental Europe, with over 16 hectares of factory floor and a work force of 2600. In addition to car bodies, HMBB turns out railway carriages, bus and tram bodies and other items.

1926: • General Motors Australia (GMA) is formed with headquarters in Collins St, Melbourne, and assembly plants in all mainland states. As well as using Holden bodies, GMA purchases tyres, springs, batteries, paint and many other parts from Australian suppliers. In the ensuing years, GMA will capture 30 per cent of the Australian market and lift local content for some models to over 65 per cent.
• The year proves Holden's best to date for car body production, with 36 171 units built.

1927: • Holden's output dips slightly, but the company still builds more than 34 000 bodies.

1928: • Holden's famous 'lion-and-stone' symbol, representing the legend of man's invention of the wheel, is first used. Designed in plaster by sculptor Raynor Hoff, it is adapted to a pressed metal nameplate and is fixed to all Holden bodies. (Although updated, this symbol is still used on all Holden cars, including the VN.)

1930: • The full force of the depression hits and Holden's, which has just completed a major expansion, is caught off-guard.

1931: • The economic situation continues to deteriorate and Holden's Motor Body Builders is closed for much of the year. The company fills just 1651 car body orders, compared with 36 000-plus five years earlier.
• The GM Corporation buys the entire Holden's Motor Body Builders operation and merges it with GMA to form General Motors-Holden's (GM-H).

1932: • Australia's total vehicle sales continue to drop. From a 1928 high of 88 815 units, they barely top 14 000 in 1932. General Motors' sales for the same period drop nearly 90 per cent, from 31 543 (for GMA) to 3674 (for GM-H).

1934: • Corporate troubleshooter Larry Hartnett is sent to Australia. Hartnett, a former Vauxhall director, is told that if GM-H cannot be made profitable, it is to be closed down.
• GM-H produces its first coupe-utility.

1935: • GM-H sales are lifted to 23 129 for the year and a $1.5 million profit is declared.
• GM-H produces its All-Enclosed Coupe body for Oldsmobile, Pontiac and Chevrolet chassis. Dubbed the 'sloper', this uniquely Australian design is the forerunner of the hatchback, with an upward lifting tailgate and a fold-down rear seat to increase the luggage area. Local and overseas body builders will later produce their own renditions of the theme.

1936: • GM-H sets up new headquarters and a new assembly plant on 20 hectares of land at Fishermans Bend, Melbourne. The layout includes provision for a foundry and engine shop.
• Hartnett and GM-H executives start discussing the manufacture of a complete car within Australia. The company has a talented managerial staff and a highly skilled team of workers with body-building and assembly experience. They are guaranteed massive technical support from GM.

1937: • GM-H builds its first all-steel bodies (for Plymouth chassis), beating GM in the USA by a full year.

1938: • GM-H fits all-steel bodies to GM chassis in Australia.

1939: • WW2 puts the brakes on the fast-crystallising plan for an Australian car. By 1940 all GM-H's factories are working for the war effort. During the course of WW2 GM-H becomes the first company to mass-produce internal combustion engines in Australia, producing the Gypsy Major aeroplane engine, the Gray Marine engine and a four-cylinder radial torpedo engine. GM-H also builds aeroplane frames, bomb cases, anti-tank guns, machine guns, armoured cars, semitrailers, troop carriers, boats, pontoons and other military hardware.

1943: • With the winding down of military contracts in sight, GM-H begins to revive plans for an Aussie car. Engineers start designing 'Project 2000' — the car they believe the company is best set up to build.

1944: • GM-H's first 'Project 2000' prototype is completed using Willys mechanic components. Dozens of variations, alternative designs and mock-ups follow.
• The Comptroller-General of Trade and Customs issues a formal invitation for submissions from companies interested in producing an Australian car. In response, GM-H undertakes to manufacture a complete car without subsidy or tariff protection. In late 1944 GM Corporation approves the project in principle.

1945: • GM-H emerges from WW2 with a full-scale foundry and the ability to make engine blocks and other mechanical components 'in-house'.
• Design work on an Australian car starts in the USA, but the Australian Project 2000 continues, eventually developing into Project 2200.

1946: • GM-H recommences car production with the assembly of Vauxhalls. Before the year's end, Chevrolets, Buicks and Pontiacs come on stream.
• A working prototype of the preferred Project 2200 design, which aims at simplicity in tooling and construction, is completed. This design is based on a styling mock-up completed in 1945.
• GM-H engineers are sent to Detroit, Michigan, USA, with their styling models, drawings and engineering ideas. They start work on the US design proposal and receive instruction on setting up the manufacturing operation.
• The joint team in Detroit produces three handmade prototypes which are virtually identical in appearance to the car eventually produced. In late 1946 the three cars are shipped to Fishermans Bend, accompanied by the Australian arm of the design team and 22 US technicians.

1947: • The Detroit-built prototypes are extensively tested on rough dirt roads outside Melbourne. The steering and suspension are among the many components modified after an exhaustive period of testing.

1948: • A production run of ten cars is secretly conducted in April to 'clear the line'.
• Amid great fanfare, the first production car, named 'Holden' after the original company, rolls off GM-H's Fishermans Bend production line. The date is 29 November and James Robert Holden, the Resident Director of GM-H in Adelaide, represents the Holden family.
• A total of 112 examples of the Holden car, designated 48-215, are completed by year's end. Thousands of orders are taken.

1949: • The demand for Holden cars astounds everybody. GM-H advertises that the 'Holden is worth waiting for' and makes every effort to increase the production capacity as quickly as possible.
• GM-H continues to import chassis and components to assemble various British and US cars and trucks.

1950: • Holden production is lifted to 80 units a day.
• GM-H employees exceed 10 000 and during the year more than $43 million is paid to outside suppliers for materials, components and services.

1951: • All GM-H plants expand and the company purchases 60 hectares of land at Dandenong, Victoria, for future development.
• Holden production reaches 100 units a day. The total production (since 1948) passes 50 000.

1952: • The demand for Holden cars continues to grow and plans are laid for further expansion of production facilities.
• Holden sales for the year reach 32 000.

1953: • The first model Holden, denoted 48-215 (but later commonly called FX), is replaced by the facelifted FJ.

1954: • The first Holdens are exported to New Zealand. By year's end 321 have been shipped.

1955: • More expansion plans are implemented, including the building of a plant at Dandenong. This gives GM-H a production capacity of 72 000 units per annum.

1956: • The 250 000th Holden, an FJ, is built.
• The third Holden model, the FE, is released.
• The Dandenong plant opens. With a floor space of over five hectares, it has the capacity to build 152 bodies and assemble 168 vehicles a day.
• Further expansion takes place to lift production to 400 Holdens a day – 100 000 a year!
• 870 hectares of land is purchased at Lang Lang, 90 km from Melbourne, to establish Australia's first automotive testing and proving ground.
• The first CKD (completely knocked down) Holden packs are shipped to New Zealand for local assembly.

1957: • The one millionth car body is produced at the Woodville plant.
• 4500 Holdens are exported during the year.

176

1958:
- The fourth Holden model, the FC, is announced.
- Sales for the year exceed 100 000 units for first time. The total number of Holdens produced reaches 500 000 and export territories number twenty-seven.
- Work begins on a four-lane banked circular test track at Lang Lang.

1959:
- Assembly of Holden commercial vehicles begins overseas.

1960:
- The fifth Holden, the FB model, is announced after more than $15 million was spent on development work.
- Holden sales top 12 000 per month and the 750 000th Holden is built.
- Production of left-hand drive Holdens (for export) begins. The first shipment to Hawaii follows.

1961:
- The sixth Holden model, the EK, is released with optional automatic transmission.

1962:
- The EJ, the seventh Holden model series, goes on sale.
- A new body assembly plant is opened at Elizabeth, South Australia, and a new engine plant nears completion at Fishermans Bend.
- The millionth Holden is built, only four years after the 500 000th. Production is now 600 units a day with cars going to every corner of Australia and 46 overseas territories.

1963:
- The eighth model Holden, the EH, is unveiled. It is fitted with a completely new locally-made six-cylinder engine.
- GM-H produces 166 274 Holdens during the year. Of these, 10 798 are shipped to 55 overseas markets.

1964:
- GM-H's fast-expanding Design and Engineering group moves into the new Technical Centre at Fishermans Bend. This houses approximately 900 designers, engineers, draftsmen, modellers and technicians, giving the company state-of-the-art facilities for virtually every aspect of designing new vehicles.

1965:
- The ninth Holden, the HD, is unveiled.
- GM-H achieves its best sales month on record, with over 19 000 HDs sold during May.
- Nearly 20 000 Holdens are exported.

1966:
- The HR Holden, the tenth new model series since 1948, goes on sale.

1967: • The first small Holden, called Torana, is introduced. Taking its name from an Aboriginal word meaning 'to fly', it is based on the English Vauxhall Viva. Between 1967 and 1969, 36 561 are produced.

1968: • Holden HK, the eleventh full-size Holden, brings the first V-8 engine, the first Monaro coupe and the extended Brougham luxury sedan.
• Torana bodies are made in Australia for the first time and work progresses on a V-8 engine plant at Fishermans Bend.
• Bruce McPhee and Barry Mulholland, driving a Monaro, win the Hardie-Ferodo 500, giving Holden its first victory in the annual Bathurst endurance race.

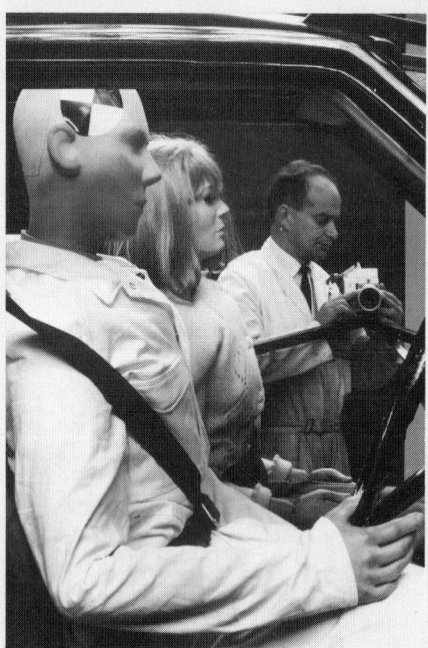

1969: • The twelfth family-sized Holden, the Holden HT, introduces an Australian-made V-8, which had earlier been exhibited in the futuristic mid-engined Holden Hurricane experimental car. The engine has been developed at a cost of $20 million.
• The original Torana HB is replaced by the Australian-designed LC, available with an imported 'four' or locally made six-cylinder engine. Between 1969 and 1972, 74 627 are sold.
• A new Safety Design Centre opens at Lang Lang with an impact sled and a 10 tonne concrete barrier for crash testing.
• The two millionth Holden is produced.

• Colin Bond and Tony Roberts, in a Monaro, win the Hardie-Ferodo 500, giving Holden its second consecutive Bathurst victory.

1970:
• The HG, full-size Holden number 13, is announced. It brings the first automatic transmission mass-produced in Australia.
• The stunning GTR-X Torana coupe is exhibited to an enthusiastic response, but the car does not go into production.
• Total GM-H vehicle sales for the year top 200 000.
• Norm Beechey drives a Monaro to victory in the Australian Touring Car Championship.

1971:
• The completely new HQ Holden range is announced. It is the fourteenth full-size model since 1948. Extensive market research is used for the first time to establish design criteria.
• The first long wheelbase luxury Holden derivative, the Statesman, goes on sale in six-cylinder and eight-cylinder versions.
• The first car-based Holden 'Cab and Chassis' light truck is announced as part of the HQ range.
• A De Luxe version of the four-cylinder LC Torana is released with a 1.6-litre engine.
• Colin Bond drives a Torana to victory in the Australian Rally Championship.

1972:
• The LJ Torana, the third small Holden, is launched. Between 1972 and 1974, 81 453 are built.
• Colin Bond drives a Torana to victory in the Australian Rally Championship.
• Peter Brock tastes his first victory in the annual Bathurst enduro, winning the Hardie-Ferodo 500 in a Torana.

1973:
• GM-H celebrates the 25th anniversary of Holden manufacture in Australia.
• Peter Lang drives a Torana to victory in the Australian Rally Championship.

1974:
- The three millionth Holden is produced.
- The fifteenth family-sized Holden — called HJ — is announced.
- A more upmarket Statesman luxury car, available in De Ville and Caprice variants, joins the GM-H stable.
- The fourth Torana — the bigger LH model — is announced. Available only in four-door form, it is one of the few cars ever offered with a choice of four-cylinder, six-cylinder and eight-cylinder engines. Between 1974 and 1976, 71 408 are built.
- The TA Torana — basically a facelifted LC — is offered with a choice of 1.3-litre and 1.76-litre four-cylinder engines. By year's end, 9288 are sold.
- Peter Brock drives a Torana to victory in the Australian Touring Car Championship.
- Colin Bond drives a Torana to victory in the Australian Rally Championship.

1975:
- The Holden Gemini TX — based on GM's first world car — is announced in two-door and four-door versions. Designed in Germany, it is assembled in Australia from local and Japanese components. The Gemini soon becomes Australia's most popular four-cylinder car and 42 792 TX models are built.
- Colin Bond drives a Torana to victory in the Australian Touring Car Championship.
- Peter Brock and Brian Sampson win the Hardie-Ferodo 1000 (formerly Hardie-Ferodo 500) in a Torana.

1976:
- GM Australia celebrates its 50th anniversary.
- The sixteenth full-sized Holden — the HX series — goes on sale.
- The HX series Statesman luxury sedan, available in De Ville and Caprice versions, is announced.
- The LX Torana range is unveiled, with a sedan body and the first locally produced hatchback. There is also a choice between four-cylinder, six-cylinder and eight-cylinder engines. Just under 50 000 LX Toranas are produced, including 8527 hatchbacks.
- Production of Monaro coupes is wound up with 600 highly specified 'LE' (Limited Edition) models.
- Late in the year the four-cylinder LX Torana is revised and relaunched as the Holden Sunbird. Sedan and hatchback variants are offered. Radial Tuned Suspension (RTS) was added to the Torana from early 1977.
- Bob Morris and John Fitzpatrick win the Hardie-Ferodo 1000 in a Torana.

1977:
- The HZ, the last of the traditional-sized Holdens (until the VN) and the seventeenth family Holden since 1948, hits the market. The big sales feature is Radial Tuned Suspension.
- The TC Gemini is announced. During 1977 and 1978, 17 257 are built.
- The Torana range is expanded with the release of the A9X performance equipment package. Available with sedan and hatchback bodies, this turns the 5-litre V-8 Torana into one of the most potent road cars ever built in Australia.
- The HZ Statesman is released.

1978:
- GM-H celebrates its 25th straight year of overall market leadership.
- The six-cylinder UC Torana and four-cylinder UC Sunbird are released, both built with a choice of sedan and hatchback body styles. Later in the year, the Opel-built four-cylinder Sunbird engine is replaced by the Australian-made Starfire 1.9-litre 'four'. A total of 53 007 UC Toranas and Sunbirds are sold.
- The Gemini TD is announced with sedan, coupe, three-door station wagon and panel van variants. During the model's life, 42 396 TDs are sold.

- The smaller and lighter Holden Commodore VB, which uses a German Opel as the basis of its body design, supplements the HZ range. The eighteenth new family-sized Holden, it soon becomes Australia's best-selling car.
- The Holden production tally (at release of Commodore) stands at 3.6 million.
- Peter Brock drives a Torana to victory in the Australian Touring Car Championship.
- Peter Brock and Jim Richards win the Hardie-Ferodo 1000 in a Torana.

1979:
- A $300 million GM-H expansion program, which includes a new engine plant for Fishermans Bend, is announced.
- The TE Gemini sedan goes on sale (a wagon and panel van follow in early 1980).
- A 'De Luxe' version of the UC Sunbird sedan is unveiled. The hatchback body style is discontinued.
- The last Torana is sold after 11 years of production, six series of models and more than 370 000 sales.
- The HZ series Statesman 'SL/E' is announced.
- Bob Morris drives a Torana to victory in the Australian Touring Car Championship.
- Peter Brock and Jim Richards win the Hardie-Ferodo 1000 in a Torana.

1980:
- The facelifted Commodore VC, full-sized Holden number 19, is announced. The range is later expanded to include a four-cylinder version — Holden's first 'four' in a family-sized car.
- 'WB' versions of the Statesman De Ville, Statesman Caprice and Holden's car-based commercial vehicles are launched. Plans for a WB series Holden sedan and wagon — a bigger family Holden to complement the Commodore — reach advanced stages but are not pursued.
- A high-performance version of the Commodore VC V-8 is produced in partnership with HDT Special Vehicles. The car is quickly dubbed the 'Brock' Commodore, after the owner/director of HDT, racing driver Peter Brock.
- The Holden Rodeo light commercial range goes on sale with two-wheel drive and four-wheel drive cab/chassis models and a choice of petrol and diesel engines. The Rodeo is sourced from Isuzu in Japan.
- Peter Brock drives a Commodore to victory in the Australian Touring Car Championship.
- Peter Brock and Jim Richards complete a hat-trick of Hardie-Ferodo 1000 victories. This time they drive a Commodore.

1981:
- The four millionth Holden, a VC Commodore, is produced.
- A third refinement of the VB Commodore, called the 'VH', is announced, bringing the model count of Holden's family sedans up to twenty.
- A new version of the Gemini TE sedan, with a 1.8-litre diesel engine, reaches the market. It is the first diesel passenger car manufactured locally.
- The Holden Jackaroo wagon, Holden's first four-wheel drive passenger vehicle, is announced with a choice of petrol and diesel engines. Like the Rodeo, the Jackaroo is built to Holden's specifications by Isuzu, Japan.
- The new engine plant at Fishermans Bend, announced in 1979, is commissioned and starts producing 'Family II' four-cylinder engines for export.

1982:
- The Holden Shuttle, Holden's entry into the forward-control van market, is unveiled. Built in Japan, it offers a choice of petrol and diesel engines and long and short wheelbase models.
- The Camira JB sedan, Holden's version of GM's new world 'J-car', is released with a 1.6-litre engine. The first front-wheel drive car produced by GM-H, it is powered by the local Family II 'four'.
- The TF Gemini goes on sale with a choice of 1.6-litre petrol and 1.8-litre diesel engines.
- A nine-seater 'LS' coach version of the Holden Shuttle van follows the Shuttle models released earlier in the year.
- Peter Brock and Larry Perkins win the James Hardie 1000 (formerly Hardie-Ferodo 1000) in a Commodore.

1983:
- The Statesman Series II is released in De Ville and Caprice versions.
- An upgraded Holden Rodeo range includes new utilities and crew cabs.
- The 4WD Jackaroo wagon is upgraded.
- The TG Gemini is announced with 1.6-litre petrol and 1.8-litre diesel variants.
- Production at the Fishermans Bend engine plant reaches 1000 units a day. A milestone is passed when the 200 000th engine is built at the new plant; by year's end the 250 000th engine is exported.
- An Australian-developed station wagon joins the JB Camira range. Component sets for this wagon are exported for use in several overseas 'J-cars'.
- The Holden Shuttle forward-control van is updated with the LT model.
- Peter Brock, Larry Perkins and John Harvey join forces to win the James Hardie 1000 in a Commodore.

1984:
- The Commodore VK, family Holden number 21, goes on sale with an upmarket Calais version complementing the range. As with the VC and VH series, an acclaimed range of high-performance 'Brock' versions of the VK (including the SS Commodore Group 3) is produced by HDT Special Vehicles.
- The four-door Holden Astra hatchback — Holden's first hatchback since the Torana/Sunbird UC — is launched with a 1.5-litre, four-cylinder engine. Built for Holden's by Nissan Australia with some components manufactured by GM-H, it represents the first example of local model-sharing.
- The half-millionth Family II four-cylinder engine comes off the Fishermans Bend line.
- GM-H's exports for the year exceed $1200 million.
- A new 4WD Rodeo pick-up is released.
- Peter Brock and Larry Perkins (Commodore) win the James Hardie 1000. The victory gives Brock his second 'Holden hat-trick', his sixth win in seven consecutive Bathurst enduros and his eighth Bathurst victory in total.
- The JD Camira introduces distinctive front-end styling and is offered with a 1.8-litre fuel-injected engine.
- GM-H announces that Statesman models and Holden's car-based light commercials will be discontinued.

1985:
- The five-door Holden Barina hatchback, 4WD Holden Drover off-roader and Holden Scurry delivery van are announced. These small four-cylinder models are imported from Suzuki in Japan (a company in which GM Corporation has a shareholding).
- A single-point tool body assembly shuttle is introduced at GM-H's Elizabeth plant.
- The all-new front-drive Gemini RB sedan rolls off the line at Elizabeth. It is the first completely new Gemini since 1975.
- New Jackaroo 4WD wagon and Rodeo light commercial models are introduced.
- The high-performance 'Brock' Commodore Group A V-8 is unveiled.

1986:
- Family Holden number 22, the Commodore VL, is announced. A more luxurious Calais version, with distinctive styling, is announced at the same time. Both cars are powered by a completely new 3-litre imported engine. A turbocharged version of this engine and a new 'unleaded' version of Holden's 5-litre V-8 follow.
- The original Holden Astra is replaced by the updated Astra LC hatchback with a 1.6-litre, four-cylinder engine.
- The fully imported two-plus-two Piazza sports coupe goes on sale with a 2-litre, four-cylinder turbocharged engine.
- The small Barina hatchback is updated with the ML model, powered by a 1.3-litre, four-cylinder engine.
- A limited edition, high-performance Group A version of the VL Commodore V-8 is announced with a five-speed manual gearbox. Eagerly snapped up, it is the last product of the six-year collaboration between Holden's and Peter Brock's HDT.
- Allan Grice and Graham Bailey win the James Hardie 1000 in a Commodore.
- GM-H is restructured with two new companies — Holden's Motor Company (HMC) and Holden's Engine Company (HEC) — replacing the former company. The old name lives on in the subsidiary, General Motors-Holden's Sales Pty Ltd.

1987:
- Holden's Motor Company severs its links with Peter Brock's HDT organisation.
- The Camira is updated with the JE model, featuring a fuel-injected 2-litre engine.
- A completely new, 1.8-litre Astra hatchback joins the Holden range. It is the result of a historic joint development program with Nissan Australia, with both companies contributing to the car's design, engineering and testing. Nissan also markets a version (called Pulsar) which, like the Astra, is powered by the Holden Family II four-cylinder engine. Sedan versions of both cars follow.
- A revised Jackaroo 4WD wagon is announced.
- Peter Brock, driving a Commodore, is third across the line in the James Hardie 1000 but is declared the winner when the first and second competitors are disqualified. It is Brock's ninth Bathurst victory and Holden's 13th in 20 years.
- The formation of a new joint-venture company is announced by Holden's Motor Company Ltd, AMI/Toyota Ltd and Toyota Manufacturing Australia Ltd. The new company is to coordinate the design, engineering and product-sharing strategies to ensure the most efficient use of existing production facilities. The Holden-Toyota statement says: 'The foundation laid by this decision will offer consumers wider product choice, provide a strong volume base for improved cost competitiveness, achieve higher quality and open up wider access to, and investment in, the latest technology while achieving the benefits envisaged by the government plan [the "Button" passenger motor vehicle manufacturing plan]'. The Holden and Toyota product ranges continue to be marketed separately, with the sharing of local models scheduled to start by the end of the 1980s.

1988:
- The fuel-injected V-8 Holden VL Group A supercar is announced following joint development by Holden's and racing driver Tom Walkinshaw's TWR operation. It is built by Holden Special Vehicles.
- The one millionth Holden Family II four-cylinder engine is exported.
- The Holden's/Toyota joint venture company is formalised with the signing of agreements to create United Australian Automotive Industries Ltd. The GM arm of the new company — General Motors-Holden's Automotive Ltd — brings back to the fore the best known name on the local motoring scene.
- The Commodore VN goes on sale. It is the twenty-third new full-sized Holden model built in Australia in the 40 years since the 48-215 was launched.

Forty years of family Holdens
... models leading to the VN

1948 HOLDEN 48-215

The first Holden, designated the 48-215 and later commonly called the FX, was Australia's first successful mass-produced car. Its arrival caused the biggest excitement in Australia since V-J Day. People queued to look at it and the newsreel of the official launching ceremony (performed by Prime Minister Chifley) was shown in every cinema in the country.

The four-door, six-seater 48-215 was adapted from an American design but built almost entirely in Australia.

4.4 metres long and weighing 992 kg, it featured a lightweight body of unitary construction and offered exceptional performance for a low-cost family car. Buyers boasted of '80 mph and 30 mpg' and the dust sealing and rough road ride were exceptional. The 45 kW 'grey engine' (named after the colour of its painted block) proved a remarkably durable unit.

As the word spread, the waiting list grew longer and longer. A legend was born.

INTRODUCTION: November 1948.
ENGINE: 2.15-litre six-cylinder.
TRANSMISSION: Three-speed manual gearbox.
MODEL LINE-UP: Sedan, Business sedan and utility.
TOTAL NUMBER BUILT: 120 402.

1953 HOLDEN FJ

Holden number two — the famous FJ model — was a facelifted and updated version of the original 48-215 design. It was the car that cemented Holden's position as the country's most popular car and it is now a celebrated piece of 'Australiana'.

The FJ used the same power train as the 48-215 but had some small mechanical refinements, a new grille, different hubcaps and bumpers and new bright metal body decorations including small chrome fins on the rear guards.

The accessory list was greatly expanded and the choice of colours lifted to twelve. The new Special model featured armrests and a cigarette lighter and was available in a two-tone finish.

Production was raised to 200 units per day. For the first time Holdens were shipped to New Zealand — the start of an export trade which continues today.

INTRODUCTION: October 1953.
ENGINE: 2.15-litre six-cylinder.
TRANSMISSION: Three-speed manual gearbox.
MODEL LINE-UP: Standard sedan, Business sedan, Special sedan, panel van and utility.
TOTAL NUMBER BUILT: 169 969.

1956 HOLDEN FE

By the mid-1950s, Holden was an institution.

The FE range featured a more modern, Australian-designed body and introduced the first Holden station wagon. The car was bigger and roomier than its predecessors, with a longer wheelbase and wider track. It had a lower roofline and flatter bonnet and boot.

Improvements included a one-piece curved windscreen, larger rear window, 12 volt electrical system, hydraulically operated clutch and a slightly more powerful (53 kW) version of the well-proven 'grey engine'.

Many new colour schemes were available and the sales figures went from strength to strength.

INTRODUCTION: July 1956.
ENGINE: 2.15-litre six-cylinder.
TRANSMISSION: Three-speed manual gearbox.
MODEL LINE-UP: Standard sedan, Special sedan, Business sedan, Standard station wagon, Special station wagon, panel van and utility.
TOTAL NUMBER BUILT: 155 161.

1958 HOLDEN FC

The FC replaced the FE at a time when Holden sales figures had reached dizzy new heights. The market was booming, as was Holden's market share, which hit an incredible 50.3 per cent in 1958.

Holden had already established the practice of introducing a model then following with an improved version and the FC continued this practice. Exterior changes to the grille and body decorations were complemented by a redesigned interior and several mechanical refinements.

The torque qualities of the 'grey engine' were improved by means of an improved camshaft. Minor improvements were made to the suspension, brakes, gear-change linkages and steering box.

Before the FC bowed out, the 500 000th Holden had been produced and the 10 000th exported.

INTRODUCTION: May 1958.
ENGINE: 2.15-litre six-cylinder.
TRANSMISSION: Three-speed manual gearbox.
MODEL LINE-UP: Standard sedan, Special sedan, Business sedan, Standard station wagon, Special station wagon, panel van and utility.
TOTAL NUMBER BUILT: 191 724.

1960 HOLDEN FB

Holden's brilliant success had not escaped the attention of its competitors, who at that stage were mostly importing or locally assembling European cars.

Ford was known to be preparing for the full-scale manufacture of the US Falcon and Chrysler Australia was also looking to the States for a medium-priced family car. Holden launched a pre-emptive strike with its own American-influenced model, the FB.

Mechanically, the new model was a further refinement of the FC but the appearance was significantly changed with a wraparound windscreen, a lower bonnet line and finned rear guards. The length was increased by 14 cm (although the wheelbase remained the same) and the 'grey' engine was slightly enlarged to produce 56 kW.

The FB was the first Holden with acrylic paintwork. It incorporated upgraded brakes, heavier front coil springs and a reworked interior. The range included six models (the Business sedan was dropped). The basic price was unchanged and Holden's amazing 50 per cent share of the Australian market was maintained. For the first time, left-hand drive export versions were produced.

INTRODUCTION: January 1960.
ENGINE: 2.26-litre six-cylinder.
TRANSMISSION: Three-speed manual gearbox.
MODEL LINE-UP: Standard sedan, Special sedan, Standard station wagon, Special station wagon, panel van and utility.
TOTAL NUMBER BUILT: 174 747.

1961 HOLDEN EK

The EK brought Holden's first automatic transmission.

The exterior changes were minute: badges and mouldings were changed and a redesigned grille featured wider-spaced parking lights/flashers. But the introduction of the optional three-speed Hydramatic transmission was significant as it provided the first taste of automatic motoring for hundreds of thousands of Australians.

The power of the Holden engine was not increased but the Hydramatic still allowed the automatic Holden to maintain respectable performance figures.

EK refinements included revised interior trim, an electric wiper motor (replacing the vacuum unit) and a new fresh-air heating unit.

The EK stayed in production for just over a year.

INTRODUCTION: May 1961.
ENGINE: 2.26-litre six-cylinder.
TRANSMISSIONS: Three-speed manual gearbox and three-speed Hydramatic automatic transmission.
MODEL LINE-UP: Standard sedan, Special sedan, Standard station wagon, Special station wagon, panel van and utility.
TOTAL NUMBER BUILT: 150 214.

1962 HOLDEN EJ

The Holden EJ range introduced a completely new body and the name 'Premier' which, for the greater part of two decades, would be identified with luxurious Holdens.

The first Premier was based on the Standard/Special sedan and featured leather-covered bucket seats, a heater, wool pile carpet, whitewall tyres, a floor console and other luxury features. It had additional body ornamentation and was the first Holden with metallic paint and automatic transmission as standard.

The EJ design incorporated a lower profile, a flatter bonnet, a squarer rear end and an overall appearance widely considered the best to date. In spite of the new 'low-line' look, the traditional Holden virtues of ruggedness, high ground clearance and good interior room were equalled or improved on. The wagon had a rear cargo tray over two metres long.

The previous Holden drive train was carried over on all models but mechanical improvements included new Duo Servo brakes, strengthened front suspension and an improved Hydramatic transmission.

The EJ production run included the millionth Holden.

INTRODUCTION: July 1962.
ENGINE: 2.26-litre six-cylinder.
TRANSMISSIONS: Three-speed manual gearbox and three-speed Hydramatic automatic transmission.
MODEL LINE-UP: Standard sedan, Special sedan, Premier sedan, Standard station wagon, Special station wagon, panel van and utility.
TOTAL NUMBER BUILT: 154 811.

1963 HOLDEN EH

Two new engines, better-than-ever styling and a knock-out price. This was the formula which made the EH the most spectacularly selling Australian car ever. The EH was the eighth Holden since 1948 and, in just 18 months, more than 250 000 were built and sold.

Based on the popular EJ, the EH incorporated a new-look roofline and clever styling which improved its looks from every angle.

The biggest change, however, was under the bonnet. A completely new six-cylinder engine, available in two capacities, gave up to 53 per cent more power. Dubbed the 'red engine' (after the colour of the painted block), this unit replaced the 'grey engine' used in all previous Holdens.

The bigger '179' engine, which developed 86 kW, was standard in the upmarket Premier (now available in wagon form) and in a limited edition 'S4' sports model,

with upgraded brakes and a bigger fuel tank. Despite all the new features, the EH was the same price as its predecessor and markedly cheaper than the Holden of ten years earlier.
INTRODUCTION: August 1963.
ENGINES: 2.45-litre six-cylinder '149' (a low-compression version of this engine was also available) and 2.95-litre six-cylinder '179'.
TRANSMISSIONS: Three-speed manual gearbox and three-speed Hydramatic automatic transmission.
MODEL LINE-UP: Standard sedan, Special sedan, Premier sedan, Standard station wagon, Special station wagon, Premier station wagon, panel van and utility.
TOTAL NUMBER BUILT: 256 959.

1965 HOLDEN HD

The early demand for the HD was so great that sales for the first few months outstripped even those of the record-breaking EH.

The HD had a restyled body, wider and longer than previous Holdens. It offered substantial increases in passenger and load space. Equipment levels were higher and self-adjusting brakes were fitted.

The Hydramatic was replaced by the Powerglide automatic transmission but the most interesting mechanical feature was the announcement of the powerful 'X2' engine. Available as an option for all models, it developed 105 kW (19 kW up on standard) by virtue of twin carburettors, modified camshaft, new manifolds and a low-restriction exhaust system.

With a choice of three engines, two gearboxes and an options list which included front-wheel disc brakes and a vinyl roof, the HD offered the Holden buyer the greatest choice yet. Unfortunately, the new model's early promise was not realised. A downturn in the market was compounded by a general cooling off of public affection for the HD.

INTRODUCTION: February 1965.
ENGINES: 2.45-litre six-cylinder '149', 2.95-litre six-cylinder '179' and 2.95-litre six-cylinder 'X2'.
TRANSMISSIONS: Three-speed manual gearbox and two-speed Powerglide automatic transmission.
MODEL LINE-UP: Standard sedan, Special sedan, Premier sedan, Standard station wagon, Special station wagon, Premier station wagon, panel van and utility.
TOTAL NUMBER BUILT: 178 927.

1966 HOLDEN HR

A refinement of the HD, the HR proved to be one of the most popular Holdens of all. Although the body changes looked mild, they involved reworking the roofline and changing almost all exterior panels to give a sleeker, more modern profile.

Changes were also effected at both ends, with a new grille with squared-off headlight surrounds at the front and 'tower-type' lights at the rear.

The Holden's performance was improved with enlarged versions of the 'red engine'. From June 1967, a new 'X2' engine became available as an option. Producing 109 kW, it incorporated Holden's first automatic choke. Other HR changes included a slightly widened track, a wider rear windscreen and a woodgrain finish for the Premier's interior.

Options included power steering, front-wheel disc brakes and a limited-slip differential.

Six months after release, all HRs were given a safety upgrading with the addition of front seat belts, windscreen washers and a shatterproof interior rear-vision mirror. The fitting of seat belts as standard was the forerunner of many significant safety-related features pioneered by Holden in Australia.

INTRODUCTION: April 1966.
ENGINES: 2.65-litre six-cylinder '161' (a low-compression version of this engine was also available), 3.05-litre six-cylinder '186' and 3.05-litre six-cylinder 'X2'.
TRANSMISSIONS: Three-speed manual gearbox and two-speed Powerglide automatic transmission.
MODEL LINE-UP: Standard sedan, Special sedan, Premier sedan, Standard station wagon, Special station wagon, Premier station wagon, panel van and utility.
TOTAL NUMBER BUILT: 252 352.

1968 HOLDEN HK

The all-new Holden HK series was a sensation, bringing a plethora of new models and mechanical features including an imported V-8 engine.

The HK was bigger, lower and more rounded in appearance. The two major model additions were the Brougham luxury variant and the Monaro sports coupe. The V-8, available on all models, proved such a success that a significant number of Holden buyers were still specifying 'bent-iron' engines 20 years later.

The base model HK sedan was called Belmont and the model formerly called 'Special' became 'Kingswood'. The upmarket Premier was retained but, in July 1968, an extended version of the HK sedan, the Brougham, was released. It was over 20 cm longer than the Kingswood and featured the Chevrolet-built '307' V-8 engine, automatic transmission, power steering and the most plush Holden interior yet.

July 1968 also brought the Monaro sports coupe. Based on the HK sedan, with which it shared its wheelbase and overall length, the pillarless Monaro was the first local vehicle of its type and won GM-H a whole legion of new fans. The three Monaro models included the potent GTS 327, fitted with a US-built, 5.3-litre V-8 engine.

With the HK, GM-H offered a larger choice of models, engines, transmissions and options than had previously been seen in a mass-produced Australian car. Safety features included an energy-absorbing steering column (another industry first) and a dual circuit braking system.

INTRODUCTION: January 1968.
ENGINES: 2.65-litre six-cylinder '161', 3.05-litre six-cylinder '186', 3.05-litre six-cylinder '186S', 5-litre V-8 '307' and 5.3-litre V-8 '327'.
TRANSMISSIONS: Two three-speed manual gearboxes, four-speed manual gearbox and two-speed Powerglide automatic.
MODEL LINE-UP: Belmont sedan, Belmont station wagon, Belmont panel van, Belmont utility, Kingswood sedan, Kingswood station wagon, Kingswood utility, Premier sedan, Premier station wagon, Brougham sedan, Monaro coupe, Monaro GTS coupe and Monaro GTS 327 coupe.
TOTAL NUMBER BUILT: 199 039.

1969 HOLDEN HT

The HT Holden was the first Australian car to offer a locally designed V-8 engine.

Although styling changes were minor, the model brought wraparound rear light clusters, a new instrument panel, a new grille and a wider back window. Other features included an increase in track width, improved suspension and synchromesh on all forward gears. The HT model choice included sedans, wagons, Monaro coupes, the stretched Brougham, plus utility and panel van versions.

The locally designed and built V-8 came in two versions — the '253' (4.2 litres) and the '308' (5 litres). In August 1969, the extremely potent 5.74-litre Chevrolet '350' V-8 was offered with the 'Bathurst Pack' Monaro GTS.

The long list of options gave buyers a choice of five engines and four gearboxes, a limited-slip differential, 'Superlift' shock absorbers, front-wheel disc brakes, power steering, power windows, bucket seats, reclining seats, refrigerated air-conditioning, 'rally' wheels and a vinyl roof.

INTRODUCTION: May 1969.
ENGINES: 2.65-litre six-cylinder '161', 3.05-litre six-cylinder '186', 4.2-litre V-8 '253', 5-litre V-8 '307', 5-litre V-8 '308' and 5.74-litre V-8 '350'.
TRANSMISSIONS: Three-speed manual gearbox, two four-speed manual gearboxes and two-speed Powerglide automatic transmission.
MODEL LINE-UP: Belmont sedan, Belmont station wagon, Belmont panel van, Belmont utility, Kingswood sedan, Kingswood station wagon, Kingswood panel van, Kingswood utility, Premier sedan, Premier station wagon, Brougham sedan, Monaro coupe, Monaro GTS coupe and Monaro GTS 350 coupe.
TOTAL NUMBER BUILT: 183 402.

1970 HOLDEN HG

The Holden HG was the final refinement of the HK/HT series, most notable for introducing the Australian-built, three-speed Trimatic automatic transmission.

The Trimatic was standard on the Brougham and available on all other models, except the Monaro GTS 350, which was offered with four-speed manual or the regular two-speed Powerglide automatic.

As well as an ABS plastic grille and 'cleaner' body decorations, the HG had new safety features, colours and trim designs.

Improved disc brakes were now fitted to all V-8 models. The Monaro GTS had a modified suspension system for greater comfort.

INTRODUCTION: July 1970.
ENGINES: 2.65-litre six-cylinder '161', 3.05-litre six-cylinder '186', 4.2-litre V-8 '253', 5-litre V-8 '308' and 5.74-litre V-8 '350'.
TRANSMISSIONS: Three-speed manual gearbox, two four-speed manual gearboxes, two-speed Powerglide automatic transmission and three-speed Trimatic automatic transmission.
MODEL LINE-UP: Belmont sedan, Belmont station wagon, Belmont panel van, Belmont utility, Kingswood sedan, Kingswood station wagon, Kingswood utility, Premier sedan, Premier station wagon, Brougham sedan, Monaro coupe, Monaro GTS coupe and Monaro GTS 350 coupe.
TOTAL NUMBER BUILT: 155 787.

1971 HOLDEN HQ

The completely new HQ Holden was hailed as the most significant Holden since the original 48-215.

As well as introducing new versions of the previous Holden sedans, wagons and coupes, it included a new long-wheelbase luxury model called Statesman. The HQ's six-cylinder engines were carried over from the HG, but with a longer stroke to increase the capacity.

Two versions of the local V-8 were offered with the imported Chevrolet '350' available in the Monaro. The HQ was the first Holden built with a semi-chassis frame (to improve rigidity and reduce noise and vibration) and it introduced other new features including flowthrough ventilation and four-wheel coil springing.

During the three years the HQ series stayed in production, various 'specials', such as the 'Vacationer' option package, were announced. The sporty Holden SS V-8 sedan featured a four-speed manual gearbox and many Monaro details. In

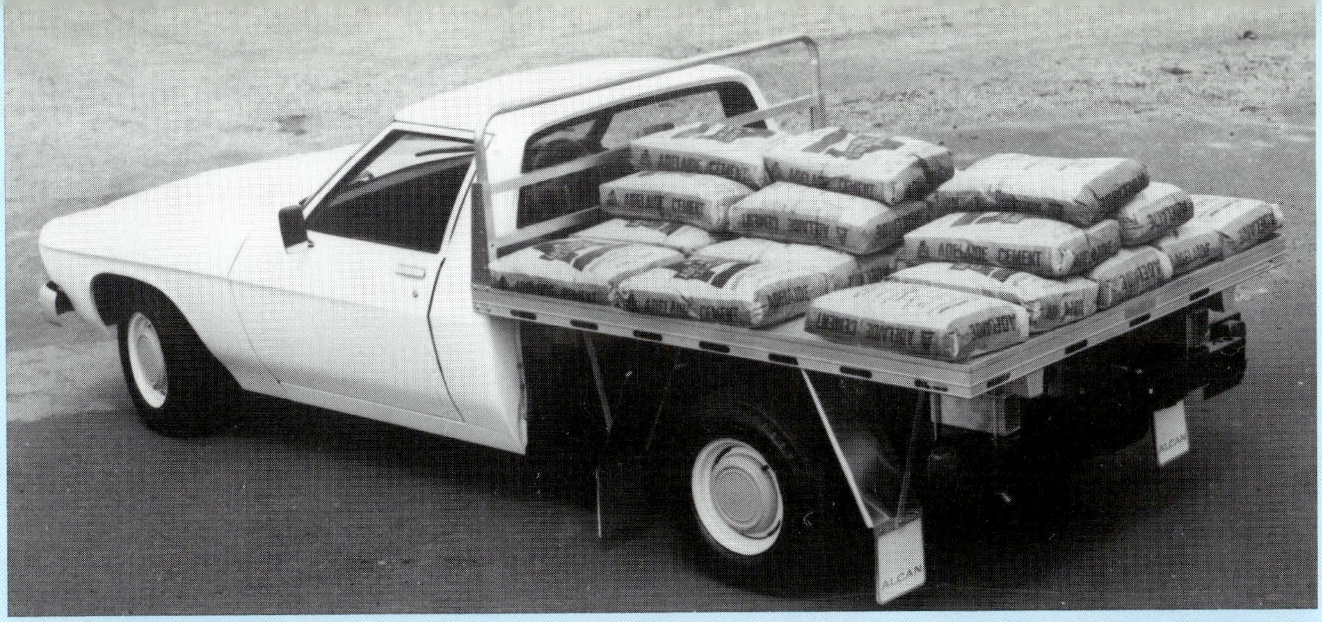
ADELAIDE CEMENT
ALCAN

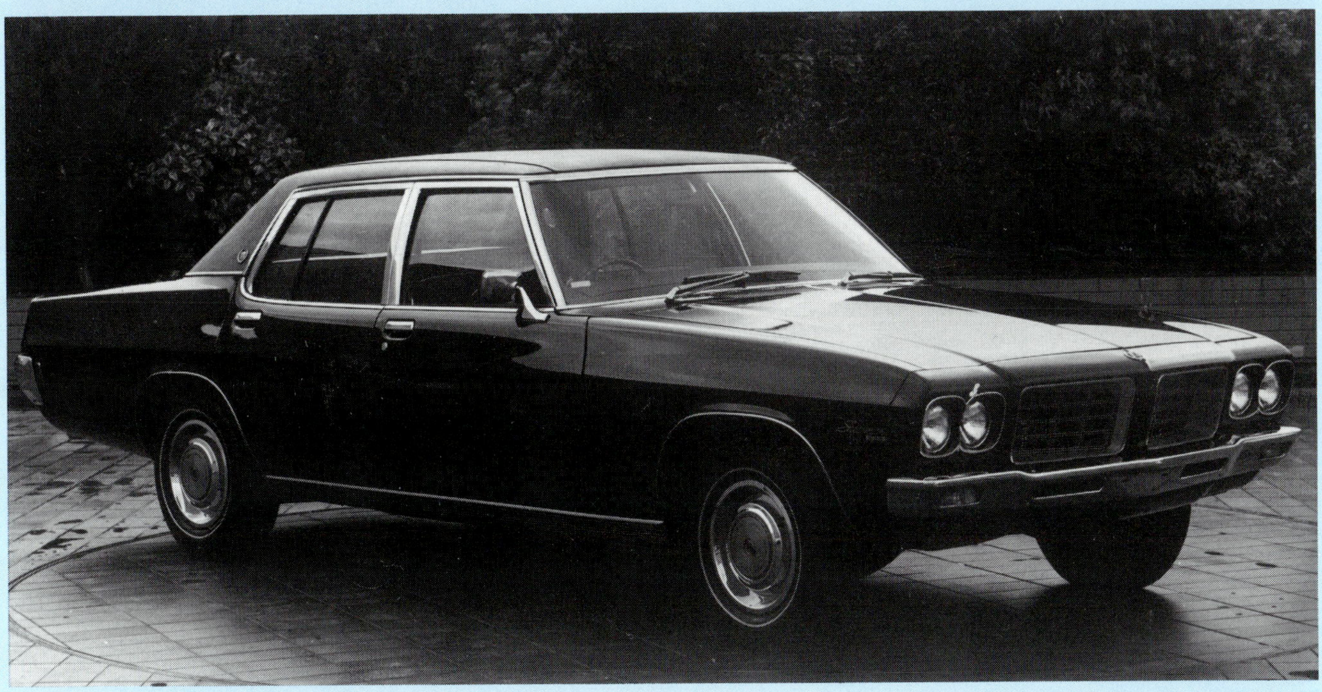

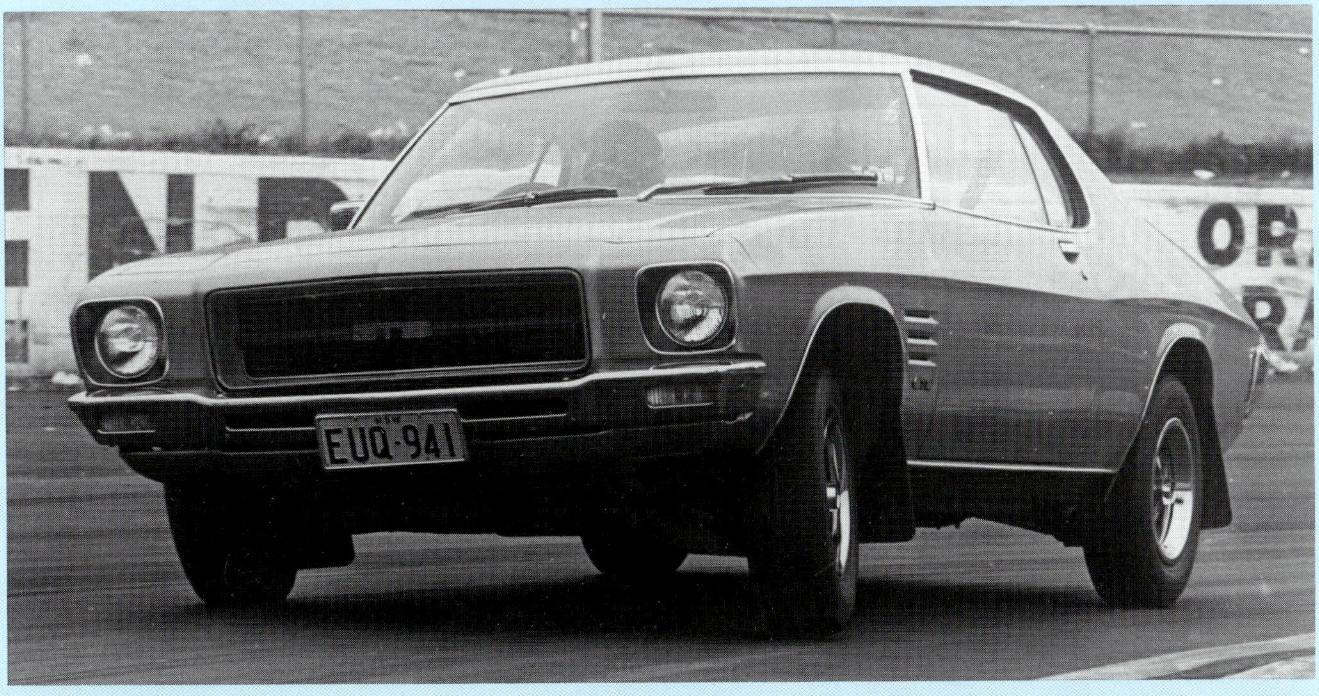
EUQ·941

March 1973, a four-door Monaro GTS sedan, with virtually the same specifications as the GTS coupe, was released. That same year, a silver Holden Premier commemorated the 25th anniversary of the Holden car.

The Statesman, built on the extended wagon wheelbase, was 26 cm longer than the other sedans and available in Custom and De Ville versions. The HQ range also included utilities, panel vans and Holden's first cab/chassis truck. The HQ design placed a considerable emphasis on safety. Nearly half a million HQs were sold, making it easily the biggest-selling single Holden model range.

INTRODUCTION: July 1971.
ENGINES: 2.84-litre six-cylinder '173', 3.3-litre six-cylinder '202', 4.2-litre V-8 '253', 5-litre V-8 '308' and 5.74-litre V-8 '350'.
TRANSMISSIONS: Three-speed manual gearbox, two four-speed manual gearboxes, three-speed Trimatic automatic transmission and three-speed Turbohydramatic 400 automatic transmission (only with the '350' V-8).
MODEL LINE-UP: Belmont sedan, Belmont station wagon, Belmont panel van, Belmont utility, Kingswood sedan, Kingswood station wagon, Kingswood utility, SS sedan, Premier sedan, Premier station wagon, Holden chassis and cab, Monaro coupe, Monaro GTS coupe, Monaro GTS 350 coupe, Monaro LS ('Luxury Sports') coupe, Monaro GTS sedan, Statesman sedan and Statesman De Ville sedan.
TOTAL NUMBER BUILT: 485 650.

1974 HOLDEN HJ

The facelifted HJ was an improved version of the enormously successful HQ.

It was distinguished by different grilles, wraparound front and rear lights, larger bumper bars and slight revisions of the front-end sheet metal. Interior changes included full-foam seats, a new instrument panel, a revised ventilation system and upgraded equipment levels.

The biggest-selling model, the Kingswood, had a 3.3-litre engine and power-assisted disc brakes as standard equipment.

Later in the year, the 'HJ' Statesman (GM-H's Holden-based extended luxury sedan) was announced with a Caprice version boasting more luxury equipment than any car GM-H had previously produced.

INTRODUCTION: October 1974.
ENGINES: 2.84-litre six-cylinder '173', 3.3-litre six-cylinder '202', 4.2-litre V-8 '253' and 5-litre V-8 '308'.
TRANSMISSIONS: Three-speed manual gearbox, four-speed manual gearbox, three-speed Trimatic automatic transmission and three-speed Turbohydramatic 400 automatic transmission (only with 5-litre '308' V-8).
MODEL LINE-UP: Belmont sedan, Belmont station wagon, Kingswood sedan, Kingswood station wagon, Kingswood utility, Kingswood Sandman utility, Premier sedan, Premier station wagon, Holden chassis and cab, Holden panel van, Holden Sandman panel van, Holden utility, Holden Sandman utility, Monaro coupe, Monaro GTS coupe, Monaro GTS sedan, Monaro LS ('Luxury Sports') coupe, Statesman De Ville sedan and Statesman Caprice sedan.
TOTAL NUMBER BUILT: 167 251.

1976 HOLDEN HX

The Holden HX was a further refinement of the HQ/HJ series and introduced a low-emission version of each Holden engine.

These modified – and less powerful – engines were fitted to ensure all Holdens met the new anti-pollution standards required by Australian Design Rule 27A.

Externally the HX had a new grille, revised hubcaps and other minor modifications. The biggest improvement from a driver's viewpoint was a steering column stalk (in all models) giving fingertip control of the wipers, washers, turn-signals, headlight dipper and flasher.

Toward the middle of 1976, a run of 600 Monaro 'LE' (Limited Edition) luxury coupes wrapped up eight years of Monaro coupe production. Powered by the 5-litre V-8, the LE was fitted with air-conditioning, a quadraphonic cartridge tape player, power windows, automatic transmission, front and rear spoilers, metallic paint with gold pinstriping, honeycomb polycast wheels and other special features.

Late in 1976, a silver HX sedan marked 50 years of General Motors in Australia. Sandman versions of the panel van and utility were released with the HX range to increase Holden's presence in the fast-expanding recreational market.

INTRODUCTION: July 1976.
ENGINES: 2.84-litre six-cylinder '173', 3.3-litre six-cylinder '202', 4.2-litre V-8 '253' and 5-litre V-8 '308'.
TRANSMISSIONS: Three-speed manual gearbox, four-speed manual gearbox, three-speed Trimatic automatic transmission and three-speed Turbohydramatic 400 automatic transmission.
MODEL LINE-UP: Belmont sedan, Belmont station wagon, Kingswood sedan, Kingswood station wagon, Kingswood utility, Kingswood panel van, Premier sedan, Premier station wagon, Holden chassis and cab, Holden panel van, Holden Sandman panel van, Holden utility, Holden Sandman utility, Monaro GTS sedan, Monaro LE coupe, Statesman De Ville sedan and Statesman Caprice sedan.
TOTAL NUMBER BUILT: 110 669.

1977 HOLDEN HZ

The Holden HZ was the first full-sized Holden with GM-H's acclaimed Radial Tuned Suspension system.

So successful was RTS, that it forced Holden's competitors to introduce their own improved suspension systems. Aside from dramatic improvements to ride and handling, the new Holdens incorporated minor interior and exterior changes, including upgraded interior trim.

The Belmont sedan was dropped from the range and the Kingswood SL added. As well as sedan and wagon versions of the Kingswood, Kingswood SL and Premier, there was an HZ GTS sports sedan and a light commercial range with Sandman van and utility variants, both featuring 'GTS' exterior treatment and trim and a 4.2-litre V-8 as standard.

New Statesman sedans were announced shortly after the rest of the HZ range.

The HZ stayed in production until 1980 and was the last traditional-sized Holden until the 1988 release of the VN. The HZ range was supplemented – and then replaced – by the smaller and lighter Commodore.

INTRODUCTION: October 1977.
ENGINES: 3.3-litre six-cylinder '202', 4.2-litre V-8 '253' and 5-litre V-8 '308'.
TRANSMISSIONS: Three-speed manual gearbox, four-speed manual gearbox, three-speed Trimatic automatic transmission, three-speed Turbohydramatic 350 (later 400) automatic transmission.

201

MODEL LINE-UP: Kingswood sedan, Kingswood station wagon, Kingswood SL sedan, Kingswood SL station wagon, Kingswood panel van, Kingswood utility, Premier sedan, Premier station wagon, Holden chassis and cab, Holden panel van, Holden Sandman panel van, Holden utility, Holden Sandman utility, Monaro GTS sedan, Statesman De Ville sedan, Statesman Caprice sedan and Statesman SL/E sedan.
TOTAL NUMBER BUILT: 154 155.

1978 HOLDEN COMMODORE VB

The original Holden Commodore sedan quickly became Australia's top-selling car.

Launched after GM-H had spent more than $110 million on development, the Commodore was a 'ground up' new design, combining a German Opel body design with an Australian engine and local mechanical components.

Importantly, the Commodore was significantly smaller than previous Holdens and signalled that GM-H was following the trend toward smaller cars sparked by the fuel crises of the 1970s.

In addition to the base Commodore, there was an SL and a luxurious SL/E. A Commodore wagon appeared eight months after the sedan.

The HZ Holden range of sedans, wagons, utilities, vans, trucks and Statesman saloons continued to be produced alongside the VB and sold well.
INTRODUCTION: October 1978.
ENGINES: 2.85-litre six-cylinder, 3.3-litre six-cylinder, 4.2-litre V-8 and 5-litre V-8.
TRANSMISSIONS: Four-speed manual gearbox, four-speed Torquemaster manual gearbox, three-speed Trimatic automatic transmission, three-speed Turbohydramatic 350/400 automatic transmission.
MODEL LINE-UP: Commodore sedan, Commodore station wagon, Commodore SL sedan, Commodore SL station wagon and Commodore SL/E sedan.
TOTAL NUMBER BUILT: 95 906.

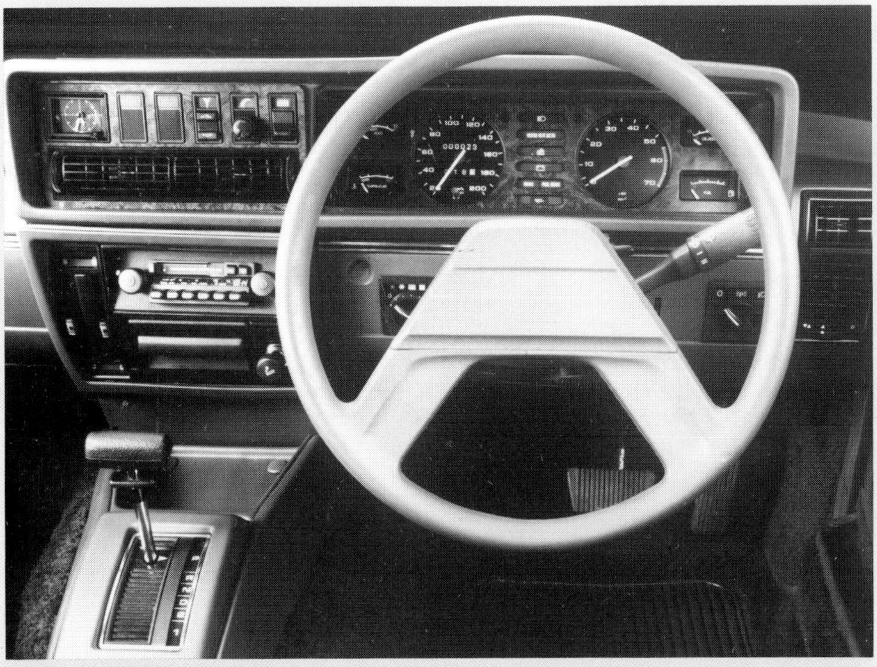

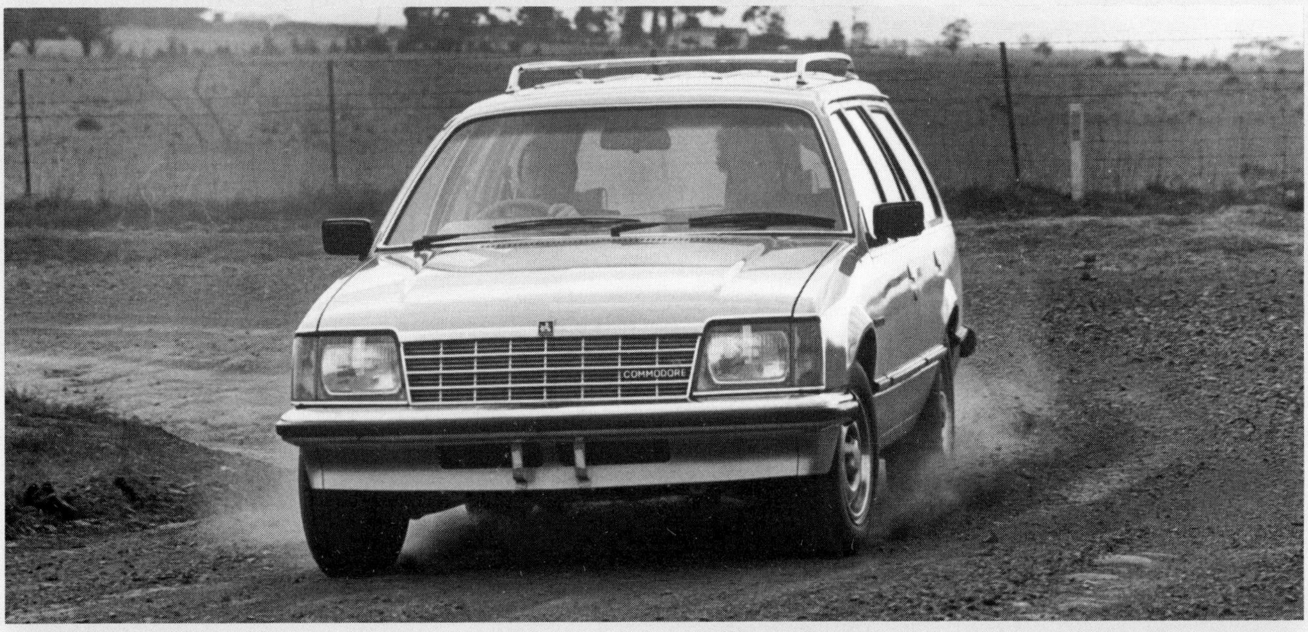
COMMODORE

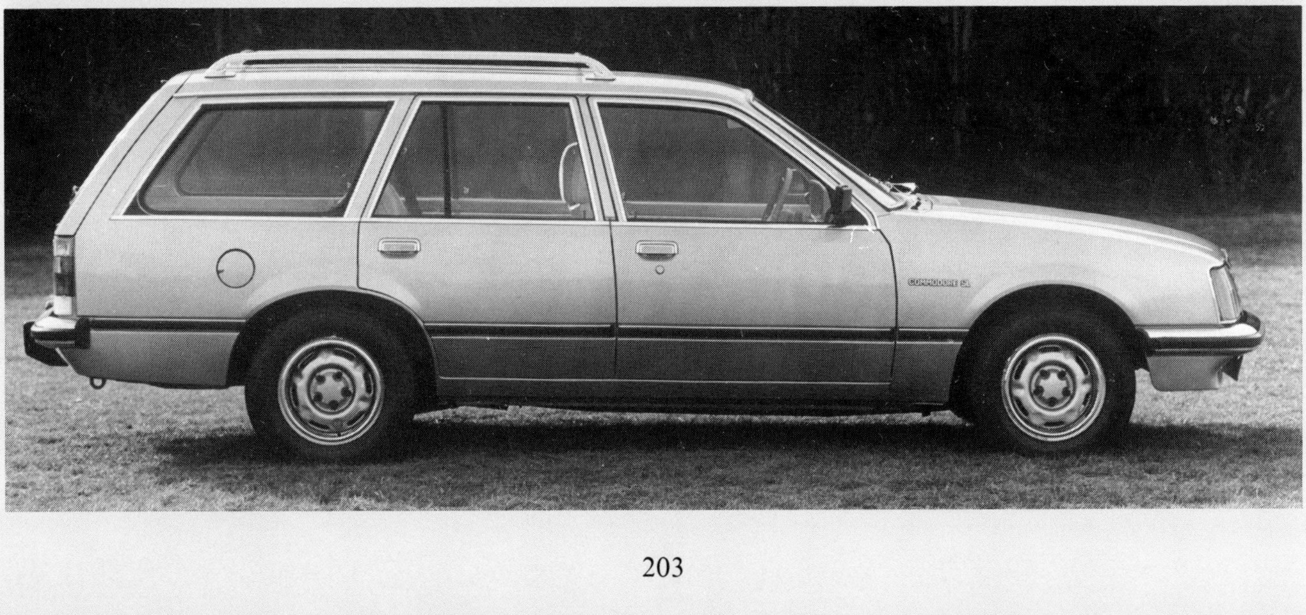

1980 HOLDEN COMMODORE VC

A refinement of the 1978 model, the VC kept Commodore in its place as Australia's top-selling car. It also offered buyers a four-cylinder engine in addition to the 'six' or V-8.

The four-cylinder model, launched four months after the rest of the range, was powered by a 1.9-litre unit based on the Starfire engine fitted to the Holden Sunbird. Changes were made to improve the fuel economy and quietness.

The six-cylinder and eight-cylinder VC engines were revised 'XT5' versions, which were up to 25 per cent more powerful and 15 per cent more economical than before. This was achieved with a redesigned cylinder head, camshaft, carburettor, inlet manifold and exhaust manifold and electronic ignition.

The VC range reintroduced 'shadow tone' paint work, a feature not seen on a new Holden for 20 years. Another new Commodore option was cruise control.

Soon after the VC was announced, production of the Holden HZ range, which had continued alongside the Commodore, was discontinued. A WB range of light commercials and Statesman sedans was announced at the same time.

INTRODUCTION: March 1980.
ENGINES: 1.9-litre four-cylinder, 2.85-litre six-cylinder, 3.3-litre six-cylinder, 4.2-litre V-8 and 5-litre V-8.
TRANSMISSIONS: Four-speed manual gearbox, four-speed Torquemaster manual gearbox, three-speed Trimatic automatic transmission and three-speed Turbohydramatic 350 automatic transmission.
MODEL LINE-UP: Commodore L sedan, Commodore L station wagon, Commodore SL sedan, Commodore SL station wagon and Commodore SL/E sedan plus WB Statesman sedans and light commercials.
TOTAL NUMBER BUILT: 109 231.

1981 HOLDEN COMMODORE VH

The VH was the third Commodore series in four years, representing a program of regular refinement rather than drastic change.

The range comprised five models, with five engine options and four transmissions, including a five-speed manual gearbox.

The body styling was similar to the previous VB/VC models but a subtle reworking at the front gave the Commodore a longer and lower appearance. The four-cylinder version was retained, alongside the six-cylinder and eight-cylinder models.

Creature comforts, including climate control air-conditioning and cruise control, were part of a lengthy options list. The VH brought about the first local fitment of advanced computer electronics to a mass-produced passenger car. One such feature was the SL/E model's trip computer.

INTRODUCTION: October 1981.
ENGINES: 1.9-litre four-cylinder, 2.85-litre six-cylinder, 3.3-litre six-cylinder, 4.2-litre V-8 and 5-litre V-8.
TRANSMISSIONS: Four-speed manual gearbox, four-speed Torquemaster manual gearbox, three-speed Trimatic automatic transmission and three-speed Turbohydramatic 350 automatic transmission.
MODEL LINE-UP: Commodore SL sedan, Commodore SL station wagon, Commodore SL/X sedan, Commodore SL/X station wagon, Commodore SS sedan and Commodore SL/E sedan plus WB Statesman sedans and WB light commercials.
TOTAL NUMBER BUILT: 126 823.

1984 HOLDEN COMMODORE VK

The VK brought major changes in styling and mechanical specifications.

New features included an advanced computerised engine management system and optional electronic fuel-injection which lifted the six-cylinder Commodore's power output to 106 kW without loss of fuel economy.

Extensive exterior changes introduced six-window styling and enhanced the longer, lower look introduced with the VH. A new louvered grille was integrated with a polypropylene bumper and wrapapround side body mouldings. There were other changes and the VK series introduced new model names: SL, Berlina and Calais.

The Calais, which was top-of-the-line, was fitted with an Australian-made digital/analogue electronic instrument panel claimed to be the most advanced in the world. It incorporated an electronic odometer and tripmeter.

By the time the VK was announced, a swing back toward big cars had caused the Commodore to lose its position as Australia's best-selling car. The VK did not win back total market leadership for 1984 but it made strong gains and, in some months, was the top seller.

INTRODUCTION: February 1984.
ENGINES: 3.3-litre six-cylinder, 3.3-litre fuel-injected six-cylinder and 5-litre V-8.
TRANSMISSIONS: Four-speed manual gearbox, five-speed manual gearbox, three-speed Trimatic automatic transmission and three-speed Turbohydramatic 350 automatic transmission.
MODEL LINE-UP: Commodore SL sedan, Commodore SL station wagon, Commodore Berlina sedan, Commodore Berlina station wagon, Commodore SS sedan and Calais sedan plus WB Statesman sedans and WB light commercials (the WB series continued until the end of 1984).
TOTAL NUMBER BUILT: 133 125.

1986 HOLDEN COMMODORE VL

The VL was the first — and perhaps the last — family-sized Holden to be powered by an imported six-cylinder engine.

It brought with it major styling changes including a new lowered front-end appearance and integral air foil at the rear. The remodelled interior had a new binnacle-style instrument panel.

The use of a Japanese engine made the VL a controversial model at first but, when the fuss died, the public discovered not only a more refined and much improved Commodore but a sensational drive train. In spite of the 1986 switch to unleaded fuel, the high-tech 3-litre engine — coupled to a four-speed automatic or five-speed manual transmission — gave the base model Commodore 33 per cent more power and 15 per cent better fuel economy than previously.

The VL was the model which enabled Holden to regain its former position as the number one choice of private buyers. In July 1986, an optional turbocharger lifted output to 150 kW, making the already quick Commodore even more lively. Three months later a revised version of Holden's V-8 was announced.

For the first time, the top-of-the-line Holden, the Calais, had significantly different styling to the rest of the range. Its front-end treatment made use of semiconcealed headlights and a transparent grille.

INTRODUCTION: February 1986.
ENGINES: 3-litre six-cylinder, 3-litre turbocharged six-cylinder and 4.9-litre V-8.
TRANSMISSIONS: Five-speed manual gearbox, five-speed heavy-duty manual gearbox (for turbo), four-speed automatic transmission, four-speed heavy-duty automatic transmission (for turbo) and three-speed Trimatic automatic transmission (for V-8).

MODEL LINE-UP: Commodore SL sedan, Commodore SL station wagon, Commodore Berlina sedan, Commodore Berlina station wagon, Commodore SS sedan and Calais sedan.
TOTAL NUMBER BUILT: 148 412 (estimate).

Index

Advertising 134, 143, 144, 145, 146
Aerodynamics 18, 21, 23, 43, 44, 46, 61, 154, 146
AeroVironment Inc 126
Arizona Proving Ground 84, 125
Audi 21, 38, 133
Australian Design Rules (ADRs) 50, 52, 55, 66, 68, 72, 73, 77, 82

Balance shaft 96
Barrier test 66, 67, 83
Bench seat (front) 31
Black box 23, 40
BOC (Buick-Oldsmobile-Cadillac) 32, 91, 94, 98
Borg Warner 56, 57, 60
Bosch 97, 100
Buick 17, 18, 43, 94, 123, 126
Button Plan 31

CAD/CAM 32, 90
Cadillac 28, 121
Chevrolet 121
Chisholm Institute 58
Clay modelling 41, 42, 51, 52, 130, 131
Clinic (see styling clinic)
Cobra security system 56
Cockpit module 62, 70, 99, 116, 117
Colours 48, 49, 50
Confederation of Australian Motor Sport (CAMS) 99, 156
Control teams (NDCT) 55, 56, 74, 75, 106
Coordinate measuring 41, 51, 105, 113
Corrosion testing 83
Cressida 130
CSIRO 119

Daewoo Motor Company 123
Dandenong plant 120
Dealer launch 143, 144, 145
Dealer network 143, 144
Delco 97, 98, 100, 126
Design Objective Manual 47, 55
Digitising 41
Di-nocing 42
Do-nothing study 17

Elizabeth plant 57, 76, 104 to 120
Electro Magnetic Compatibility (EMC) 63, 73
Electronic Data Systems 121

Family II engine 31, 56, 93, 98, 102
Fanuc 110
Fibreglass models 42, 43, 50, 52
Fisher Body division 51
Fishermans Bend plant 15, 17, 25, 57, 58, 69, 70, 71, 84, 102, 106
Fleet market 146, 147
Flush window glass 17, 30, 44, 51, 61, 135
Ford 20, 21, 24, 25, 27, 131, 147
Ford Falcon 15, 16, 17, 19, 20, 21, 23, 26, 27, 28, 39, 59, 130, 131, 134, 146

Gerotor oil pump 98
General Motors Australia 121
General Motors Corporation 28, 38, 51, 121
General Motors Institute 58, 90
GM70 car 18, 22, 27
GM Advanced Engineering Staff (AES) 124, 126, 127
GMF Robotic Inc. 110
GM-H 90, 91, 102, 104
GM Overseas Corporation 120

GM Research Laboratories (GMR) 123, 124, 126, 127
GM Technical Centre 30, 33, 123
'Grey' motor 91
Group A racing 78, 100, 151, 152, 154, 156, 159, 160, 161, 162

Hardie-Ferodo 99
Hitachi Zosen 104
Holden Dealer Team 151, 152, 153, 159, 160, 162
Holden Engine Company (HEC) 91 to 102
Holden models:
  48-215 91
  Astra 31, 36
  Camira 31, 35, 37, 44, 57, 58, 130, 131
  Commodore VB 15, 16, 18, 53, 58, 60
  Commodore VH 17
  Commodore VK 25, 58, 74, 151
  Commodore VL 17, 20, 21, 23, 28, 30, 35, 37, 38, 45 to 49, 55 to 61, 64, 66, 70, 74, 75, 78, 84 to 88, 94, 96, 99, 100, 130, 131, 134, 146, 147, 154
  Commodore VM 18
  Gemini 62
  HD 130
  HK 66
  HT 91
  HQ 35
  HX 89, 130
  WA 130
  HQ-HZ series 36, 39, 53
  Kingswood 55
  Monaro 53,
  Torana 54, 90
Holden Motor Sport (HMS) 152, 153, 155, 156, 157, 159, 161
Holden National Leasing (HNL) 147
Holden's Motor Body Builders 68, 121
Holden Special Vehicles (HSV) 153 to 162
Honda 133
Hughes Aircraft Company 121, 126
Hydramatic Division 32

Industrial Design Council 46
Isuzu 123

Jaguar 17
James Hardie 1000 99, 151
Just-in-time (JIT) 56, 117

Kirby 60

Lang Lang 32, 57 to 59, 65 to 67, 74 to 77, 82 to 85, 87 to 90, 125
Lotus 121, 123, 126

Marketing campaign 134, 135, 143, 144, 145, 149
Master Timing Document 50
Mazda 131
Mercedes 40
Merchandising campaign 134, 143, 144, 145, 146, 150
Milford Proving Ground 125
Mitsubishi 131, 147
Moulded trim 47, 64, 65, 118

N.A.S.A. 126
New Design Control Team (NDCT) see Control teams
Nissan 17, 20, 22, 27, 31, 32, 56, 57, 59, 87, 114
Noise-vibration-harshness (NVH) 65, 66, 77, 82, 83, 86, 99

Okaya, Miic and Mori 105
Oldsmobile 18, 94, 123
Opel 16 to 27, 30, 38 to 41, 44, 51, 54 to 62, 87 to 91, 123
Orchestrated technology 56

Pentax World Solar Challenge 126
Piezoelectric 66, 97
Pontiac 18, 58, 91, 94, 123
Press launch 148, 149,
Price Review Committee 148
Product Policy Committee 27, 30
Product Strategy Committee 15, 17, 18, 23, 24, 32
Public relations 134, 148

Radial Tuned Suspension 58 to 59
'Red' motor 91
Reliability audit 75
Rig testing 69, 70, 72, 77
Roger's Report 74
Royal Melbourne Institute of Technology (RMIT) 44 to 46, 54, 61, 150
Run-out campaign 134, 146

Sealed House for Environmental Determination 82
Seating Buck 24 to 27
Shuttle Assembly 113
Sigma 130, 131
Silcraft 65
Simultaneous Engineering (SE) 55, 56, 76, 83, 106
Single Point Tooling 106, 113
Slam Rig 69
Solar Car (SunRaycer) 125, 126
Space frame 22
Styling clinic 28, 52, 128, 130
SunRaycer 126
Suzuki 123

Tape drawings 38, 39
Tom Walkinshaw Racing (TWR) 153 to 161
Total Quality Control (TQC) 46, 49, 109, 119, 120
Toyota 22, 74, 121, 131, 147
Tubemakers Australia 60
Turbohydramatic 700 32, 57, 60, 99

Unit Checking/Parts Checking Fixture 109
University of Melbourne 33, 150

Vauxhall 33, 56, 91
VDO Australia 62

Wind tunnel tests 61, 73
Woodville Plant 68
Wylie, W.H. & Company 68

Zincrometal 61

---

* As this book is specifically about the Holden VN and the people around it, this index is confined to firms, facilities, processes, organisations, committees, car models and special equipment.

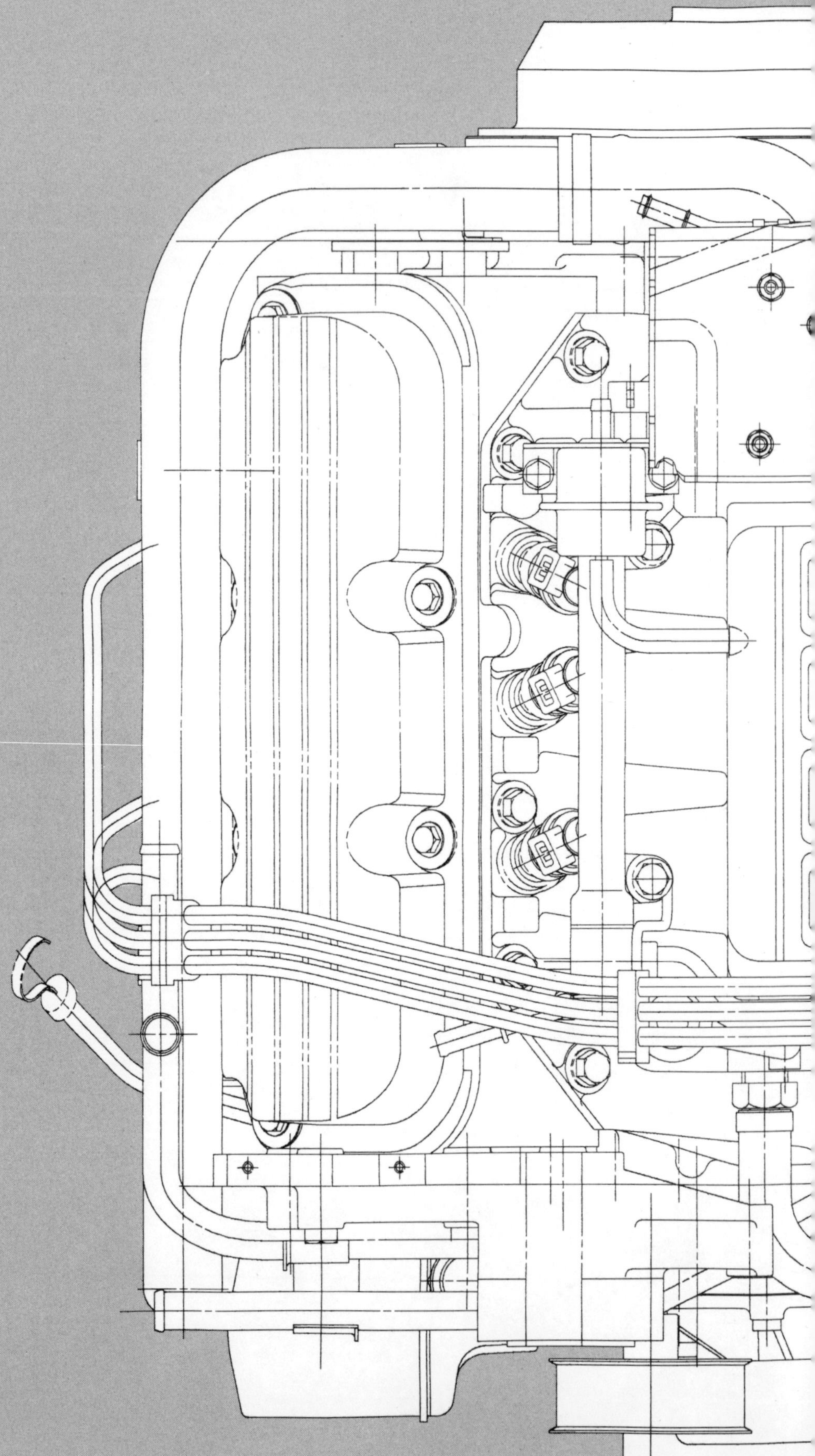